D0768946

DISCARD

PHYSICIANS
of the SOUL

PHYSICIANS
of the SOUL

The PSYCHOLOGIES
of the WORLD'S GREAT
SPIRITUAL TEACHERS

Robert M. May

Foreword by Jean Houston

CROSSROAD · NEW YORK

TO ALL OF MY TEACHERS

1982

The Crossroad Publishing Company
575 Lexington Avenue, New York, NY 10022

Copyright © 1982 by Robert M. May

All rights reserved. No part of this book may be reproduced, stored in a retrieval system, or transmitted, in any form or by any means, electronic, mechanical, photocopying, recording, or otherwise, without the written permission of The Crossroad Publishing Company.

Printed in the United States of America

Library of Congress Cataloging in Publication Data

May, Robert M.
  Physicians of the soul.

  Bibliography: p.
  Includes index.
  1. Religion—Biography.   2. Spiritual life.
3. Psychology, Religious.   I. Title.
BL72.M39   1982   291.6'3'019   82-4689
ISBN 0-8245-0511-5

Acknowledgments

(*EXCEPT* for the Moses Chapter), The Scriptural quotations in this publication are from the *Revised Standard Version* of *The Bible*, copyrighted 1946, 1952 © 1971, 1973 by the Division of Christian Education of the National Council of the Churches of Christ in the U.S.A. and used by permission.

Excerpt from page 3, *The Gospel According to Thomas*, translated by A. Guillaumont, et. al., copyright © 1959 by E. J. Brill, reprinted by permission of the author.

Excerpts from THE HOLY SCRIPTURES *According to the Masoretic Text*, © 1955. This material is copyrighted and used through the courtesy of The Jewish Publication Society of America.

Reprinted with permission of Macmillan Publishing Company, Inc. From THE KORAN INTERPRETED approximately 4 pages (from pp. 30, 31–33, 39, 42, 45, 65–66, 71–72, 344) by Arthur J. Arberry, Translator. © George Allen & Unwin, Ltd., 1955 (U.S., territories, and dependencies).

THE KORAN INTERPRETED (approximately 4 pages) by Arthur J. Arberry, Translator. © George Allen & Unwin Ltd., 1955. Reprinted by permission of George Allen & Unwin Ltd. (World Rights outside U.S., territories, and dependencies).

Excerpts totalling approximately 270 words from MEMORIES, DREAMS, REFLECTIONS by C. G. Jung, translated from the German by Richard & Clara Winston, Copyright © 1963 by Random House, Inc. Reprinted by permission of Random House, Inc.

Excerpt from page 17, THE PROPHET by Kahlil Gibran. Copyright © 1951 by Administrators C.T.A. of Kahlil Gibran Estate, and Mary G. Gibran. Reprinted by permission of Alfred A. Knopf, Inc.

Excerpts from THE SON OF GOD *Bhagavad Gita*. Copyright © 1972 by The Vedanta Society of Southern California. Reprinted by permission of The Vedanta Society of Southern California.

Excerpts from *Tao Te Ching*, translated by Ch'u Ta-Kao, published by Samuel Weiser, Inc., York Beach Maine. Reprinted by permission of Samuel Weiser, Inc.

Extracts from THE TEN PRINCIPAL UPANISHADS translated by Shree Purohit Swami and W. B. Yeats. Reprinted by permission of Benares University and Michael and Anne Yeats.

"Man is born in Tao" from Thomas Merton, THE WAY OF CHUANG TZU, copyright © 1965 by The Abbey of Gethsemane. Reprinted by permission of New Directions Publishing Corporation.

From THE WAY OF LIFE by Lao Tzu, as translated by Raymond B. Blakney. Copyright © 1955 by Raymond B. Blakney. Reprinted by arrangement with The New American Library, Inc., New York, New York.

From *The Way of the Sufi* by Idries Shah. Copyright © 1968 by Idries Shah. From *Tales of the Dervishes* by Idries Shah. Copyright © 1967 by Idries Shah. Reprinted by permission of the publisher, E. P. Dutton, Inc. (U.S., dependencies, and Philippines).

From "The Tale of the Sands" from TALES OF THE DERVISHES © 1967 by Idries Shah. "The Seed of Sufi Knowledge" and "The Way" from THE WAY OF THE SUFI © 1968 by Idries Shah. Reprinted by the permission of Idries Shah and Jonathan Cape Limited (World Rights excluding U.S.A.).

Koan on page 253 of ZEN COMMENTS ON THE MUMOKAN by Zenkei Shibayama, translated by Sumiko Kudo. Copyright © 1974 by Zenkei Shibayama. Courtesy of Harper & Row, Publishers, Inc.

Contents

They that are whole have no need of the physician,
but they that are sick. . . .

Jesus of Nazareth

And when a man is oppressed with sickness,
there being a physician who can heal him,
and he does not avail himself of the physician's help,
that is not the fault of the physician.
Even so when a man oppressed by the malady of wrong-doing
does not seek the spiritual guide of enlightenment,
that is no fault of the evil-destroying guide.

Gotama the Buddha

Foreword

*S*OULMAKING is not necessarily a happy thing. Critical parts of it are not. It almost always involves a painful excursion into pathos wherein the anguish is enormous and the suffering cracks the boundaries of what you thought you could bear. And yet the wounding pathos of your own human story may contain the seeds of healing and transformation in the larger mythic story that it reflects. As one notes in the Greek tragedy, the gods force themselves symptomatically into consciousness at the time of pathos. And by "gods" I mean not only the archetypal dimensions of the psyche, but also the constellation of psychophysical potential and psychospiritual patterns which charge the human self with evolutionary possibilities. This is why pathos can open the doors of our sensibility to a reality that often remains closed to a normal point of view. When we feel our minds and our hearts breaking, this sometimes pushes us into a different topography, a different extension of reality. Thus in high tragedy pathos is a divine process working in the human soul, ennobling the self and rendering us capable of being healed and filled with the giftings of spirit.

Robert May has the gift of complex suffering. His own long dark night of the soul has made him wise in the ways of inward journeys and given him a compassion for wounded souls that is as healing as it is instructive. Like Dante lost in the dark woods of an unacceptable reality, he seeks the Guide through the hells and purgatories of the decaying social and internal domains. Unlike Dante, his Virgils are many and many are the paths which he uses and explores, each ending however in the same Paradise of Self-realization. With lucid commentaries and deeply personal reflections, he takes the reader back and forth between the cutting edge of modern psychological theory and the high practice of the perennial philosophies. Lao Tzu and Moses, Jesus, Krishna, Buddha and Muhammed emerge as the great sacred psychologists helping the modern seeker to wage holy war against the enemies within. May discovers the field of unity within the cultural diversity of each illumined spiritual master and finds striking parallels between them in their use of parable and allegory. Indeed, they are frequently found to be telling the same story, and they certainly tell of the same consummation. Since such a one's visions, ideas, and inspirations emerge from the Source levels of reality, they redeem the disintegrating orders of psyche and society and tap us directly into the eternal springs through which self and society are reborn. In joining them on their path, one transcends cultural and familial conditionings and undertakes the extraordinary task of dying to one's modernity and being reborn to one's eternity. But there is still more. By serving as the lure of becoming, the great sacred psychologists give us the courage to cleanse, purify, and prepare ourselves for doing the difficult work of becoming the channels, the instruments through which the One can enter into time and culture and civilization can join a larger ecology of Being. We become, therefore, the agents of the entelechy, joining the complexity of our local space-time to the eternal domain of consciousness, risking the uncovering of painful knowings and self-destructive patterns so as to be able to transmute these to higher and more integrated patterns of human consciousness and culture.

In offering us his experience of the cartographies of these spiritual paths, Robert May gives us glimpses of a new practice of soul craft deriving from the once and future profession of *therapeia*—the doing of the work of the gods.

JEAN HOUSTON

Preface

THIS book is the product of an Inner Journey, my own, of ten years' duration (which seems to be traditional!). My Journey began in the summer of 1971 when I resigned my college teaching position in psychology, and somehow felt called to "enter the Path." That was the summer I was twenty-nine. In truth, my search began many years earlier in the summer of 1962, when I was twenty, and I experienced what Christian mystics would call the "Kingdom." It was not an "alone experience," but one I shared with the woman I loved. Not long afterward, I experienced its opposite, and, unprepared for this test, I received a deep wound to my soul. Mystics call this the "Fisher Wound." My lifelong goal was hence set at twenty: to find again the Wholeness I briefly knew, and, at the same time, to find the Healing I needed for the wounds to my soul. This is the Holy Grail Quest; the Grail is the only thing which heals such wounds.

From ages twenty to twenty-nine, I sought the Grail, but in the *wrong places:* in academic psychology and philosophy. These were the years of my "intellectual quest." In the process, there was a Ph.D. candidacy in psychology, as well as two years of teaching at a state college in Connecticut. One subject, personality theory, had more relevancy for my quest, as it dealt with the depth psychologies of such as Freud and Jung. Later, I explored these *in depth* in the Journey through my own Unconscious.

During the summer of 1970, when I was twenty-eight, I met by "chance" an enlightened master of the Path, named Pierre, in rural France. Pierre seemed to *live* what I briefly experienced at the age of twenty. After one more year of teaching, a year of growing frustration with the narrowness and sterility of academia, I resigned my assistant professorship and "threw myself open" to whatever powers that be that lead one on the Path to Self. Three days after I made this commitment to "the Path," the first mystical school presented itself to me in the form of the "Arica training" of Oscar Ichazo. Following a year with the "Aricans," I pursued more traditional spiritual paths. The teachers and teachings seemed to virtually "present themselves" to me, or I was "led" to them, one after another. The outer side of my Journey was somewhat correlative to the inner side, and I essentially found what I needed at the time. The territories of the inner side are almost indescribable; they can be experienced, but hardly spoken about. As for the outer side, or the traditions I studied and practiced, they were, in roughly this order, as follows (including both "distant" teachers and "person to person" teachers): Arica training—Oscar Ichazo; Sufism—Adnan Sarhan; Tai Chi Chuan (applied Taoism)—William C. C. Chen; Yoga—Swamis Vishnu Devananda, and Satchidananda, Tantra—Sri Bhagwan Rajneesh; Tibetan Buddhism—Chogyam Trungpa; Rimpoche, Kabbala—Rabbis Joseph Gelberman, Zalman Schacter, and Schlomo Carlebach; Jungian analysis in Christian mystical context—Robert Johnson; Incan Indian teachings—Tupacc Amaru; and the *Course in Miracles,* a modern Christian mystical teaching—Doctors "Helen" and "Bill." Besides these ten traditions, there were other teachers who had an influence upon me. Among these were a very enlightened psychiatrist, Dr. Richard Phillips, who told me to "keep a journal;" a Congregationalist minister, the Reverend Jeff Belcher, who was a friend and counselor; a Lutheran pastor, Dr. James Laughlin, who was an unfailing friend and helper in a most difficult time in my life; Dr. Jean Houston, whose very presence has an enlightening effect; and the Reverend John A. Sanford, Episcopal priest and Jungian analyst, who was my "writing therapist" who helped me break a two-year writing block. Other teachers too affected me greatly, even on quite brief meetings, such as Pierre, a mendicant and Christian mystic; the Reverend Stanley Gross, a World War II combat pilot turned priest; and Seung Sahn, a Korean Zen master. Last, but not least, Margie Lee, a gifted artist, was my "cotraveler," as well as "reading aloud editor," during the last two years of my Journey.

The book itself was born in my mind during the summer of 1974, the third year of my Journey. Following a two-year long Dark Night of the Soul, I called upon "the aid" of Christ, Buddha, Lao Tzu, Krishna, Muhammed, and Moses, all at once. A month later, this thought came to me, as recorded in my diary:

My real work is to write my book: *Physicians of the Soul.* It is my work to (1) follow the spiritual path, and (2) write said book (related). It is purity of heart to will one thing.

My first thoughts about the book were these, still in 1974:

The Ways of the Higher Religions—these are certainly "psychologies" of the *whole person*. This is practically nonexistent in either academic psychology, which studies behavior in abstraction, part processes, and sometimes generalizes incorrectly to the whole man—or—in psychoanalysis which studies abnormal and neurotic behavior, and also often generalizes incorrectly to the whole man. The Religions (Ways of Near and Far Eastern Masters of the Soul) were, in a real sense, *psychologies of the whole man.* They knew the Laws of Man and Life in general.

That was how the book came to be. Special thanks to my editor, Richard J. Payne, for his faith and encouragement, and for his advice to "personalize, personalize."

ROBERT M. MAY

Prologue

The Search for Self

THE "Search for Self" is a classic theme in the Western mythological, literary, and spiritual traditions. From Parcival's Quest for the Holy Grail to Goethe's pursuit of value in *Faust*, the theme repeats itself many times. The East had its questors too, from Siddhattha Gotama, who became the Buddha, to Shankara, the author of the *Crest-Jewel of Discrimination*. The Grail seemed at hand at many times in human history and in many different cultures. It is the Grail which can heal the wounded soul.

My old teacher Robert Johnson wrote a little book entitled *HE*, which is all about the Grail Quest. To quote him:

Our story begins with the Grail castle. The Grail castle is in trouble. The Fisher King, the King of the castle, has been wounded. His wounds are so severe that he cannot live, yet he is incapable of dying, he groans, he cries out, he suffers all the time. In fact, the land is in desolation. The cattle do not reproduce, the crops won't grow, knights are killed, children are orphaned, maidens weep, there is mourning everywhere—all because the Fisher King is wounded.[1]

It is not the Fisher King, but the innocent youth Parcival who must make the Quest for healing. The "Fisher King," "Parcival," and even the "Grail castle" are terms for different parts of ourselves. The Fisher King is that part of oneself which has been grievously wounded by some injustice, and we have all suffered grievous injustices in the process of growing up in this world. Parcival is that part of oneself who has the courage and innocence to make the Quest. The Grail castle is the place within us where the Holy Grail (true Self) is kept,

1

but the Fisher King in us is unable to touch the Grail because of his wound. We need to call upon the Parcival within us to make the Quest.

This vision of the "Quest for the Holy Grail" nourished Western man's soul for at least a thousand years. Eastern man had his visions of the Quest for Enlightenment as well. There were even those in Western and Eastern history who attained the Grail! These men (or women) became teachers to others on the Path.

What happened to Western man's vision of the Grail in the last hundred years or so? What happened to the soul of Occidental man that the "leading lights" of psychology and psychiatry, the presumed disciplines of the soul or psyche, routinely deny the existence of the human soul? Has the god of "scientific materialism" so thoroughly corrupted modern man? Have the materialistic philosophies of such latter nineteenth-century "savants" as Darwin in biology, Helmholtz in physics, Marx in socioeconomics, and Freud in psychology so thoroughly blinded our vision? The ancient Hebrews said the "idolatry blinds the eye." It also kills the soul.

To our age, Sigmund Freud is almost synonymous with "psychology," although he himself was not a psychologist or psychiatrist, but a neurologist, thoroughly imbued with the scientific materialism of his day, which would reduce hysterical neuroses to "brain lesions" and the like. Freud did break away from the dominant materialism of his time sufficiently to discover the very real realm of *unconscious mental life*, which he called "the repressed." His psychoanalytic method gave some hope of "uncovering" these repressions and recovering for the ego some measure of its lost control. His discoveries notwithstanding, Freud never gave up his "project for a scientific psychology," with its biological reductionist bias. This is reflected in Freud's view of the ego itself, which he considers a realm of the "id." The "id" is the inherited, the biological, that which is present at birth, above all, the somatic instincts, such as sexuality, aggression, hunger, thirst, pain avoidance, and tension reduction. Originally, according to Freud, "everything was id." "Id" is the Latin word for "it." The "id" is not yet a person, but merely an organism, seething with excitations seeking discharge. How can an ego arise from the id? Freud states:

Under the influence of the real external world which surrounds us, one portion of the id has undergone a special development. From what was originally a cortical layer, provided with organs for receiving stimulation, a special organization has arisen which henceforward acts as intermediary between the id and the external world. This region of our mental life has been given the name of ego.[2]

If the ego arises from the id, what Freud calls the "superego" arises from the ego. The superego is the "precipitate" from the long period of socialization of human beings in childhood. It amounts to the "inner parents." These three, then, id, ego, and superego, are all that we are "composed of" in the view of Freudian psychology. But the "really basic" reality is not the ego, but the id. Id is the "energizer" for Freud's theory:

The power of the id expresses the true purpose of the individual organism's life. This consists in the satisfaction of its innate needs.[3]

Do you get the picture? In Freud's psychology, the most influential psychology of the twentieth century, we are basically biological "stuff " in search of bodily satisfaction in a "real," hard, external world. Only this exigency forces the development of an "ego," and social contingencies eventuate in the emergence of a "superego." It is a very neat deterministic system, and it obviously has some truth in it. But there is not much room for real love, or genuine moral values, much less would the spiritual quest be tolerated in such a "system." The experiences of the saints and sages would be "explained away" as cases of "regression to the womb," or some such thing. Real explanation ultimately means biological explanation in the Freudian scheme of things. Yet, this is the psychological thought frame (or some near version of it) of most psychiatrists, clinical psychologists, and social workers of our time. Sure, the "neo-Freudians" emphasize the "role of society" above "mere biology," and the "ego psychologists" grant the ego some "autonomy" in its own right, but they, no more than Freud, believe in, or care about, the ancient quest of the human soul for liberation and enlightenment. To these "lights" of our age, the soul is an "outmoded concept" of a "bygone age." It does not answer to the role call of the Great God Science!

Academic psychology, particularly in its American and Russian versions, is even far worse off than clinical psychology and psychoanalysis. Since the turn of the century, it has been dominated by the behaviorists. The most "notable" American behaviorist of the early twentieth century was John Watson. He and his followers "banished" mind and consciousness from the curriculum of American psychology departments for more than a half century. The hope of William James for a spiritual psychology was replaced with the "Skinner box," the "reinforcement schedule," and the "cumulative recorder." Mind and consciousness were supplanted by "stimulus" and "response." B. F. Skinner, the most important behaviorist of our time, has truly created a "psychology" without a psyche! To Skinnerians, even such Freudian concepts as "id," "ego," and "superego" would be considered "metaphysical fictions." In Russia, Pavlov, and his teachings of "respondent conditioning," became the "orthodoxy" of the Marxists. Our capitalists have not ignored the teachings of Skinner and his "operant conditioning" school of thought.

Europe, in the twentieth century, produced more "humanistic" trends in psychology from existentialism to structuralism. The brilliant Piaget developed his theories of "genetic epistemology" in the quiet dignity of his native Switzerland. Continental European psychology from the Gestaltists to the Piagetians never became as grossly materialistic as the psychology laboratories of the U.S.S.R. and U.S.A. with their strapped-in dogs salivating to the sounds of a bell or albino rats and pigeons pressing bars to obtain the delivery of food pellets. For European psychologists, the human mind's structure and development was a "legitimate issue." The existentialists, such as Boss and Binswanger, even cared about the "phenomenal worlds" of their patients. Real creativity, however, issued forth from the series of "defectors" from the Freudian camp. We will look at three of these, in particular: Adler, Jung, and Rank.

Alfred Adler was Freud's first "defector," who formed his own independent school of thought which he called "individual psychology." Adler's contributions were many, and included such discoveries as the "inferiority complex," "striving for superiority," and "style of life." Whereas Freud considered the id's "pleasure principle" to be the basic motivating force (relegating the ego's "reality principle" to secondary status), Adler said:

In a word, I am convinced that *a person's behavior springs from his idea*. We should not be surprised at this, because our senses do not receive actual facts, but merely a subjective image of them—a reflection of the external world. *Omnia ad opinionem suspensa sunt*. This saying of Seneca's should not be forgotten in psychological investigations. How we interpret the great and important facts of existence depends upon our style of life.[4]

Adler's psychology obviously grants far more significance to the ego, and its "ideas," as a determining force in life than do the Freudians. Adlerian man can do more than simply seek to reduce biological tensions, or even learn, explore, and adapt to society; Adlerian man can create ideas! What's more, he can choose to live by them. One's idea may even override merely biological instincts, the dangers of reality, or even societal rewards and punishments. One's idea of oneself may be based, for example, on the ideals of the Franciscan monk in search of God, or the lonely and dedicated research scientist in search of Truth, or the true artist in search of Beauty. None of these relates directly to "id gratification," nor are they the most "realistic means" of achieving instinctual satisfaction, and sometimes, they may put one in direct confrontation with one's society, as was the case with certain scientists during the Inquisition, or was (and is) the case with well-known writers in Communist countries in this century, etc. These are behaviors guided by ideals. To be sure, however, these ideals are considered by Adler to be "compensations for felt inferiorities" of childhood. The polio victim becomes a track champion, the hard-of-hearing becomes a great composer, and the stutterer overcomes his or her problem by becoming a master orator. "Compensation" is the dynamic of Adlerian psychology, and the ego is the "great compensator." Healthy compensation, in Adler's view, is one that leads to "social interest." Adlerian man reaches beyond neurotic selfishness to social fellowship. Beyond "social good," however, there is no place to go in Adler's world.

Carl Gustav Jung was by far the most brilliant of Freud's early circle. Freud himself clearly recognized this, and even fancied Jung as his successor. However, due to increasingly wide differences with his old teacher, Jung resigned his presidency of the International Psychoanalytical Association. This break with Freud precipitated Jung's own "confrontation with the unconscious," as he calls it in his autobiography, *Memories, Dreams, Reflections*. For the next several years, Jung followed the Inward Journey where it led him. He emerged from it with an immensely enriched conception of the human psyche. The soul was rediscovered, one might say, by Dr. Jung in the years of his Night Sea Journey. He also discovered the "archetypes of the collective unconscious." These racial archetypes relate to the mythologies of all times and cultures, and include such inner figures as the anima, the animus, the wise man, the wise woman, the shadow, and the centralizing archetype of the Self. Jung says this about the Self:

During those years, between 1918 and 1920, I began to understand that the goal of psychic development is the self. There is no linear evolution; there is only a circumambulation of the self. Uniform development exists, at most, only at the beginning; later, everything points toward the center. This insight gave me stability, and gradually my inner peace returned. I knew that in finding the mandala as an expression of the self I had attained what was for me the ultimate. Perhaps someone else knows more, but not I.[5]

In Jung, the archetype of the Self, well known to all mystical traditions, was rediscovered for psychology and psychiatry. This was no mean achievement, but the fruit of Jung's own five-year-long Inner Journey, as well as his prodigious studies of mythologies. Jung confirmed his findings in his life's work with hundreds of patients and his analyses of thousands of dreams. Jung's psychology is becoming increasingly popular in our time, as can be seen in literature, films, art, etc. Jung's concepts are even slowly making their impact upon the "mental health" professions. But does Jung's "archetypal psycholology" contain the whole truth about the Journey to Healing? Jung says, "Perhaps someone else knows more, but not I."

Otto Rank was the last of the defectors from Freud's "inner circle." Rank protested Freud's determinism, which deprived man of the very qualities which make him human, above all, ". . . the human phenomenon par excellence, the individual will."[6] Rank also opposed Freud's reductionism, which would reduce artistic creativity to "sexual sublimation." Rank claimed that there is a distinct "artistic type" who differs in fundamental ways from the "neurotic" and the "normal." Rank made the interesting observation that men everywhere seek what is greater than themselves; i.e., salvation: "Freud sees it in sex, Adler in social fellowship, and Jung in racial collectivity."[7] All of these, Rank noted, fell short of the "cosmic unity" that the man of antiquity knew and expressed in his religions but that modern man has lost, a loss that accounts for the widespread malaise of neurosis.

Perhaps Rank intuited the Cosmic Conscious or Spiritual Rebirth experience of the mystics and masters reported in mankind's religious scriptures, from the "burning bush" episode in Moses' life to the "descent of the holy dove" in the account of Jesus' baptism, to the "enlightenment" of the Buddha under the Bodhi tree. It is to these *physicians of the soul* that we will turn in our search for a truly spiritual psychology, a "science of the soul."[8]

NOTES

1. Robert Johnson, *HE*, Harper & Row, New York, 1977, p. 8.
2. Sigmund Freud, *An Outline of Psychoanalysis*, W. W. Norton, New York, 1940, p. 15.
3. *Ibid.*, p. 19
4. Alfred Adler, *Social Interest*, Capricorn Books, New York, 1964, p. 19. ("Omnia ad opinionem suspensa sunt" means "Everything depends upon opinion.")

5. C. G. Jung, *Memories, Dreams, Reflections*, Vintage Books, Random House, New York, 1963, pp. 196–197.

6. Otto Rank, *Beyond Psychology*, Dover Publications, New York, 1958, p. 34.

7. *Ibid.*, pp. 36–37.

8. "Psychology" is an ancient Greek word which means "the study of the soul." The Greek word "psyche," translated "soul," means "inner essence" or "inner self." The closest Hebrew equivalent to this concept is the term, "Nephesh," which means "that which breathes or has life." The Hindus' soul concept was "Atman," which is usually translated "Self." Every culture of mankind has some version of the soul idea. American Indians believed that all living beings have a soul, or "manitou," which is also their word for the Supreme Being, the "Great Manitou."

Chapter One

Lao Tzu, the Old Sage

THE great philosopher and moralist Confucius, who lived in China of the sixth century B.C., came to Honan province to consult with his contemporary, the Old Sage, Lao Tzu, who was the historian and keeper of the secret archives of the Chou Court, on matters of ritual, and to speak with him about the heroes of old. Lao Tzu had this to say to Confucius:

All of those of whom you speak long since mouldered away with their bones. Only their words remain. When a capable man's time comes, he rises, if it does not, then he just wanders wearily around. I have heard that good merchants keep their goods buried deeply to make it look as if they had none and that a superior man whose character is perfected will feign stupidity. Give up, sir, your many wishes, mannerisms, and extravagant claims. They won't do you any good, sir! That's all I have to tell you.

Confucius went off and said to his students: I know that birds can fly and fish can swim and beasts can run. Snares can be set for things that run, nets for those that swim and arrows for whatever flies. But dragons! I shall never know how they ride wind and cloud into the sky. Today I saw Lao Tzu. What a dragon![1]

Lao Tzu lived a humble life in Honan province. When he retired, he decided to leave for parts unknown. When he reached the frontier, as legend has it,[2] the border official, Yin Hsi, would not allow Lao Tzu to pass until he had written a book for posterity. Lao Tzu wrote a book of his wisdom in the form of short aphorisms, eighty-one in number, in just over 5,000 words, and then he went away, never to be seen again. What he left, the *Tao Te Ching*, or "The Way of Life," became the sacred scriptures of Taoism, a major influence on Ch'an

(Zen) Buddhism, and one of the seminal masterpieces of all religious literature. Today, the *Tao Te Ching* is translated into almost as many different languages as the *Bible*.

One subject permeates the *Tao Te Ching* and that is what Lao Tzu calls the *Tao*. It is a word that is as indefinable as God, and it is, in fact, used in similar ways. For Lao Tzu the essence of existence is the Tao, as for Moses and Jesus it is God (YHWH). This is what Lao Tzu says about the Tao (I take the liberty of giving the poems names; Lao Tzu merely numbered them):

The Eternal Tao (I)

The Tao that can be expressed is not the eternal Tao;
The name that can be defined is not the unchanging name.

Non-existence is called the antecedent of heaven and earth;

Existence is the mother of all things.

From eternal non-existence we clearly see the apparent distinctions.

These two are the same in source and become different when manifested.

This sameness is called profundity. Infinite profundity is the gate whence comes the beginnings of all parts of the Universe.

"The Tao that can be expressed is not the eternal Tao." One thinks of the prohibition against the pronunciation of the divine Name, YHWH, in the Jewish tradition. The second commandment, which forbids idolatry, or the making of "graven images," makes the same point. The modern philosopher Ludwig Wittgenstein put it as follows: "What we cannot speak about we must pass over in silence."[3]

"Nonexistence is called the antecedent of heaven and earth . . . . " This is the Taoist expression of the Mystery of the Source of the Universe. In the Hebrew mystical Kabbala, the highest form of the Godhead is known as "Ain," which is translated "Void." To scientific astronomy for which the evidence points overwhelmingly to the "Big Bang" theory of the origin of the Universe, as well as for metaphysical and religious thought, the "brute fact" stands: we are a *creation ex nihilo*. The astronomer Robert Jastrow states:

Now we see how the astronomical evidence leads to a biblical view of the origin of the world. The details differ, but the essential elements in the astronomical and biblical accounts of Genesis are the same: the chain of events leading to man commenced suddenly and sharply at a definite moment in time, in a flash of light and energy.[4]

From nothing did everything arise. What kind of *no thing*? We need only look around us to conclude: a *no thing* of extraordinary creativity! "His" thought gives birth to an expanding Universe of billions of stars, each of these of immense size, power, and longevity. Perhaps among the countless billions of stars of the known Universe are many that have developed planetary systems, and among these some which have evolved higher forms of life, even civilizations. I personally believe that our Universe is teeming with life, some as highly subtle and complex as human beings, who are, in our Judeo-Christian tradition, said to be created in the Divine image. Who or What is the Source of such a Living Universe? Lao Tzu calls this the Tao, and views it in a somewhat impersonal sense. Moses was vouchsafed the name: "I Am That I Am." Jesus spoke of the Source of Existence as "Abba," or "Father." Our English word "God" comes from the German root word which means "Depth." Once I consulted the *I Ching*, the ancient Chinese "Book of Changes," and "asked" the question, "What is God?" The "reply" (what the random coin tosses revealed) was: a "Well" and an "Abyss."

Does this Cosmological Mystery of the origin of existence in nonexistence have relevance for our individual lives? I think so. If our true origin is God or Tao, and we have fallen into "Exile" through "eating of the Tree of Knowledge of Good and Evil," thus forming a limited self-concept, and losing contact with true Self, then Salvation is the regaining of this connection with the Source of our being. The Buddhists of the Rinzai school have a Koan (riddle) which is: "What was my Original Face before my parents were born?" The student meditates upon this Koan day after day until he or she receives an "answer." This "answer" may not even be in the form of words or images; it may just be a state of *awareness*. It is certainly nothing that the rational intellect can conceive of. The intellect tells us that we did not exist before our parents were born, and that there is no possible answer to such a question. But the intuitive mind and soul has an intelligence and wisdom of its own. It is to these deeper sources that the meditative experience leads.

An "experiment" for you as "irrational" as it seems: Sit for fifteen minutes a day, for three days in a row, and meditate on the "Original Face" Koan. When your mind wanders, just bring it back to the question: "What was my Original Face before my parents were born?" Don't "think about it," or "ratiocinate," or "philosophize," or "introspect." Introspection is not meditation. Meditation is not "doing" but "nondoing." It is entering the state of pure awareness. In the case of the "Original Face" Koan, await an answer. It will come in due time from your Deep Unconscious. It may be a word, image, or altered state of consciousness that is different from your usual ego consciousness in an indefinable way. You may experience in this way something of the *no thing* which preceded existence. Lao Tzu called this the Tao.

Teaching without Words (II)

When all in the world understand beauty to be beautiful, then ugliness exists.

When all understand goodness to be good, then evil exists.

Thus existence suggests non-existence;

Easy gives rise to difficult;

Short is derived from long by comparison;

Low is distinguished from high by position;

Resonance harmonizes sound;

After follows before.

Therefore the Sage carries on his business without action, and gives his teaching without words

Lao Tzu's poem suggests the post-Exile condition of human beings. Prior to the Exile, Adam (Adam = "man" in Hebrew) did not know of any distinctions. He lived in the original state of Unity. When he ate of the Tree of Knowledge of Good and Evil proffered him by the serpent, the world became split and divided into "pairs of opposites." We pay a heavy price for "beauty and goodness," namely, "ugliness and evil!"

All wars in history tend to be the struggle to defend what one side considers "good" against the "enemy" who is adjudged "evil." It is, doubtless, what the Crusaders had in mind in their war to win back the Holy Land from the Saracen "infidel." The Moslem defender viewed the Christian invader as "infidel" as well. The two sides saw "the enemy" as each other. This same thing is seen in its most brutal terms in history, in the attempt in this century of the Nazis to first defame, and then exterminate, their "arch enemy" the Jew. What was "Aryan" was seen in terms of "goodness" and "light" and what was "Jewish" was associated with "darkness" and "evil." When you make these kinds of distinctions, the unthinkable becomes the actual! On the other hand, there is the Jewish correlative tendency to project the Shadow as well, e.g., on the "goyim." Shadow projections tend to be reciprocal. Capitalists see Communists as the "archenemy"; Communists see Capitalists as "imperialist war mongers." Mass murder can be the result of such mutual Shadow projections. This dividing of people and things into opposites is not indigenous to any group or people; we are all heirs to the universal disease of splitting the original unity into duality. C. G. Jung spoke about the division that happens within us in terms of the "ego" and "Shadow." The ego, or conscious self, is all that *we think we are* and aspire to be; the Shadow is all that is repressed and rejected and denied about ourselves. The Shadow, unconscious in most people, tends to be projected on some "enemy," whether the enemy be individual or collective. Facing the Shadow side of ourselves is the first step in the Inner Path following the break-down of the "persona," or mask personality. Ego and Shadow is like the story of Dr. Jekyll and Mr. Hyde. Dr. Jekyll is the upstanding doctor and good citizen, liked and admired by all. He is the "daytime" personality (he is the conscious self). Mr. Hyde comes out "at night" (alluding to the unconscious).

We are all Dr. Jekyll and we are all Mr. Hyde. Most of us identify with our Dr. Jekyll side and remain unaware of the Mr. Hyde who lurks within. It is the almost universal human tendency to "cast one's Shadow." That is, the Shadow side of ourselves tends to be projected upon others, usually quite unconsciously. Do you have an "enemy" whom you just loathe? I think we all do beginning sometime in childhood past the age of innocence. When I was seven or eight years old, in summer camp I had such an "enemy," and his name was "Schneck." I hated his guts! Later in life, at the age of twenty-nine, I met this "fellow" again while taking the Arica training in the person of someone named "Eckhart." I found him so "negative" a fellow. Later, in the "encounterlike" sessions of the Arica training, I discovered that I embodied the very same thing to him, as he did to me. What a revelation of mutual Shadow projection! What "Schneck" and "Eckhart" represented to my psyche was the perfect projection foil for my own unconscious Shadow (and I to them apparently). At a later point in my Journey, I experienced the Shadow more directly in terms of a "dark beast" in a dream. Shakespeares's "Caliban" in *The Tempest* is a literary Shadow figure. The recognition and integration of the Shadow side of oneself, and the concomitant withdrawal of projections, is the first, and one of the most difficult, moral barriers of the Inner Journey. It is an essen-tial step in the Alchemy of regaining one's lost Wholeness.

Is this the "acceptance of evil," you are asking? On the contrary, the failure to take responsibility for one's own Shadow is the psychic force behind the bloodshed and evil of human history. If the "pure Aryan"

Nazis had accepted and assimilated the "Jewish side" of themselves, the bloodiest chapter in human history might have been avoided. If the Southern bigot of the heyday of the Ku Klux Klan could have realized the "black side" of himself, how many murders and lynchings would have been averted! And likewise with individual hate, revenge, and murder. These are the social (or should I say antisocial?) consequences of the nonassimilation of the Shadow. The personal consequences are as weighty. Prior to the integration of the Shadow, one lives in inner warfare between the "good" and the "bad" sides of oneself. This inner warfare, if too overwhelming, is known in psychological parlance as "neurosis." We may succeed in suppressing, or even repressing, our Shadow side, but it expresses itself in all manner of symptoms and manifestations from phobias and anxiety attacks to psychosomatic disorders such as hives and asthma, and everything in between. The Freudian psychologist seems content to make conscious to the ego of his patient his unconscious urges, and help strengthen the patient's ego in keeping these impulses under control. The Jungian goes one great step beyond this, and actually leads his patient in the Alchemical process of integrating and assimilating the Shadow side. This is the crucial first stage on the Journey to Wholeness. This integration of the light and dark is perfectly symbolized in the Taoist "Tai Chi" symbol.

What does it mean to integrate your Shadow side? Integration is not acting out. If your Shadow contains murderous or lascivious elements, it does not mean that you will become a murderer or a rapist when you integrate your Shadow. It may mean, however, that you may now be able, for the very first time in your adult life, to express healthy aggression that you were unable to express before, so blocked were you in your healthy aggressiveness, and it does mean you may become unblocked and freer in your sexual life, so repressed were you in your healthy sexuality, and so on. You see, when the normal instincts are long repressed, they become "monsters." They usually form a symbolic image figure, generally of the same sex as we are, which Jung called the "Shadow." Freud would have merely called this "the repressed"; and the lifting of repressions, and the strengthening of the ego, is the beginning of "cure" in the Freudian sense. Another step beyond this is the integration of the Shadow with the more conscious side of ourselves which both Freud and Jung called the "ego." This integration process is the "minor work" of the inner path, and results in a wholeness not before experienced (at least not since the age of original innocence in early childhood). This new wholeness may be experienced in symbolic forms by the psyche, for example, as a "white stone." Because of the possibility of integration, both Jung and the Alchemists said that the Shadow contains "gold." This "gold" is the potential for the reintegration of the two sides of ourselves leading to wholeness. No longer is the world divided into "beautiful" and "ugly," "good" and "bad"; it has become Whole again. The "Tao" is now found even in the lowliest of things when the opposites have embraced each other.

Lao Tzu says that the Sage conducts himself "without action" and "gives his teaching without words." This is hard to understand except if you have met someone like that. The most enlightened one I have ever known was a wandering mendicant named Pierre whom I met in rural France. He embodied this idea of "teaching without words." I actually met Pierre while driving along the road in rural France with my friend, John, who is a photographer. We were overwhelmed by the beauty of the French countryside. As we drove along, we saw a most beautiful dark-haired young woman, standing by the road, hitching a ride. We stopped, and out from behind a bush came the most Christlike man I have ever met in my life; barefoot, and tattered, but shining with a certain inner light which was unmistakable. He said very little during the twenty-four hours that we spent together, and what little he did say was in French, and my French was rudimentary to say the least. Yet, I learned more of the greatest value to me from the look of Pierre's eyes, and his presence, than I learned in more than a decade's study of "academic psychology" which led me to Ph.D. candidacy. This man's Christlike being I shall never forget. This single meeting was enough to start me out on a Journey of a lifetime. Never have I met a higher master than Pierre; one who "gives his teaching without words."

The Mystic Mother (VI)

"The valley and the Spirit never die."
They form what is called the Mystic Mother,
From whose gate comes the origin of heaven and earth.
This (the origin) seems to endure.
In use it can never be exhausted.

This poem of Lao Tzu's makes me think of the Virgin Mary in our Western tradition who is regarded in Christianity as "the mother of God." I discovered, one fall day in Central Park in New York a few years ago, that the Mystic Mother can be interceded with in prayer, as in the Rosary: "Hail Mary, full of Grace, the Lord is with thee; blessed art thou among women, and blessed is the fruit of thy womb, Jesus."

Walking through the park that day, I repeated the Rosary to myself again and again. To my astonishment, I had a vision of the "birth" of a "fur-covered ball" from Mother Earth herself. In the vision, I "peeled off" the "fur," and it revealed a new-born baby. The baby transformed into a white stone, and then into a symbol of the Holy Grail. What I experienced so overwhelmed me emotionally for the next few weeks, I cannot describe it. Jungians might speak of the "Self "; the Christian mystics would speak of the "Christ."

A couple of years later, following a period of dark tribulation, I experienced the intercession of the Mystic Mother in another form. I encountered Kwan Yin, the far-Eastern Bodhisattva of Universal Compassion, through the person of a bisexual woman whom I will call "J" who said the words, "I love you," and meant them, in this dark time in my life. "J's" love vouchsafed me a vision of Kwan Yin, the lifegiver. "J" wrote something very beautiful to me, the last line of Dante's *Divine Comedy*: "The Love that moves the sun and other stars."[5] From such as Kwan Yin and the Virgin Mary, perhaps two versions of the same archetype, we can experience this *healing love*. It can also be expressed through people who love us.

In the Kabbala, the feminine aspect of the Divine is known as the "Shekhinah." *She* is the Creation itself, or "matter," which comes from the same root word as "mother." The material universe, in the eyes of the Kabbalists, is not "dead matter," or "blind atoms," but the *very embodiment of God*. Modern physics itself, as opposed to the atomism and materialism which dates from ancient Greece through the nineteenth century, is not really that far from the mystical view of the Kabbalists, judging from the writings of physicists such as Fritjof of Capra, author of *The Tao of Physics*. To quote Capra:

Relativity theory has had a profound influence on our picture of matter by forcing us to modify our concept of a particle in an essential way. In classic physics, the mass of an object had always been associated with an indestructible material substance, with some "stuff " of which all things were thought to be made. Relativity theory showed that mass has nothing to do with any substance, but it is a form of energy. Energy, however, is a dynamic quantity associated with activity, or with processes. The fact that the mass of a particle is equivalent to a certain amount of energy means that the particle can no longer be seen as a static object, but has to be conceived of as a dynamic pattern, a process involving the energy which manifests itself as the particle mass.[6]

$E = MC^2$, the creation of matter from pure energy, this is the legacy of the Einsteinian physics of the twentieth century. What, indeed, we may ask is "pure energy"? The physicist Capra turns to the metaphor of the "cosmic dance" which finds expression in Hinduism. The Hindus view this world as the manifestation of the dancing god, Shiva. It is Shiva's "dance" which sustains the Appearance of a Material Universe. This is, in truth, closer to the view of modern physics than it is to the older view of "static matter" which dates from Democritus, the ancient Greek atomist, to nineteenth-century classic Newtonian physics. What we take to be a "static piece of matter" is, in reality, a "creation" of our sensory-perceptual apparatus. A *plain little stone* I am looking at consists of a relatively stable configuration on the macroscopic level of a dance of energy at the subatomic level, that, if we could see it, would make the Bolshoi Ballet look like very dull stuff indeed. The concept of this world as "dance" or "song" is not unique to Hinduism. It is to be found in our Judeo-Christian tradition as well, if we investigate beneath the surface. In the original translation for the Aramaic of the Lord's Prayer, the text states: "For Yours is the Kingdom, and the Power and the Song, from Ages to Ages . . . ."[7] God's song, His dance, is the Material Creation. "He" Himself sustains the "existence" of "solid matter." This is a rather different world-view from the usual dualism of Western theology which views Creator and Creation as radically separate and apart (this may have little relation to the world views of either Moses or Jesus). It also differs fundamentally from the materialistic monistic view of "hard matter" as the basic reality. It is a "nondual" view of God and the World as essentially two aspects of One Reality. In the Spiritual, or "energy" aspect, we can speak of "Spirit Father," and in the Earthly, or "material" aspect, we can speak of "Earth Mother." These "two" are, in reality, "Not two." "Not two" is a Zen Koan, I am told. Jesus, in the *Gospel According to Thomas*, also speaks about "making the two one." It is the meaning of the sacred name: YHWH. If you know the Kabbalistic code, it refers to the fact that Spirit and Matter, God and Creation, Shaddai and Shekhinah, Yang and Yin, are "Not two." This is the Cosmic Unity. Pierre Teilhard de Chardin *knew* this when he spoke of "the Diaphany of the Divine at the heart of a glowing Universe . . . ."[8]

The Tao Is like Water (VIII)

The highest goodness is like water. Water is beneficent
to all things but does not contend. It stays in places
    which others despise. Therefore it is near Tao.

In dwelling, think it a good place to live;
In feeling, make the heart deep; In friendship, keep on good terms
with men; In words, have confidence;

In ruling, abide in good order;
In business, take things easy;
In motion, make use of the opportunity.
Since there is no contention, there is no blame.

In this, and in many other places, Lao Tzu uses the metaphor of
water for the Tao. In keeping with this metaphor, the American
orientalist Alan Watts entitled the last book of his life, *Tao: the Watercourse Way*. Watts says that "Tao is the flowing course of nature and
the universe . . . and water is its eloquent metaphor."[9] He goes on
to say that we can never find an "aesthetic mistake" in water, from the
flowing of a mountain stream, to the dashing of waves upon a beach,
to the merest trickle of rainwater on a rooftop. It is always *just right*.
But artificial things and activities from "business" to "baseball," while
they may be interesting for a while, would become a Mephistophelian
hell if they went on and on without cease. Faust found this out in
Goethe's classic. There is something about human artifice which goes
"against the grain" of the human soul. But can the ocean bore you, or
a lake, or a river? I can return many times to the Cove in La Jolla,
California, and walk along the "Coast walk," or just sit on a rock and
watch the ocean waves coming in and out; it never bores me. It is a
refreshment to my soul. H. D. Thoreau spent two years by his little
Walden Pond in rapt enthusiasm as anyone who reads his book,
Walden, can plainly see. I visited Walden Pond for two summers in a
row, and it is just an ordinary little pond. In Herman Hesse's novel, *Siddhartha*, the protagonist finds his enlightenment, after many
years of previous searching in everything from sexual pleasures to
ascetic disciplines, by working as a riverman, crossing back and forth
the river, day after day, month after month, year after year, until he
became at one with the river, and the All. To become waterlike is to
become attuned to the Tao.

The Tai Chi "dance" which was invented by the Taoist monk
Chang San-fung 1,000 years ago during the Sung dynasty in China,[10]
is indeed "waterlike" in its continuous and flowing motion. Tai Chi is
one of those Oriental arts, like Sumi painting, calligraphy, flower
arrangement, etc., in which a person strives for "oneness with nature." Tai Chi is "applied Taoism" at its best. It is very much like a
flowing stream in its naturalness and effortlessness. It seems "easy,"
but this kind of "easiness" is very difficult to attain, and takes many
years of practice. It eventually becomes an exercise not so much in
"doing" as in "nondoing." At the point at which you are not so much

moving of your own effort as you are being "moved by" the Tao, the Tai Chi art gains its uncanny power. Like water, it can be as peaceful as a mountain lake or as forceful as a tidal wave! At its best, it is "near Tao."

Lao Tzu asks his reader to apply the "Tao principle" to all aspects of his life. He advises you to "dwell in the Tao," to "make your heart deep in it," to "allow the Tao to speak through you," etc. This egolessness of which Lao Tzu speaks is paradoxically the true meaning of confidence. It reminds me of what Jesus said to his disciples about not worrying about what to say, but rather to let the "Spirit of the Father" speak through them. In my experience as a college teacher, I found that the less I worried about prepared notes and the more I simply said "whatever came into my head," the better my lectures were. This applies to writing, too, and to just about any creative activity. There is the necessity of preparation, true, but the creative act takes place spontaneously. Creativity is to allow the Greater Unconscious to express itself. Taoists call this, *P'u*, the "Uncarved Block."

Lao Tzu says an interesting thing in his last line: "Since there is no contention, there is no blame." Our "modern" Western world of the twentieth century is certainly full of contention on all levels, between nations, between groups in the same nation, between individuals, and within individuals; our world is one of continual and nerve-wracking contention leading all the way from world wars to nervous breakdowns! Our Capitalist "free enterprise" system even recommends it: "Competition is the American way." Not that the Communists believe in noncontention either; their very world view is based upon the idea of "class struggle" and "dialectics" which implies struggle and contention at all levels of nature from animals competing for the same food supply to social classes competing for the means of survival. Mao Tse Tung, the spirit behind the Chinese Communist revolution, favored "continuous revolution." Struggle without end! Mao Tse Tung's predecessor in the history of ideas, Lao Tzu, preached quite a different idea: noncontention! When you do not contend, no one will blame you, and you can go about your business in peace. If individuals and nations were to follow this, we would live in a far happier and more peaceful world.

What about the inner world of the psyche? How does noncontention apply here? Neurosis, as I have said earlier, is a state of continuous inner warfare within ourselves. Ego versus id, superego versus ego, and superego versus id, the war rages on in the Freudian tripartite system of psychodynamics. There is more hope in the Jungian system of finding the *deep center*, or the Self, which is the "still point in a turning world." This is the point of noncontention where one can *let be*, or to say it another way, "let go, and let God."

The Use of Non-Existence (XI)

Thirty spokes unite in one nave,
And because of the part where nothing exists we have the
use of the carriage wheel.

Clay is moulded into vessels,
And because of the space where nothing exists we are able
to use them as vessels.

Doors and windows are cut out in the walls of a house,
And because they are empty space, we are able to use them.

Therefore, on the one hand we have the benefit of existence,
and, on the other, we make use of non-existence.

This poem of Lao Tzu's is reminiscent of the Buddhist teaching about form and emptiness: "Form is emptiness, and emptiness is form." To consciously realize this is to attain "satori" or "awakening." I experienced something of this while driving all day long through Canada with a Chinese friend, Paul. We were talking and talking endlessly on "philosophical subjects" such as the "mind-body problem" and the "nature of reality," and the like, when we both simultaneously *broke through* to a state of mutual satori in which we realized that all the "boundaries" and "concepts" through which we usually view the world were merely mental fictions created by our egos. All we saw was form and emptiness, emptiness and form. It was a great joy! In this state, we drove all the way to Cambridge, Massachusetts, to Harvard University where we walked around laughing and laughing at all the pretensions of academia. Then we drove home to Connecticut where we both taught at a state college, and returned also to the ego consciousness of subject-object. Our satori was just for the day.

The Western world, it can be said, emphasizes the value of thought and ratiocination: look at the history of philosophy, theology, and science dating back to the ancient Greeks. It is a history of endless rational and intellectual disputation on what is the "nature of reality." The empiricism of Aristotle and the idealism of Plato were the two poles in this history of Western ratiocinative thought. The Eastern world, throughout its history, has valued more than the "thought" the "emptiness" in which the thoughts took place. This very emptiness is enlightenment in the Zen Buddhist and the Taoist sense. A Zen story may illustrate this:

A great professor visited a humble Zen master in his small hut in the mountains in search of enlightenment. The Zen master offered the professor a cup of tea. While the professor held the cup, the Zen master poured the tea, but he kept pouring, and did not stop, until the tea had spilled all over the professor's clothing and the floor. The professor was puzzled about this strange behavior. The Zen master said, "How can you come to me in quest of enlightenment when your head is already so full of opinions? There is no room to add anything. Empty yourself first, and then come back to see me."[11]

The anonymous author of the Christian mystical classic *The Cloud of Unknowing* must have had something very similar in mind when he exhorted his reader:

Let go of this "everywhere" and this "everything" in exchange for this "nowhere" and this "nothing." Never mind if you cannot fathom this nothing, for I love it surely so much the better. It is so worthwhile in itself that no thinking about it will do it justice.[12]

Both the humble Zen master and the author of *The Cloud of Unknowing* understood the same mystery of "emptiness" of which Lao Tzu speaks in his poem. It is the predecessor to spiritual peace.

He Who Attains the Tao (XVI)

Attain to the goal of absolute vacuity;
Keep to the state of perfect peace.
All things come into existence,
And thence we see them return.
Look at the things that have been flourishing;
Each goes back to its origin.
Going back to the origin is called peace;
It means reversion to destiny.
Reversion to destiny is called eternity.
He who knows eternity is called enlightened.
He who does not know eternity is running blindly into miseries.
Knowing eternity is all-embracing.
Being all-embracing he can attain magnanimity.
Being magnanimous he can attain omnipresence.
Being omnipresent he can attain Tao.
He who attains Tao is everlasting.
Though his body may decay he never perishes.

Lao Tzu is speaking of the enlightened ones who have attained what he calls "absolute vacuity." They are empty of ego, and thus can see through the dark "cloud of unknowing" to the spiritual light which is the true giver of peace. It is here that you go back to "the origin" and revert to your destiny. It is here that you leave the ways of your worldly conditioning. I recall, in the beautiful motion picture about St. Francis of Assisi, *Brother Sun, Sister Moon*, when Francis, who had attained enlightenment and had become a child of God, took off all his clothes, and handed them to his rich merchant father, and said, "these are yours." He walked out of the city into the woods to the amazement of all, including his parents, and the bishop to whom his father had brought him for judgment (Francis had given away a great deal of his father's merchandise to the poor). This is what it is like to return to your origin and revert to your destiny! Francis went on to build a new monastic order which swept through Europe reviving the simpler traditions of early Christianity.

The last stanza of the poem is remarkable in its similarities to the sayings of Jesus. Lao Tzu says that "He who attains the Tao is everlasting/Though his body may decay he never perishes." Jesus said "He who believes in me, though he die, yet shall he live."[13]

Wholeness (XXVIII)

He who knows the masculine and yet keeps to the feminine
Will become a channel drawing all the world toward it;
Being a channel of the world, he will not be severed from the eternal
    virtue,
And then he can return again to the state of infancy.
He who knows the white and yet keeps to the black
Will become a standard to the world;
Being the standard of the world, with him eternal virtue will never falter,
And then he can return again to the absolute.
He who knows honour and yet keeps to humility
Will become a valley of the world, with him eternal virtue will be complete,
And then he can return again to wholeness.
Wholeness, when divided, will make vessels of utility;
These when employed by the Sage will become officials and chiefs.
However, for a great function no discrimination is needed.

"He who knows the masculine and yet keeps to the feminine. . . ." Lao Tzu is speaking to the necessity for the male to come to consciousness of his hidden or inner feminine side if he is to come to wholeness (analogously for the woman and her inner masculine side). The Jungians speak of the feminine in the unconscious of a male as the "anima." *She* is always personified and is usually known in projection as "the woman we fall in love with at first sight." This goes far beyond merely sexual attraction; it is a numinous experience as all archetypal experiences are. It is an experience of the soul.

Let me speak of some of my own experiences of the anima; they may remind you of yours. I think my first anima figure, in adolescence, was Joan Baez (I have vague reminiscences of the anima in early childhood). She represented the *mysterious feminine* to me. Margaret was my first love. We shared an experience of the Holy Grail when we were twenty. Ours was the true love of which the poets speak. It lasted for one blessed summer of 1962. *I shall never forget.* Ten years passed before I met another "anima female" in the person of Gabrielle, who was a dancer. She was, to me, awesomely beautiful. I saw Gabrielle for the very first time in a restaurant in San Francisco, and I just instantly "flipped out." That was at age thirty. It was not until more than two years later, while I was in analysis with Robert Johnson (the author of *HE* and *SHE*), that I came to consciousness of the *anima within.* This is quite a hard thing to come to consciousness of, and it usually follows the moral barrier of Shadow integration. When you come to know your own inner feminine side (or correspondingly in the woman, the inner masculine side), it is quite an extraordinary thing. *She* is the "mediator," as it were, between your ego and the Greater Unconscious. Whereas the Holy Sage can open the door, the Inner Maiden can lead you all the way to the Holy of Holies. In the *Divine Comedy* of Dante Alighieri, when Virgil bowed out as a guide, Beatrice "descended from heaven" (arose from the Unconscious) to guide Dante on the rest of the Journey to the Heavenly Jerusalem. This is an allegory of the Journey to Self.

While I was in analysis with Robert Johnson, and was coming to consciousness of the anima within, an extraordinary synchronicity took place. I heard for the first time from Gabrielle, the dancer from San Francisco, who was for me the "anima without." She had never written to me before, nor had we any contact for a couple of years. This is Gabrielle's letter (it was written on green paper—the color of love!):

Dearest Bob,

The path of the warrior is a lonely one until we totally surrender to the moving spirit.

Love my brother and thank you for sharing your process with me. I left the school over a year ago and after a period of total disintegration and illness embraced and nurtured my broken spirit.

Back on the souls of my feet again dancing and singing with humanity. A new-age nun of the church but not in the church happy to have a friend in San Diego willing to share—that is what you must do—share—giving people the space to be more and more of who they are. Stay in action, my friend. Our stay is so brief, our capacity so enormous.

Recommend the SETH books and a lovely little book TO A DANCING GOD—Sam Keen.

Being mother to my little Zen master, travelling working giving readings growing changing praying cause deep down I know we are truly one and our common link is our uniqueness.

Love and Peace,
Gabrielle

This letter from Gabrielle, who had never written me before (although I had written her), truly overwhelmed me. This synchronicity of inner/outer anima called forth in me the "hero image." I was filled with images of Sir Lancelot of the Lake, Samurai warriors, American Indian war chiefs, and the like. I wanted to become a "true Knight . . . deserving of the hand of the fair maiden!" It is incredible how closely linked are the anima and animus archetypes in the psyches of both male and female alike. One will surely arouse the other into awakening. For the male, where the Holy Sage leaves off (Robert Johnson who is a monk and analyst was a Holy Sage figure to me), the Holy Maiden appears to lead you on your way.

Corresponding in function to the anima in the male is what Jung calls the "animus" or inner male figure in the female psyche. I believe that both anima and animus exist within both men and women, but in differing relations to the ego. The anima in the male is his "dearly beloved"; his soul figure. The animus in the female is her "knight in shining armor" who will awaken her from her sleep, as in the tale of *Sleeping Beauty. He* is a spirit figure. Yet, the male relates to the animus too in terms of the "hero" with whom he identifies. And, in the opinion of some, the anima is the soul figure in women as well as men. The soul, since the time of the ancient Greek myths, has been pictured as a maiden. The spirit, on the other hand, has been portrayed as a masculine potency.

I have spoken of the anima already, and some anima figures of mine, so let me give some examples of animus figures in the popular culture. They are obvious and many. Children's literature, television, and movies seem to be the first place where these archetypal figures appear. The rebirth of the old comic book hero, Superman, in the recent film is one such example. Do you recall the "flight" that Superman took Lois Lane on through the evening sky? It was pure "magic." It connoted somewhat of the feeling of awe which the female feels toward her "animus figure." The immense popularity of the motion picture, *Billy Jack,* about the half-breed American Indian Vietnam veteran who comes home to take on the whole town and all its toughs and villains at once, is explainable in terms of animus numinosity. Older examples of animus figures in world literature include Sir Lancelot, Robin Hood, and Tarzan.

"And then he can return to the state of infancy." Does Lao Tzu mean infancy literally? Jesus also said, "Unless you become converted and become as little children, you will not enter the Kingdom of Heaven." Notice that Jesus does not say that you must become little children, but you must become "as little children." I think that what both Jesus and Lao Tzu had in mind by the words "infancy" and "little children" is the state of Original Wholeness and Innocence that we have all experienced once, and inevitably lose in the course of the "socialization process." I have a photograph of myself at two years of age, sitting on a hill, holding a large ball. It is the "picture of wholeness."

The state of Original Wholeness is what we have all lost in "the Fall" and subsequent "Exile," however we may interpret this to mean. Original Wholeness was the Edenic state of man before he ate of the "Tree of Knowledge of Good and Evil" and fell from Grace. Man now knows the difference between good and evil, but in gaining this, he has become split from Original Unity and loses his Innocence. Man now walks the earth aware of his "nakedness" and in "shame." It is an exceedingly painful state, this state of Exile, and we try to cover it up in many ways from drugs and alcohol to achievement and worldly success to the search for pleasure. But, for some, the Exile is so horribly painful that they are compelled to "enter the Path." And they find that they must make the most difficult Journey in the world from the state of "Exile" to what St. John called the "Heavenly Jerusalem." Really speaking, the Garden of Eden and the Heavenly Jerusalem are the same, but with one difference: the Garden of Eden is the place of Unconscious Wholeness, the world of early childhood; the Heavenly Jerusalem is the place of Conscious Wholeness, the realm of the enlightened adult. *Consciousness* is the crucial difference. It seems that in order to attain consciousness in the first place (to attain an ego), it is man's destiny to eat of the fruit of the "forbidden tree." In so doing, Original Wholeness is inevitably lost. It is lost for the sake of developing an "I." The cost is sundering oneself from Original Unity. Most people wander through life like this in Conscious Unwholeness, as Adam did after he left Eden. Some feel "the call," and make the agonizing Journey back. It is no "rose garden path." One passes through trials and tribulations undreamed of by most. The fires of "purgation" are intense indeed! There are many allegories of this Journey in Western literature. One of the best is Dante's *Divine Comedy*. The final vision of Heaven is a fully conscious one; Original Eden was unconscious. It is consciousness we have gained in the process of making the Journey, as the travellers in *The Wizard of Oz* have gained, respectively, their brains, heart, and courage. The Journey, however, has been a circle, and you will be "startled" at first to discover your "Original Face" at the end of the Path. Welcome Home!

Lao Tzu speaks of the one "who knows the white and yet keeps to the black. . . ." Robert Johnson said one day during our work together that "the Christ is light within, darkness without," but "the anti-Christ is light without, darkness within." The *I Ching* says the same thing about peace versus its opposite. "Ta'i," or peace, is Yin, or darkness without, and Yang, or light within. Its opposite, "P'i," or stagnation, is Yang, or light without, and Yin, or darkness within. Is this unclear? It was to me at first. Some examples might clarify it.

Charlatans, "gurus," and false prophets seem to abound in our time. They "promise you the world," and deliver something quite different. They seem to "shine" with the light of self-glorification. An obvious and notorious example was the Reverend Jim Jones who proclaimed himself "Messiah" and even "God" to his followers. He established a "utopia" in Jonestown, Guyana. He was the "beneficent one." Where did he lead his followers? To mass suicide and death. He wore his "white" on the outside, and kept his "black" within—until it manifested itself! A classic "wolf in sheep's clothing," in Jesus's words.

Jones is not the only false prophet of this type by any means; most are still extant. We have the "benevolent and smiling" Reverend Sun Myung Moon, and his "happy" young disciples selling carnations in the streets to increase the empire of their arms manufacturer self-proclaimed "messiah." Reverend Moon's people operate under many false fronts on campuses promoting such things as "community development," "educational utopias," and "scientific research." "Divine deception" is one of Reverend Moon's own terms. Speak of light without, darkness within!

There are many subtler frauds in the vast industry of "pop therapies" which proliferate more rapidly than hotel chains in America and feature everything from "rebirthing" from hot tubs to "primal screaming" to "getting it" to anything you can think of. It's all "therapy" today as Thomas Szasz, M.D., has so disarmingly pointed out in his iconoclastic book *The Myth of Pychotherapy*. Many of these "therapies" (unlike their more established predecessors such as Freud, Jung, and Adler) claim "100 percent success." They back their claims with specious "scientific reasoning." It is astonishing how seriously they are taken as they emanate from the West Coast one after another. All of these "saviors" (who shall go unmentioned) wear their "light" on their sleeve. What is within is another story. The sacred profession of healing has become big business with each of the "money changers" sellings his or her "wares." Light without, darkness within.

I spoke of the enlightened master named Pierre whom I met in France. He was penniless and wore the most tattered and humble clothes. He walked mostly barefoot. He was devoid of possessions save a tea kettle and a burlap-covered Bible. He walked in most humble ways. I have never met a more illumined one. His light was within. This is perhaps what it means "to know the white and yet keep to the black. . . ."

In the Jewish mystical tradition, there are said to be thirty-six holy men, or "Tzaddekim," who uphold the world. Without them, humanity would lose all contact with the Divine. Yet, they are the most ordinary men imaginable! Rabbi Zalman Schacter tells a story about the meeting of a famous Rabbi with one of these hidden Tzaddekim who was a poor and humble tailor. That tailor "sewed together" the Rabbi's soul that day! Darkness without, light within.

"He who knows honor and yet keeps to humility. . . ." The Taoist sages greatly stress the value and importance of humility. They will never brag or boast, nor are they concerned with "image" or "appearance." They keep their treasures secret; they are men who can "bow low." Yet the Tao raises them up! As in the "poor in spirit" in Jesus' saying about those who inherit the Kingdom. The greatest people are the most humble. Lao Tzu himself led a humble and practically anonymous life. Jesus was an unknown Galilean carpenter until he began his life's mission. He never "raised himself up," although the Devil tempted him to do so. In the end, he died in disgrace upon a cross, only to be "raised up" by God Himself. The humble carpenter turned preacher became the central figure of the Christian religion. The reclusive historian of the Chou court became the standard for Chinese religion. The humble seem to be "raised" by some mysterious force, but the arrogant who raise themselves up, tend to take a terrible fall! Look at the arrogant dictator Mussolini, who proclaimed himself the "new Caesar," and tried to build a "new Roman Empire."

He was hung upside down by his heels by his countrymen in a public square in Milan. The infamous tyrant Hitler died by a self-inflicted bullet wound in his underground bunker in Berlin, a fitting end to his "thousand-year Reich." The little emperor Napoleon, who tried to conquer Europe, spent his last years in exile in Waterloo, a tiny island. The examples could go on. The arrogant fall, the humble are raised. There is a moral order in this Universe. It may not seem so in the "short run," but it is so.

"Wholeness, when divided, will make vessels of utility. . . ." My intuition is that Lao Tzu is speaking of the "One and the Many." When the Tao, the One, becomes the Many, it becomes the sun, and moon, and stars, and trees, and rocks, and birds, and flowers, and butterflies, and human beings, and so on. . . .

Lao Tzu says that "These when employed by the Sage will become officials and chiefs." It makes me think of Plato's concept of the "Philosopher King." The latter appoints those below him to their appropriate positions, i.e., "officials and chiefs."

"However, for a great function no discrimination is needed." This is a very Zenlike statement. The enlightened state comes when you stop judging, stop dividing the world into "good" and "bad," stop making discriminations into "this" and "that." All becomes one at this stage. Action in this state is really perfect. Of all places, I met a wandering Zen master in San Diego's Balboa Park last summer. He did not advertise himself as a "master," but I know one when I see one. He was a Japanese who was travelling 100 miles a day throughout the world, supporting himself in a most unusual way. He did a dance while at the same time sculpting "dream image" figures out of a lump of resinlike substance on a stick. Within less than a minute each, he completed a "dragon," an "elk," an "eagle," and so on. He gave these out at random, or so it seemed, to various people gathered around him. He handed me a beautiful unicorn. I felt it stood for freedom! How we would wish to attain the freedom of this man. He is like the ones born of the Spirit of whom Jesus spoke.

Knowing Thyself (XXXIII)

He who knows others is wise;
He who knows himself is enlightened.
He who conquers others is strong;
He who conquers himself is mighty.
He who knows contentment is rich.
He who keeps on his course with energy has will.
He who does not deviate from his proper place will long endure.
He who may die but not perish has longevity.

"Gnothi seauton," or "know thyself," was the teaching of the Delphic Oracle of ancient Greece. It was also the teaching of the Buddha, who said "Be thou a lamp unto thyself." Jesus said the same thing when he said, "You shall know the truth, and the truth shall set you free." It is the teaching of the Old Sage, Lao Tzu, as well. To know others may be wisdom, it is true, but to truly know yourself is the meaning of enlightenment. And what is "enlightenment" but the discovery of *the light* that was always there within you. It is what Jesus meant by "You are the light of the world." You can actually *see* this light in the faces of the illumined masters.

Lao Tzu says that the conqueror of others is "strong." But the truly "mighty" are those who conquer themselves. Alexander the Great was surely a "strong man," he conquered nations. But he was hardly a man of Self-knowledge, and he died in a drunken orgy at a young age. In a Sioux Indian prayer to Manitou, the Great Spirit, one line is as follows: "I seek strength, not to be greater than my brother, but to fight my greatest enemy—myself."

Contentment, not material wealth, is what makes one truly "rich" in the words of Lao Tzu. Robert Johnson once said that "content" comes from the same root as "contain," and that gives a clue to its meaning. To be content is to be contained. That is, to be in harmony with one's environment. Robert said that glassblowers he saw in Tijuana, Mexico, seemed content in a way that Americans rarely are: they were "contained." Most people in our culture seem to "fill a job"; they "clock in" and "clock out," and the time in between is that of "quiet desperation" in the words of Thoreau, the nineteenth-century mystic who saw the beginnings of "modern technocracy" even in his rural Concord, Massachusetts. I have always admired people whose work is also their joy. One such person I know is my friend Doris, the librarian of the C. G. Jung Institute in New York. She is more bibliotherapist than librarian. Whenever I came in, I would say a few words about "where I was at," and Doris would immediately recommend the appropriate book to me and she was astonishingly accurate in her intuition. Doris was "content," or "contained," in her profession and role in life; this is a rare thing in this day and age.

"Keeping on one's course with energy." Have you ever heard a more perfect definition of will power? It is applying all of one's energy to one's chosen course. It is so rare today that it is a marvel when you see someone like that. An example of this is the incredibly gifted violinist Yitzak Perlman. He devotes himself to his violin art with such energy and total devotion. Picasso was like that in his painting, and he painted from boyhood to the day he died in his nineties.

Such concentration of energy is what it takes to become a master of anything. The masters of the martial arts I have known devote such energy to their art, hour after hour, day after day, until they are flawless. Then they practice some more!

When you find your "proper place," you will long endure, says Lao Tzu, the Sage. I take "proper place" to mean your "true calling." Not what your parents want you to be, or your teachers, or your culture, but what you are called to be in your heart of hearts. This is a difficult thing to listen to, the heart, in this modern materialistic age which values "things" over feelings and "logic" over the heart. How can you know what your calling is if you are not as precocious as Mozart who began composing great symphonies at the age of nine? It may come much later for you. You may have what I will call a "vocational dream." It is usually a powerful one. I had two dreams of this sort with regard to writing; both came in my thirties. One was a "visit" by the Russian novelist Leo Tolstoy. In the dream, I was first visited by various characters, including college professors (I used to teach college), and they were all "two-dimensional." They were "flat." And then came Leo Tolstoy. He was three-dimensional. He was solid! The other dream was this: there was a line of eight persons, representing eight different interests of mine. However, the first space was vacant. Walt Whitman came to fill this vacant space. My Unconscious has certainly given me high models to strive to emulate. Whether I can or not is one question, but these dreams absolutely gave me a direction.

Alfred Adler, the Viennese psychologist, and one-time disciple of Sigmund Freud, made an interesting discovery of the relationship between earliest memories and eventual vocational choice. My earliest recollection had to do with learning the meaning of a word. I was two years old at the time, and was having dinner with my parents and another couple at our rented summer house in New Jersey (I filled in some of these other details later). The other man (not my father) was serving fruit for dessert, and asked me, "Do you want an apricot?" This seemed strange to me because I already knew the word "uppercut," which my Grandpa Abe had taught me, "Give 'em an uppercut!" And this new word for fruit seemed to sound exactly like it. Curiously, during my years in academic psychology, my field of specialization was psycholinguistics, which is the psychology of language. Some years after I left academia to pursue the spiritual path, I decided to become a writer. The early memory seems to have been prophetic of future vocational interest. In the former case, the "study of" language seemed to be the thing. Later, the "use of" language as a direct means of expression of what I have to say seems to be what the Self has in mind for me.

It is often not until midlife that one finds one's "proper place," and this may involve, at times, a rather drastic change of direction. One thinks of Paul Gauguin, who quit his well-paying job as a banker at age thirty-five and left for the South Seas to devote himself to painting. It involved drastic material sacrifice, and dislocation of his life, but he *found himself* and the world was made richer because of it. Dante Alighieri only began his epic masterpiece, *The Divine Comedy,* at age thirty-five after he had been exiled from his native Florence. He begins Canto I with these words:

Midway life's journey I was made aware
That I had strayed into a dark forest,
And the right path appeared not anywhere.[14]

From this point of *utter nothingness,* Dante began his Inner Journey that he allegorized in his great work of epic poetry. Before we can find our true calling, there may be a very long period of retreat and withdrawal from the affairs of the world, a Nightsea Journey, but when we return, we may bring back with us the seeds of our future growth, a treasure that can be attained in no other way. The historian Arnold Toynbee speaks of this:

There is one characteristic that though far from being general, has been common to a number of great men. That is, some of the greatest men have been people who have had a broken career; they started off on some ordinary conventional line; they have come to grief in that; and then they've withdrawn from the world and come back in some new capacity. There does appear to be a psychological law operating here—a law that people who somehow got off on the wrong path recover themselves in the middle of life. They are twice born; and they are different from the once born. The twice born often get farther; it's like a rocket that has a second boost.[15]

Lao Tzu seems to imply that when you have found your "proper place," you may die, but you will "not perish." You will have "longevity." It brings to mind my favorite American poet, Robert Frost, up there with John F. Kennedy at his inauguration in the winter of 1961. Frost was old, in his eighties, but he had already achieved immortality! I also think of the great Pablo Casals, the cellist, who played with such virtuosity into his nineties. Or that incredible architect, Frank Lloyd Wright, who began to change the shape of America in his twenties, yet designed great buildings into his eighty-ninth year. Such people will "not perish."

On the other hand, it doesn't matter if you live to a very old age either, as long as you have found your "proper place." My old hero, Henry David Thoreau, who died at the relatively early age of forty-five, had these words to say, and they are written on the sign that marks the site of his tiny cabin on Walden Pond:

> *I went to the woods because*
> *I wished to live deliberately,*
> *to front only the essential*
> *facts of life, and see if I could*
> *not learn what it had to teach*
> *and not, when I came to die,*
> *discover that I had not lived.*[16]

To find one's true way may involve sacrifices, such as giving up a secure job, a marriage, the approval of one's parents and relatives, or even one's culture and all material comforts. It may even involve the sacrifice of one's life. But not to find one's own true path involves even greater sacrifice. We should not like to come to the end of our life, as Thoreau suggested, and discover that we "had not lived."

Your Person

Fame or your person, which is nearer to you?
Your person or wealth, which is dearer to you?
Gain or loss, which brings more evil to you?
Over-love of anything will lead to wasteful spending;
Amassed riches will be followed by heavy plundering.
Therefore, he who knows contentment can never be humiliated;
He who knows where to stop can never be perishable;
He will long endure.

Lao Tzu's poem recalls to mind the analogous saying of Jesus concerning ultimate values: "What does it profit a man if he gains the whole world, and loses his own soul?" What would you trade your soul for? Material wealth, fame, status, power? It is a Devil's bargain. Jesus of Nazareth, whom Christians regard as the Messiah, was offered all these things by Satan in his temptation in the wilderness. The final reply of Jesus to Satan was: "Begone, Satan! for it is written, 'You shall worship the Lord your God and him only shall you serve.' "[17]

How many of us in this "modern world" are asked to make the Devil's bargain of the exchange of soul for some material reward. I think almost all of us. When a student feels he must compromise his integrity, and falsify his beliefs and values, in writing a paper, in order to "please his professor," this is the Devil's bargain. In one of the saddest experiences of my college years, I wrote what I believed in a term paper for one of the archbehaviorists of our time, and my defense of the soul and human consciousness "earned me" a "D." "D," I think, for "Devil!" This "professor" demanded total compliance, on the part of his students, with his ultrabehaviorist views in order to earn the "magic A." I chose, instead, to write according to my conscience. This "D" prevented me from gaining admission to the graduate school of my choice. But is a graduate school worth your soul (or your integrity)? Is a high-paying job worth your soul? Or a promotion to a higher position, is this worth your soul? How many in this culture feel they have to sell their souls for money, power, security, or other material advantage in this age of materialism? Big government, industry, military, and academia can all be as soulless and soul-denying in this age of technocracy, or "Kali Yuga" as the Hindus would put it. We are a country who began in illumined vision, but have in the past century gone a long way toward selling our collective soul to the Devil! It is not surprising that the "unique contribution" of American psychology in the twentieth century was behaviorism, which as its first premise denied the reality of the human soul. John Watson himself, after losing his academic job in a scandal, went on to offer his services of soulless behaviorism to the Madison Avenue advertising industry. There he applied his "science" of manipulating people through "conditioning." B. F. Skinner, in his *Walden Two*, would construct his "ideal society" through the use of "operant conditioning" techniques based upon his laboratory work with pigeons and white rats in "Skinner boxes." If pigeons and white rats can be "conditioned" to perform, then why not human beings? I have seen children in public school who were put on "operant schedules" á la Skinner. How far we have come from the supreme valuation of the human soul as expressed by the Chinese poet-sage, Lao Tzu, and the miracle-working Rabbi Jesus, who lived almost two thousand years ago.

Lao Tzu says that "overlove of anything will lead to wasteful spending." It relates to the Buddhist idea of "attachment." Whatever you are attached to, you are enslaved by, whether it be the attachment to money, prestige, power, or the approval of others. True freedom is precisely nonattachment. The Taoist sages were less austere than the Buddhists, but they knew that it was not "amassed riches," but rather simple contentment which was the goal worth seeking.

Nonaction (XLVIII)

He who pursues learning will increase every day;
He who pursues Tao will decrease every day.

He will decrease and continue to decrease,
Till he comes to nonaction;
By nonaction everything can be done.

This poem of Lao Tzu's is quintessential Taoism. The pursuit of the Tao is nothing like the pursuit of "scholarly learning." The latter is a never-ending accumulation of "facts" and "theories." The Way of the Tao is just the opposite. It is a decreasing, a diminishing, a losing, a dying to all that is illusory, artificial, or unreal in yourself until you have come to the rest of nonaction, or *wu wei,* and by this "everything can be done."

What a mystery this nonaction, or *wu wei* is. Tai Chi Chuan, the Taoist martial art, actually demonstrates this power in the physical world. When the "solo-dance" becomes perfectly effortless and easy, as if you are no longer doing it, but it is being done through you, it becomes, at the same time, immensely powerful. The "light touch" of a Tai Chi master will send an opponent flying. I saw a film of the great Tai Chi master Cheng Man Ch'ing, in his seventies, doing the "push-hand" exercise with his student, my teacher William C. C. Chen, and sending his younger opponent sailing off his feet, time and again, with the softest touch. The "force" responsible for this is difficult to explain in terms of classical physics, if not impossible. There is a certain state of consciousness associated with this power, and I experienced it myself through "beginner's luck" after my first Tai Chi lesson. I went to visit a friend of mine, and I asked him if he'd like to experience the power of Tai Chi. He said, "sure." I touched him ever so lightly while "rooting" my body in the Tai Chi posture. He took off and hit the wall with tremendous force! Fortunately, there were no broken bones; he was just a bit shaken. I couldn't believe it myself, and I have never achieved anything quite like it in all my years of Tai Chi practice. You see, in my "beginner's luck," I was not really "trying." I had come, inadvertently, to this mysterious "nonaction," or *wu wei.*

This same consciousness and power upon which the Tai Chi art is based as a martial art applies to every aspect of life from making a speech to painting a picture. It is quite a different thing to make a speech with prepared notes, as politicians and professors are wont to do, and speaking through the power of the Spirit as Jesus advised his disciples to do when he said not to worry about what you shall say, but rather "let the Spirit of the Father" speak through you. One can imagine that the Apostle Paul did just this in his charismatic addresses as when he said this to his Corinthian audience: "And if I have prophetic powers, and understand all knowledge, and if I have all faith, so as to remove mountains, but have not love, I am nothing."[18]

It is one thing to paint according to "academic rules" learned in the Academy, but quite another to paint as that tragic hero Van Gogh did, as though the Spirit were moving his brush. He is my favorite painter, and I saw all 500 of his collected works at the museum in Amsterdam devoted to his work. I was moved to tears by the awesome power of his paintings. He did not paint in the manner that was customary in his day in the late nineteenth century, and as a result he sold only one painting for about $10 in his lifetime. This rejection by the artistic establishment of his time was so bitter that Vincent took his own life at age thirty-seven. If he had lived for a few more years, he would have known worldwide acclaim; today any painting of his is a priceless treasure. His personal life was a tragedy, but few painters of the West have ever painted with the spiritual power of Vincent Van Gogh.

What comes of this nonaction is of such beauty and perfection, and is quite unlike the results of ego's striving to achieve something. Many Japanese Zen arts are done in this egoless, effortless way, whether it be Zen archery, or calligraphy, or flower arrangement, or the tea ceremony, or Haiku poetry. There is a spiritual power which *moves* when the ego steps aside. It is called "Ch'i" by the Chinese, "Ki" by the Japanese, "Prana" by the Indian Yogis, "Ruach" by the Hebrew prophets, "Ruh" by the Sufi saints, "Pneuma" by the Greeks, and "Spiritus" is the Latin word from which our English word "Spirit" is derived. In all of these languages and diverse cultures, the word "spirit" relates to "breath." In most cases the same word is used for both. The Holy Spirit to the Jewish mystics is the Ruach Elohim, "the Breath of God." I was reading the account of a "born-again Christian" of his experience of the Holy Spirit, and he described it as a "rushing wind." Yoga teaches an elaborate breath discipline known as "pranayama," which is said to harness the power of "prana" or spirit. Zen Buddhists employ a similar breath discipline, known as "mi-sogi" which builds "Ki energy." The Sufi mystics have their breath disciplines. "Speaking in tongues," or "glossalalia," must relate to the same phenomena. When you are "breathed" by the Divine Spirit, what comes forth has power and truth. How to achieve it? You can't. It comes through the action of nonaction, or *wei wu wei*. Through the action of nonaction "everything can be done." Was not Jesus of Nazareth saying the same thing when he said the following: "Consider the lilies of the field, how they grow; they neither toil nor spin . . ."[19] Precisely!

Not Knowing (LXXI)

Not knowing that one knows is best;
Thinking that one knows when one does not know is sickness.
Only when one becomes sick of this sickness can one be free from sickness.
The Sage is never sick; because he is sick of this sickness, therefore he is
    not sick.

I remember the words of that charming Korean Zen master, Seung
Sahn (his book is *Dropping Ashes on the Buddha*), whose lectures I attended in New York. His favorite saying was "Go straight, don't
know!" I wish I could capture the way in which he said that: *Don't
know.* He says that the point of Zen is to attain to this "don't know
mind."

It is in this "don't know" mind, or state of "emptiness," that one can
really know reality as it is, and not as our ego's constructions project
upon it. The ego is the great "map maker" and "theoretician." Our
Western philosophical heritage is a testimony to the "productivity" of
the ego in constructing "theories of reality." A course in the history of
Western philosophy is something like a tour through the "Tower of
Babel." Nominalism, realism, materialism, idealism, rationalism, empiricism, utilitarianism, existentialism, ad infinitum, ad nauseam.
Have you seen that marvelous play, *Godspell,* with its first scene of all
the "philosophers" from Karl Marx to R. Buckminster Fuller simultaneously "spouting" their philosophies? It is babble! And do you recall
the sudden appearance of John the Baptist who says: "Prepare the
way of the Lord, make his paths straight!" One needs to clear the
mind of all the "babble" in order to perceive reality as it is. In *Godspell,*
the *sacred reality* is the appearance of Jesus. For the Zen Buddhist, it is
the coming of "satori," or enlightenment. And for Lao Tzu, the
Taoist Sage, it is the becoming "sick of this sickness" of "thinking that
one knows when one does not know. . . ."

This "thinking that one knows when one does not know" leads to
what I will call "procrustean thinking." Do you know the myth of
Procrustes? He was the giant who had a bed in his house of a certain
length, and when a guest came who was too short, he stretched him
out to fit the bed; when a guest came who was too tall, he chopped off
just enough of him to make him "fit perfectly!" This is what happens
in so much of Western thinking of whatever sort from philosophy to
biology. Everything must "fit" the theory! I am most familiar with
psychology, so I will take my examples here.

To the Freudian, everything, just everything, must be "reduced" to the vicissitudes of the sexual instinct (Freud later added a "death instinct" which was not as popular with his students). And so Freud "explains" the work of Leonardo da Vinci in terms of the "sublimation" of the sexual instinct: "If we reflect on the concurrence in Leonardo of his overpowerful instinct for research and the atrophy of his sexual life (which was restricted to what is called ideal/sublimated/homosexuality) we shall be disposed to claim him as a model instance of our third type. The core of his nature, and the secret of it, would appear to be that after his curiosity had been activated in infancy in the service of sexual interests he succeeded in sublimating the greater part of his libido into an urge for research."[20] And so the "great" Freud *reduces* the creative genius of the multifaceted Leonardo, a highest-order Renaissance man, scientist, inventor, and artist of world rank, to the "vicissitudes" of the sexual instinct! Freud's "argument" that creative genius is "sublimated sexuality" is impaired by the fact that there were other Renaissance men of the order of William Blake, the poet-artist, and Johann Wolfgang von Goethe, the scientist-man of letters, who were married men of fully active sexuality, who despite this "handicap" attained the highest levels of achievement. Freud goes on to admit that the evidence for Leonardo's sexual life (or lack of it) is very scanty indeed! Freud bases much of his speculation upon an early memory of Leonardo's in which the Italian word for "kite" is mistranslated (by Freud) as "vulture."[21] Leonardo recalled a kite falling into his baby carriage as an infant, and his sucking it (that's what babies do!). In Freud's mistranslation, a vulture presumably alighted upon the hapless infant, and he sucked its tail; ergo, passive homosexuality! To such lengths will Professor Freud go to make the "patient" fit the psychoanalytic procrustean bed. An alternative "interpretation" of the "kite episode" is that this symbolized the fact that Leonardo would attain "great heights," as well he did. In another "classic work" of Freud's, *Moses and Monotheism,* Moses is "proven" to be an "Egyptian" on the basis of the scantiest, or rather nonexistent, "evidence," such as the fact that the Egyptian word for child is "mose."[22] Freud thereby relegates one of the greatest episodes in human religious history to the Oedipal struggle between father and son. In another famous work, *The Future of an Illusion,* the Viennese physician and creator of psychoanalysis reduces the spiritual heritage of all humanity to the "infantile projection" of the "father-complex" upon the universe![23] And so the former astute scientist-explorer, Dr. Freud, who penetrated the mysteries of hysterical neuroses in the 1890's, in such cases as Frau Emmy von N. and Fraulein Elisabeth von R., becomes infected, in the 1920's and 1930's, with the disease of procrusteanism. The young scientist has become the old ideologue.

Alfred Adler, the first of Freud's early circle to defect from the "master" and form his own school of "individual psychology," hinges his core theorizing upon what he calls the "inferiority complex." True, most of us feel "little" or even "inferior" as children in the "big world" of adults, and many of us suffered specific forms of "inferiorities." True, as Adler points out, there are *some* whose adult careers are compensations for these real or felt inferiorities. There are classic examples, such as Demosthenes, the stutterer, who went on to become one of ancient Greece's greatest orators, and the American black woman, Wilma Rudolph, who overcame childhood polio to win two gold medals in Olympic track. Other examples may occur to you. But Adler's theory of individual psychology *demands* that this principle be true universally! So he makes the outlandish statement that "Signs of an inferior visual apparatus play a large part in the development of painters." Adler has to search history to find a little known fifteenth-century Italian painter, Guercino da Centa, who "squinted." He mentions another painter, Piero de la Francesca, who became blind in old age. And another, Lenbach, who had only one eye![24] To such lengths will Dr. Adler go to "support his case." Never mind that such world masters of art as Titian, Raphael, and Rembrant van Rijn had perfectly normal vision! Most artists whom I have known myself have normal 20/20 vision (writers are much more likely to be nearsighted!). Adler extends his "argument" to other fields such as actors, singers, musicians, etc., and in each case he goes to obvious lengths to select cases which "prove his hypothesis." The point is that merely one exception would disprove the "rule." Yet, quite to the contrary, Adler's "examples" are exceptional indeed! Far be it from the socialist-egalitarian Adler to conceive of the notion of a God-given gift! It is *just possible* that Mozart was endowed with a musical gift, Shakespeare with a literary gift, and Jim Thorpe, the American Indian Olympic champion, with an athletic gift, and that these and others were not just cases of "striving to overcome inferiorities."

I feel closer to the Jungians in my views, and I think they have done much to revive the ancient truths contained in the myths of all cultures. But I must differ with them too in their overextension of "Jungian theories." They too extend their "map," based upon the limited, though brilliant, career of C. G. Jung, to "explain all." All religious phenomena are, therefore, reduced to the Jungian "archetypal categories." Christ is viewed by one famous Jungian analyst as the "arche-

type of the individuating ego." Apparently, this is all. It denies by
nonstatement the possibility of a transcendent spiritual dimension,
call it God, and reduces this to the self/ego relationship within the
individual psyche. By ignoring this transcendent dimension, one denies the possibility of the *incarnation* of this transcendent dimension in
the person of a man named Jesus. It makes "merely symbolic" the
miracles and healings and even the resurrection of Christ. The Self,
or the psyche's image of "wholeness," is as far as most, if not all,
Jungians will go. They almost universally say that the God image and
the Self are "indistinguishable." This goes contrary to the history of
Western mysticism which is a history of souls in search of God. It is
true that to find God is also to find the Self, but this in no way
abrogates the distinction between transcendence and immanence, between God and Self. The orthodox Jungians seem to ignore the action
of a transcendent God in the world and in history. This is the action of
the spiritual dimension: *revelatory* and *miraculous*. It is not "reducible"
to the dimension of the archetypes of the collective unconscious; it is a
higher dimension. It is real! To close oneself to this possibility is also
procrusteanism, of a higher order to be sure than Freud's or Adler's,
but procrusteanism just the same. Like all procrusteanism, or reductionism, it has two dangers: (1) it may "mutilate" the patient, and (2) it
ignores the possibility of healing of a higher order.

Jung himself, as opposed to the "Jungians" (I heard that Jung said,
"Thank God, I'm Jung, and not a Jungian!"), cannot be faulted on
this level. In his autobiography, *Memories, Dreams, Reflections,* as an old
man in his eighties looking back at his life in its broadest patterns,
Jung reflects the sentiment of Lao Tzu, the Old Sage, when he de-
clares:

When people say I am wise, or a sage, I cannot accept it. A man once dipped a
hatful of water from a stream. What did that amount to? I am not that
stream. I am at the stream, but I do nothing. Other people are at the same
stream, but most of them find they have to do something with it. I do nothing.
I never think that I am the one who must see to it that cherries grow on stalks.
I stand and behold, admiring what nature can do.[25]

Jung repeats a Hasidic story about a student who came to a rabbi and
said: " 'In the olden times there were men who saw the face of God. Why
don't they any more?' The rabbi replied, 'Because nowadays no one can
stoop so low.' "[26]

Jung echoes the exact words of Lao Tzu on the last page of his book
when he says: "All are clear, I alone am clouded."[27] He has come to

the end of the sickness of "thinking that one knows when one does not know."

Although Jung would not claim the title for himself, Lao Tzu, I suspect, would say, "This man has become a Sage." Sagehood involves self-emptying and humility. It is the opposite of Procrustes.

The Weak Can Overcome the Strong (LXXVIII)

The weakest things in the world can overmatch the strongest things in the world.
Nothing in the world can be compared to water for its weak and yielding nature; yet in attacking the hard and the strong nothing proves better than it. For there is no other alternative to it.
The weak can overcome the strong and the yielding can overcome the hard:
This all the world knows but does not practice.
Therefore the Sage says:
He who sustains all the reproaches of the country can be the master of the land;
He who sustains all the calamities of the country can be the king of the world.
These are words of truth,
Though they seem paradoxical.

What is "weaker" and more "yielding than water"? Any hard object will pass through water unobstructed. Yet, the ocean's waves, in the course of time, will turn hard rocks upon the shore into the finest sand. A tidal wave will demolish any seaside town. Air is even "weaker" and more intangible, yet a tornado is one of nature's most powerful forces, and it will uproot anything in its path. The Tai Chi art bases itself upon this "water principle," neutralizing any "hard attack," through yielding, and delivering explosive force through the concentration and release of "Ch'i."

If water and air are "weak" and "yielding," and yet paradoxically so powerful, how much "weaker" and more "yielding" is "Ch'i," or "Spirit"? Both water and wind, it might be noted, are Biblical symbols of the Spirit. Our "modern world" has ceased almost entirely to believe in the reality of the Spirit, in its scientific and philosophical materialism, the legacy of the Age of Rationalism of the last three centuries (only now coming to its limits and ultimate demise at the threshold of a new age). Yet, a man moved by the Spirit, such as

Moses at the burning bush, or Jesus at the River Jordan, can alter the course of human history in ways that no Caesar, Genghis Khan, Adolf Hitler, or even any modern "warlord" of this nuclear age could even dream of, despite their great material power. A modern "conqueror" would only bring about mutual destruction, and would obliterate himself as well as his opponent. But the words and deeds and examples of such men of the Spirit as Lao Tzu, Moses, and Jesus live on into eternity influencing people's hearts and souls for the good.

Lao Tzu was a shy and retiring historian and mystic who shaped the course of Chinese religious, philosophical, and literary thought for two and a half millennia. Moses was the adopted son of a pharaoh, turned exile and wanderer in the desert. Yet, he was vouchsafed a spiritual vision at a "bush" which altered the course of all of human history, established a monotheistic religion which has lasted for over four millennia, and produced two offspring (Christianity and Islam), and has given Western people their ethical and moral standards in the form of the Ten Commandments. A humble carpenter, born in a stable in a small town in the Middle East, experienced a spiritual transformation following his baptism by a desert prophet named John, and went on to fulfill the "prophesy" of a Chinese Sage named Lao Tzu who lived hundreds of years earlier in a different part of the world: He sustained "all the reproaches of the country," and "the calamities of the country" were laid upon his shoulders (in the form of a cross upon which he gave up his life). In the belief of Christians, at least, he became the "king of the world." Jesus' reliance, as was true of Moses, was on the Spirit, and not on any worldly force or power. Because of this reliance upon "the weakest thing in the world," Jesus defied the laws of death itself, as Moses before him had defied all laws of nature and of man, leading a slave people to freedom across a sea, in the face of the greatest army of the world (at that time).

Throughout history, there have been people of great political, military, and economic power, who seem to have been the "movers" of events. Most of them have long since turned to dust, dead and forgotten. There have also been the much rarer kind of people who show that Lao Tzu spoke the truth when he said, "The weak can overcome the strong and the yielding overcome the hard."

Probably the greatest of the Taoist Sages following Lao Tzu was Chuang Tzu, who lived in the third century B.C. Chuang Tzu was a master of humor and wit, and he has been called the "genius of the absurd." In concluding this chapter, we could not do better than to quote the following poem by Master Chuang Tzu:

Man Is Born in Tao

Fishes are born in water
Man is born in Tao
If fishes, born in water,
Seek the deep pool,
All their needs
Are satisfied.
If man, born in Tao,
Sinks into the deep shadow
Of non-action
To forget aggression and concern,
He lacks nothing
His life is secure.

Moral: "All the fish needs
Is to get lost in water.
All man needs is to get lost
In Tao."[28]

The spiritual geniuses of history, the likes of Moses, Jesus, and the Buddha, as well as Master Lao Tzu, had one thing in common: they knew how to "get lost in Tao." In doing so, they paradoxically found themselves. Moreover, they became beacon lights to the rest of us human beings who are still "lost" out here in exile from the Kingdom of God, or the Tao. Each of these beacon lights "calls us home" in his own unique fashion. But, we should not forget that each of these enlightened ones receives *his light* from one single Source, whatever name we call this: TAO, YHWH, ABBA, TRUTH, BRAHMA, OR ALLAH. So, in the words of Chuang Tzu: "Get lost[in Tao]!"

NOTES

Primary Source:
Lao Tzu, *Tao Te Ching*, trans. Ch'u Ta-Kao, Samuel Weiser, New York, 1973, Chapters I, II, VI, VIII, XI, XVI, XX, XXVIII, XLIV, XLVIII, LXXI, LXXVIII,

Secondary Sources:
1. Lao Tzu, *The Way of Life*, trans. R. B. Blakney, New American Library, New York, 1955, p. 27.
2. There is a question among scholars as to whether Lao Tzu actually was a person or a spiritual tradition. Legends about him are wrapped in cryptic symbolism, such as the legend that Lao Tzu was never young, but was born an old man with a long white beard! The only evidence that someone called Lao Tzu, the "Old Philosopher," did exist are the reports of his meetings with Confucius, and the existence of the extraordinary little book: the *Tao Te Ching*. I favor the view that he did exist; he certainly exists for me.

3. Ludwig Wittgenstein, *Tractatus Logico Philosophicus*, Routledge & Kegan Paul, London (New York: Humanities Press), 1961, p. 151.

4. Robert Jastrow, *God and the Astronomers*, Warner Books, New York, 1980, pp. 3–4.

5. *The Portable Dante: The Divine Comedy*, trans. Clifton Wolters, Penguin Books, New York, 1961, p. 544.

6. Fritjof Capra, *The Tao of Physics*, Shambhala Publications, Berkeley, Calif.,1975, p. 77.

7. Rocco A. Errico, *The Ancient Aramaic Prayer of Jesus "The Lord's Prayer,"* Science of Mind Publications, Los Angeles, 1975, p. 59.

8. Pierre Teilhard de Chardin, *The Heart of Matter*, Harcourt Brace Jovanovich, New York and London, 1978, p. 16.

9. Alan Watts, *TAO: The Watercourse Way*, Pantheon Books, New York, 1975, p. 49.

10. William C. C. Chen, *Tai Chi Chuan*, published by William C. C. Chen School of T'ai-Chi Ch'uan, 161 West 23rd Street, New York, 1973, Introduction.

11. I heard a Zen master tell this story several years ago; I do not recall his name.

12. Author—anonymous, *The Cloud of Unknowing*, trans, Clifton Wolters, Penguin Books, New York, 1961, pp. 134–135.

13. *The Bible*, Revised Standard Version, New Testament, American Bible Society, New York, 1971, John 11:25.

14. *The Portable Dante*, p. 3.

15. I discovered this quotation by Arnold Toynbee in a clipping from a magazine in my 1976 diary; I do not know the source.

16. Henry David Thoreau, *Walden*, College & University Press, New Haven, Conn., 1965, p. 105.

17. *The Bible*, Revised Standard Version, Matthew 4:10.

18. Ibid., 1 Corinthians 13:1.

19. Ibid., Matthew 6:8.

20. Sigmund Freud, *Leonardo da Vinci and a Memory of His Childhood*, trans. Alan Tyson, W. W. Norton, New York, 1964, pp. 30–31.

21. Ibid., p. 9.

22. Sigmund Freud, *Moses and Monotheism*, Vintage Books, Random House, New York, 1967, p. 5.

23. Sigmund Freud, *The Future of an Illusion*, Anchor Books, Doubleday, Garden City, N.Y., 1961, p. 35.

24. Heinz L. Ansbacher and Rowena R. Ansbacher, eds., *The Individual Psychology of Alfred Adler*, Harper & Row, New York, 1956, p. 29.

25. C. G. Jung, *Memories, Dreams, Reflections,* recorded and edited by Aniela Jaffé, Vintage Books, Random House, New York, 1963, p. 355.

26. Ibid.

27. Ibid.

28. Thomas Merton, *The Way of Chuang Tzu*, New Directions, New York, 1965, p. 65.

Chapter Two

Moses, the Liberator

*T*HE story of Moses has been called the "greatest liberation story ever told." However, the saga of the Hebrews began centuries before, when according to Jewish tradition, and historical records tend to verify it, Abraham, the patriarch, came from Ur in Sumer (known also as Mesopotamia, or "between the two rivers") to Canaan, the "Land of Promise" in obedience to divine revelation. This was the first "exodus"; it was the exodus of Abraham from the idolatry of his Mesopotamian culture. Historians place the date of Abraham's migration at approximately 1850 B.C.[1]

Abraham and his wife, Sarah, though both were late in age, had a son whom they named Isaac. Isaac begot two sons, Jacob and Esau, with his wife Rebekah. It was Jacob who received both his father Isaac's blessing and the blessing of the Lord. Jacob was renamed "Israel," which means, "he who struggles with the Lord," after "wrestling" all night with an angel of the Lord. Jacob had twelve sons who were to become the twelve tribes of Israel. His favored son, Joseph, to whom he had given a "coat of many colors," was left in a pit to die by his jealous brothers, but then, taking pity upon him, they sold him into slavery to Midianite merchants. A slave in Egypt, Joseph rose to the rank of regent over the land after he correctly interpreted a dream of Pharaoh's of seven fat cows and seven lean cows, symbolizing seven fat years and seven lean years, thus saving Egypt from a famine. Joseph's brethren, and their aged father, Jacob, were invited to settle in Egypt. There they prospered and multiplied as honored guests of the Pharaoh.

The Israelites' good fortune did not last forever. When Joseph and

44

his generation had all died out, a new Pharaoh came into power over Egypt, who did not know Joseph, and the "honored guest" status of the Israelites was to change. The new Pharaoh, thought by scholars to be Ramses II of approximately the thirteenth century B.C.,[2] enslaved the Israelites and set cruel taskmasters over them who afflicted them with heavy burdens building the treasure cities of Pharaoh. "And they made their lives bitter with hard service, in mortar, and in brick, and in all manner of service in the field. . . ."

Many peoples who have suffered slavery have identified with this archetypcal story of liberation, among them, the blacks of the days of American slavery, who made up such songs as "Go down Moses." The cry of the Israelite and the black slave alike was "Let my people go!"

Now, suppose that we take this story, which appears to be a literal one, and for which there exists historical evidence, on another level, an allegorical level, what will it reveal to us then? Is it also the story of the struggle of every person to escape his or her own personal bondage and come to liberation? Is it the eternal quest of the human soul to be free? The metaphorical level of the story dawned upon me several years ago during the Passover season (which is the Jewish commemoration of the Exodus). It *is* an allegorical story, as well as a historical event. To those who can discern its hidden meanings, it is a *guide to liberation.*

Going with the allegorical sense of the story, do you recall feeling like an "honored guest" as a very little child of perhaps two or three in your parents' home? Was it not as if you had come from "someplace else," from some holy place, the land of the soul? In the ensuing years, did you experience your father's temper and loud voice, and your mother's anger and hysteria come upon you whenever you had "done something wrong," or had been a "bad child"? Were you always inevitably "getting into trouble" and fearing the "heavy hand of punishment?" The Golden Age of childhood somehow changes into the time of troubles and woes. Joy disappears and only the "rules" remain. "Pharaoh" and "Pharaohess" loom large in our lives, and the precious feeling of freedom of the Age of Original Wholeness has waned into practical nonexistence. In the language of the Freudians, you have "introjected" the parental authorities with their particular set, sometimes very arbitrary, of prescriptions and proscriptions. You have formed a "superego" which looms over your ego as the taskmasters of Egypt loomed over the Israelite slaves. It is the interiorized agent of parental and societal authority which not only supresses the ego, but exerts repression over the instinctual impulses, or "id," with its instincts of sexuality and aggression. In the Jungian language and level, the child has formed parental "images," and has repressed a significant portion of himself or herself into the darkness called the "Shadow." Moreover, the child has, through the impositions of the forces of social reality, withdrawn consciousness from the archetypal world we all know so well through the magical medium of fairy tales and myths. The innocent and whole little child of two or three becomes the socialized and repressed child of five or six, who is "set" in his or her learned personality traits as well as neuroses, and is now "ready" to enter the school system to become even more repressed and inhibited. "Sit straight!" "Fold your hands!" "No talking!" "I want a straight line!" Such are the demands put upon the young child in our modern school systems. This is "compulsory brain damage" according to the educator and researcher Dr. Jean Houston.[3]

I am not saying that a degree of repression or suppression of impulses and moral rule learning is not necessary in the passage from nature to culture. It is universal in all civilizations and cultures of the world as Freud laments in his book *Civilization and Its Discontents*. The difference between the neurotic and the normal is one of degree, and not of kind. The complete absence of superego is not "normal," but is usually associated with the "psychopathic personality" who has no restraints on his impulses at all. If he wishes to have sex, he rapes; if he is angry, he kills. This individual needs more, not less, superego. He needs to internalize some authority! But the neurotic personality of our time has not too little, but *too much*, superego, and it inhibits him in his normal sexuality, aggression, self-assertion, independence and autonomy, and even in the feeling that he is a person of worth and value who deserves to enjoy life and be happy. Freedom and spontaneity are almost impossible to such a person. He suffers a severe guilt complex, a manifestation of a brutally punitive superego, or interiorized parental complexes. Such a person may never regain the innate feeling of value he had about himself as a little child. He may suffer a lifelong "inferiority complex." He lacks all self-esteem and self-confidence, despite his native gifts and talents. He may fail at the tasks of life because his "inner parents" are constantly telling him "You are no good!" "You are an ingrate!" "You will never amount to anything!" And so on. Enough of this "self-fulfilling prophecy" throughout one's childhood and adolescence, and one may become just what these inner (originally outer) voices have told one that one is. One becomes a prisoner of one's own superego, or parental complexes, and walks through life as if in a strait jacket. It seems impossible *to do.* I have heard that Carl Jung called neurasthenia an "American disease." Neurasthenia is psychologically induced fatigue. Among the more severe symptoms of a severely punitive superego are phobias, anxiety attacks, sex and work inhibitions, and chronic depression. Depression, a common disorder of our era, is really self-inflicted punishment. It can lead to suicide. When you have been told you are "no good" long enough, you unfortunately may come to believe it, and choose to end it all, rather than living with such a sense of self-negation.[4] Superego can be far more punitive than the actual parents!

The punitive superego may lead to another common disorder of our time: the loss of identity, or *I am-ness.* A friend of mine, Dr. Joe Savage, a psychiatrist from Oklahoma, believes that this is the core problem of neurosis, the loss of the sense that *you are.* At best, the neurotic has a "contingent beingness," which is to say, "I am if and only if. . . ." For example, "I am if and only if people approve of me." Or, "I am if and only if I am perceived as tough and people fear me." Etc. When the contingency breaks down, and it usually will, the person breaks down as well. He has lost the basis of his "I am-ness." Contingent "I am-ness," in theological terms, is idolatry, and "idols have clay feet!" They break easily. The ego usually learns its contingencies through its socialization agents who "teach" through approval and disapproval, reward and punishment, and love and the withdrawal of love. Perhaps the latter, that is love, is most crucial, and an unconditional love can go a very long way toward giving one a strong sense of self which is relatively impervious to circumstances. But unconditional love is as rare in this world as diamonds are, actually much more rare. Most child-rearing situations are very far from this ideal, and so most children lose their original, innate "I am-ness," and form some kind of contingent beingness that ranges from the fairly normal personality who has a fairly broadbased "contingent I am-ness," to the psychotic who has lost his "I am-ness" altogether, or formulated it along purely delusional lines. Somewhere in between are the vast numbers of neurotics whose "I am-ness" has a relatively narrow base, and hence go through their lives rather defensively, fearfully, and far from freely. The enlightened one, according to this view, has found noncontingent "I am-ness" and knows that *he* or *she is,* no matter what the circumstances of life. Such a one was Moses, the Liberator, and it is to him that we relatively enslaved neurotics can turn to as a teacher of liberation.

What is slavery? From the external point of view, it is the loss of freedom to choose one's own way, as well as the devaluation of one's personhood to the point that one is treated not as a person with a soul, but as mere chattel. Such was the position of the Israelites in Egypt, such was the position of the blacks who suffered slavery in America, and such is the position of all who have lost their freedom. What is it like *inside* to have entered into slavery? The slave mentality corresponds, I believe, to a loss of being. If you are only what others *say you are,* and you come to believe what they say, and see yourself in this way, then you have lost connection with your real self. How you are treated is also a way of saying something, and you tend to get the message, either consciously or unconsciously. What could the Israelites have felt about themselves based upon being treated as if they were beasts of burden? How do you think the black slave felt as he was being auctioned off for sale as if he were "a thing"? The same can be said for those who suffered slave labor camps in Nazi Germany and Stalinist Russia in this century. What is it like to be treated *as if* you are a "thing" and not a person? Many lose their sense of being, but a few retain it, and these few may get very angry, and rebel. Anger is a beginning; it was for Moses.

All that I have said about slaves and slavery applies as well to the "universal enslavement" of childhood when most of us come to some contingent "I am-ness," which says: "I am what Mommy and Daddy say I am." Unfortunately, what they say usually has far more to do with them than it has to do with the child, and many a child is the target of the projections of parents. These *repetitive voices* of the past tend to become unconscious, and continue to "say what we are" throughout life, and moreover control us through reward and punishment, guilt and the alleviation of guilt, and acceptance or nonacceptance of our personhood in a very radical sense. We are speaking of the Freudian superego, the Jungian parental complexes, and the "inner parents" of Eric Berne's "transactional analysis." On a much deeper level than the personal, reflecting the universal and evolutionary experience of mankind, are the collective unconscious Terrible Mother and Terrible Father archetypes, rediscovered by Jung, and well-known to the mythologies of all cultures. The Terrible Mother represents Mother Nature in her most devouring sense, and she is symbolized by such figures as the Gorgon, the Dragon, and the Medusa. The Terrible Father represents universal human culture in its most repressive and negating sense, and he is symbolized by such figures as "the Pharaoh," "the Emperor," "the chief priest," and so on. It is clear that Moses takes on and overcomes the Terrible Father in the form of the Pharaoh, and he also counteracts the power of the Terrible Mother in the Red Sea episode when he causes Mother Sea to part to permit the Israelites to pass through unharmed. Moses was a man who had, through a divine revelation, regained his power to *be,* and it was he who awakened the enslaved and sleeping Israelites to their own beingness. One must *be* before one can be free.

There is the outerhistorical Moses of the Exodus story, and the evidence is that he really existed and that he really led his people, the Israelites, to freedom. How he did this, whether by natural or supernatural means, is not a question that historians can answer, but is a matter of faith. Inwardly, Moses corresponds to the appearance of the Wise Man. He can appear in a dream, or in a waking vision, at the beginning of our Journey. He is the initial guide on the Way to Freedom, as the Moses of history was the initial guide to the enslaved Israelites on their long road back to the "Promised Land." We will look at the historical Moses as a symbol of the inward Moses in all of us who can set us on the path to freedom.

As was true of Jesus of Nazareth who was born more than a millennium later, Moses survived the attempt of a tyrant in authority at the time to destroy him as a babe. Pharaoh will attempt to destroy that which is within you that will free you, but *he cannot destroy it.* Moses survived, and the Moses within you will survive the attempt of every agent of your socialization and indoctrination to destroy him, whether it be family, tribe, or culture. He survives as an archetype, which is to say, as a latency. But a latency needs to be activated in order to be realized. In the following narrative, think alternately of Moses as historical liberator of the Israelites and as the archetypal Wise Man (or Wise Woman) within. We will move between the inner and the outer, and back again.

Nothing is related in the biblical account of Moses' growing up years in Pharaoh's court (as similarly nothing is related in the Bible about the growing-up years of Jesus between the ages of twelve and thirty). We can assume that he was educated in Egyptian culture, and, no doubt, at a very high level. The Egyptian civilization of Moses' time was an advanced one with magnificent architectural achievements, highly developed sciences of astronomy and medicine, a high art and literature, and so on. Egypt was one of the two centers of civilization of the time, the other being the Sumerian, and the Hebrews were involved in both, and left both to make their own way. As Abraham left Ur in ancient Sumer in about the nineteenth century B.C., Moses was to lead the Israelite people out of Egypt in the thirteenth century

B.C. But first he was to have his own personal exodus, as we shall see.

The Bible says that when "Moses was grown up," he went out to see his brethren, and he looked upon their burdens. He apparently knew that he was an Israelite from the Bible account. When Moses saw an Egyptian smiting a Hebrew, he slew the Egyptian and hid his body in the sand. When Pharaoh heard of this, he sought to kill Moses, but Moses fled from Egypt to the land of Midian. The Bible does not mention it, but biblical scholars have deduced that Moses was forty years of age when he left Egypt on his personal odyssey to the land of the Midianites.[5] He was what we would call a "midlife" adult. The Jewish mystics, or Kabbalists, say that it was from the Midianites, and particularly from Jethro, his father-in-law, from whom he learned the ancient teachings of the Spirit known to his forefathers, Abraham, Isaac, and Jacob. Moses settled in Midian, married Zipporah, the daughter of Jethro, and fathered a son whom he named Gershom, which means "a sojourner." Moses himself was to be only a sojourner in the land of the Midianites. However, it was in this land that he had the most important experience of his life. One day, while he was tending the flock, Moses saw a bush on Mt. Horeb which, though it burned, was not consumed. Moses went up the mountain to witness this great sight.

And the angel of the Lord appeared unto him in a flame of fire out of the midst of the bush; and he looked, and behold, it was not consumed. And Moses said: "I will turn aside now, and see this great sight, why the bush is not burnt." And when the Lord saw that he turned aside to see, God called unto him out of the midst of the bush, and said: "Moses, Moses." And he said: "Here am I." And He said: "Draw not night hither; put off thy shoes from off thy feet, for the place whereon thou standest is holy ground." Moreover He said: "I am the God of thy father, the God of Abraham, the God of Isaac, and the God of Jacob." And Moses hid his face; for he was afraid to look upon God.

Moses was at this point a man of midlife who in the course of his ordinary work (i.e., tending sheep) had an experience of the *inward light*. Moses saw this inward light as if it were coming from a "burning bush," but it did not burn because *the light was within*. It is from within our souls that we experience God or the Self. When you have this experience, you are indeed on holy ground. You have reason to fear, as Moses did, because your whole accustomed way of life may be swept from beneath your feet. You may be called upon to perform tasks that you never believed yourself capable of, and you may argue with this *inward light* who is also an *inward voice*.

The Lord tells Moses that He has seen the affliction of his people, and He has heard their cry. He knows their suffering, and He intends to deliver them out of the hand of their oppressors to a "land flowing with milk and honey," to the land of the Canaanites. God tells Moses that He will send him to Pharaoh, and that it will be his task to bring forth the sons of Israel from Egypt. Moses immediately objects, "Who am I, that I should go unto Pharaoh, and that I should bring forth the children of Israel out of Egypt?" God assures Moses that "Certainly I will be with thee. . . ."

Going back to the inward sense of the story, *that* of God within you, or the Self, knows what is the suffering and alienation of your ego. He knows of your afflictions. And He wants to deliver you from your oppression to a "land of promise," the Kingdom of your true Self. If you are afraid, and you will be, He assures you that *He is with you.* It is from the discovery of the Deep Center that our deliverance begins.

Moses makes the most important inquiry to this Voice: he asks it to reveal its name. And to Moses is revealed the Highest Name of God:

And Moses said unto God: "Behold when I come unto the children of Israel, and shall say unto them: The God of your fathers hath sent me unto you; and they shall say to me: What is His name? what shall I say unto them?" And God said unto Moses: "I AM THAT I AM"; and He said: "Thus shalt thou say unto the children of Israel: I AM hath sent me unto you."

God tells Moses that I AM is His Name forever throughout all generations. The discovery of I AM is a monumental discovery on the Spiritual Path. In psychological language, it is the ego's discovery of the Self. Religious traditions tend to make this experience "unique" to such legendary figures as Moses and the prophets, but it is an experience that anyone on the Path may have, and mystics throughout history have spoken of it. I had the "I AM experience" myself at a time of insecurity and suffering while living in a cheap hotel room in San Francisco in the winter of 1974. This experience followed a long Dark Night of the Soul. Let me relate it to you in the words of my diary, including some thoughts I had preliminary to the revelation of the Voice which called itself I AM:

All concepts, Let Go. All repressions, Let Go. All defenses, Let Go. All desires, Let Go. All guilt, Let Go. All fear, Let Go. All anxiety, Let Go. All concern with achievement, Let Go. Let Go, Let Go, Let Go. Even of Life, Let Go. Of the fear of death, Let Go. Of existence itself, Let Go. The Spirit *is*. Nothing to do. You cannot earn it or get it through trying or striving after it. This keeps it away. It need only be recognized to be realized. That All There

Is is Here and Now = I AM THAT I AM = God. Nothing to fear but fear. Everything is Here and Now and Nothing is Here and Now. *This is It.*

Then the Voice spoke as follows:

Be at Peace. Shalom. Be still, and Know that I AM God. I AM the Creator of All. I AM within All Things. I AM within you. I AM you. Realize this and nothing external will disturb you. You will be *at peace.* The Baptism will come when it will. Meditate, yes, to be at peace with I AM and WHAT IS. The Baptism will come when it will. It will. Do not be concerned—for I will be with you even to the end of the World. I AM you. You are me. I AM present within All things. I AM in all things. I AM in every heart. I AM within every soul. Every atom—*I AM.* Cleave a piece of wood—*I AM* there. Lift up a stone and you will find me there. I AM not separate from anything. I AM THAT I AM. The reason I AM so difficult to find is that there is no place where I AM not. In that way I AM totally hidden. But, in fact, I AM Omnipresent.

Realize that you are a son of the Living God, and I love you. In fact, I AM you. But don't hold on to your self, your desires, or even your body. They are temporary forms. Use them, enjoy them, but then let them go. Fear not, for I AM still there. And when you let go of your old self—I will be born anew within you. That is the Baptism of the Holy Spirit. When you let go of all, as my son Jeshu did upon the Cross, I WILL BE BORN ANEW. This is the Resurrection. Peace be with you, Robert Michael.

Following this experience, and this Voice, I felt a oneness with God, and an opening of the inner worlds of imagery, or "heavenly worlds." I saw Christ on the Cross, Moses at Sinai, the Buddha, the Madonna and Child. I also saw a beautiful butterfly breaking free of its cocoon. I saw Satan, or the Trickster, through all of this. And I saw an inner image of Christ crying for the world.

It was from then on, more or less, that I learned to follow the Voice for Self, and its promptings. With fear and trepidation I left the hotel in San Francisco, and went where I felt that God was leading me. It was thus that my Journey continued, and I met the next teacher on my Path, Robert Johnson, in San Diego. He was the Wise Man figure to me.

To follow the Voice for Self is different from the world's ways. But it is not recommended that you ignore the world either. Quite the contrary, you must be very cognizant of the world, just as Moses had to be in dealing with Pharaoh, who was no "easy customer." Following the Voice for Self is not magic; it is sometimes a very difficult struggle indeed. There are many obstacles on the Path.

When Moses left the land of the Midianites, he met his brother, Aaron, and then he went before the Pharaoh, saying this to him:

"Thus saith the LORD, the God of Israel; Let My people go, that they may hold a feast unto Me in the wilderness."

The Pharaoh was not exactly compliant, and replied:

"Who is the LORD, that I should hearken unto His voice to let Israel go? I know not the LORD, and moreover I will not let Israel go."

Moses remonstrated with Pharaoh:

"The God of the Hebrews hath met with us. Let us go, we pray thee, three days' journey into the wilderness, and sacrifice unto the LORD our God; lest He fall upon us with pestilence, or with the sword."

This was not too convincing to Pharaoh, who replied:

"Wherefore do ye, Moses and Aaron, cause the people to break loose from their work? Get you unto your burdens."

Just because you have heard the Voice for Self does not mean that you are instantly free. It just means that your ego has encountered the Deep Center. You still must fight the battles with inner and outer Pharaoh. You may quote the Lord, but the Pharaoh, whether within or without, as Moses found out, does not know him. Moreover, the Pharaoh increased the peoples' burdens depriving them of the straw that they needed to make bricks, while still requiring them to fulfill the same quota, while gathering stubble for themselves throughout the land. This rings true on the personal level as well. When you begin the struggle to break free of the Pharaohs in your life, whether within or without, they tend to retaliate with increased burdens, and harsh punishments. Pharaoh tends to become more, not less, oppressive when you announce to him your wish to be free.

Let us backtrack a little, and look at what Moses has done in his reactions to the enslavement of his people, and his attempts to free them. How does Moses deal with Pharaoh? There are three levels of behavior, or three "ways" which we can discern: (1) Moses simply went along with the enslavement of his people; he was forty years old before he went out among them, and felt their suffering; (2) Moses reacted violently to the situation by slaying an Egyptian he saw beating a Hebrew; and (3) Moses tried to "justify" his case for the freedom of his people before Pharaoh, i.e., he sought for Pharaoh's "OK" to be free. G.I. Gurdjieff, the Russian-born mystic of this century, would call what Moses was doing in the third case "self-justification." None of these ways worked for Moses. None led to the freedom of his people.

Let us look at these three ways on a more personal level. I will call these three ways of behaving: (1) *Compliance*—here you merely go along submissively with the authorities in question. You can see fairly willing compliance in school-age children. Even college-level and graduate students feel "compelled" to comply with their professors. Parents of all cultures seem to value compliance in their children above all. The military inculcates compliance, i.e., the "obedience to superiors," as a paramount virtue. And in the adult world of affairs, in business, in government, in education, and so on, the "virtue" of compliance, or conformity, is highly rewarded. The "rebel" is often deprived of his job, chance for advancement in an organization, and sometimes even his very freedom in various societies of the world. Even in such "learned groups" as the early psychoanalytic association surrounding Freud in Vienna, conformity seems to be the sine qua non of worldly success. It is not difficult to observe compliance or conformity in this age of the "organization man."

(2) *Rebellion*—in this case you have gotten angry, and said "Hell, no, I've had enough!" That's what Moses did when he saw the Israelite being beaten by the Egyptian taskmaster. It's what many thousands of young men did during the Vietnam war era; they refused to serve in a war they considered to be unjust. It is what Martin Luther did in his day when he refused to go along with the corruptions he saw around him in his church. It is also what his later namesake, Martin Luther King, Jr., did when he viewed the oppressions that his people were suffering in the days of legalized segregation in the United States. It is the absolutely necessary stage that one must pass through on the road to liberty. An element of anger seems charactcristic of this stage.

One can, however, get overly carried away with the emotion of anger in this rebellion stage, and make it the end in itself. Some of the "left-wing" liberation movements of our time have made rage, and its offspring, revenge, a moral "badge of courage" of their movement. One can argue that the tyranny of Lenin easily equalled or surpassed that of the Czar. It led to the organized and "legalized" mass murder and terror of the Stalin regime. The recent "revolutionary" Pol Pot regime in Cambodia committed genocide on a proportionate scale unequaled in history. On the other hand, one reads with dismay in recent articles and books about the almost "routine" atrocities against civilian villagers, men, women, and children, committed by "our side" in the Vietnam conflict. Murder is murder, whether it be "revolutionary" or "counterrevolutionary." Clearly, the stage of rebellion, or counterrebellion, can get out of hand. There must be added to righteous indignation a level of moral principles such as those which informed our own revolutionary ancestors in our better days. When the American patriots beat their British enemy at the Battle of Yorktown, they did not exact vengeance upon their former adversaries once they surrendered. These ethics perhaps account for the long-term success of the American Revolution which did not replace tyranny with greater tyranny. Likewise, in our own lives, there comes a time when we must say, "Hell, no!" We must say "no" to the Pharaohs in our lives. But this "no" with its inevitable element of indignation must not be allowed to grow into a rage which consumes us or leads us to actions morally inferior to the behavior of those who have oppressed or enslaved us. The second stage is one to be transcended, but pass through it we must.

(3) *Self-justification*—this is the offering of rationalizations to the authorities in question as to "why" they should allow you to be free. This is like a young man or woman going to his or her parents and quoting from the Bible, "a man shall leave his father and his mother . . . ," or else quoting from a psychology book about the same thing. When you are ready for freedom, you need not justify it!

Self-justification takes some interesting turns. An art student may explain to his art teacher "why" he should be allowed to paint in the way he does. Vincent Van Gogh did not even get to this stage when he went to art school; he brought a gun to school prepared to shoot his teacher after he felt he had been unjustly criticized! Later, when he lived in Arles, France, and shared his house for a time with Paul Gauguin, Vincent used to argue incessantly with Paul "in defense of" his painting technique. It wasn't quite satisfactory. He had to say, in effect, "the hell with you, Paul," and go about his business painting in his own way. This he did eventually.

The letters of Freud and Jung provide a beautiful illustration of the progress through these levels. Jung was the younger man, and Freud was his mentor, a kind of father figure. The first letters of Jung to Freud indicate a compliant kind of "pupil to teacher" relationship. Later as Jung came into his own as a psychologist, there were elements of anger and rebelliousness in his letters to "Profesor Freud." When his views began to diverge considerably from those of Freud, Jung did some obvious self-justifying in his attempt to convince his old teacher of his "right" to think for himself. This really couldn't work, and Jung finally declared his independence from his former teacher in one of his last letters to him. In this letter, Jung stated that he did not "thrust his friendship on anyone," and ended with, "the rest is silence."[6] It was only after his separation from Freud that Jung went through his own Inner Journey, and developed his unique contribution to Western psychology. There is the suggestion here of something beyond self-justification. What, we may ask, is the fourth way?

Let us look at this progress through the "levels" in its most purely archetypal form in the story of Moses. We left Moses pleading his case before Pharaoh and being flatly rejected. In the Bible, one sees Moses returning rather sheepishly to God and asking Him why He has "dealt ill with this people," and "why is it that Thou has sent me?" Moses goes on to say that since he came to Pharaoh to speak the Lord's name, "he hath dealt ill with this people; neither hast Thou delivered Thy people at all." The Lord assures Moses that *He can be relied upon.* And He says: "Now shalt thou see what I will do to Pharaoh. . . ." God renews His covenant with Moses, and reveals his most sacred name, YHWH, which means "He who causes to be." On the inner level, we can see ego sheepishly going back to Self and telling of its failure to achieve freedom. The Self reassures the ego; there is a strengthening of confidence.

Moses enters into a long series of negotiations with the Pharaoh which can be viewed as "intermediary steps" between the third and the fourth way. Moses performs "wonders," such as changing his rod to a serpent to show Pharaoh God's power. But Pharaoh's magicians easily perform the same thing, and Pharaoh does not relent. Next, the Lord instructs Moses to visit a series of ten plagues upon Egypt. In each case, up to the last, the Pharaoh's heart "was hardened," and he did not let Israel go. Finally, when all the first-born of Egypt are slain by the "angel of death," and grief is great in all the land, Pharaoh at last relents, and tells Moses to take his people and "go!"

So Moses and the Israelites, 600,000 men, women, and children, packed their belongings, and with their flocks of sheep and cattle left Egypt. While the Israelites were encamped by the Red Sea, Pharaoh's heart was hardened once again, and he ordered his chariots and armies to pursue the Israelites and re-enslave them. When the people saw the pursuing Egyptians with their horses and chariots, "they were sore afraid." I think that you and I would be too. The children of Israel lost faith, fearing death, and they told Moses, ". . . it were better for us to serve the Egyptians than that we should die in the wilderness."

Their fear and lack of faith in themselves is what kept the Israelites in slavery in the first place, and it is what keeps anybody enslaved. It is not just "the tyrant" who keeps people enslaved; the people themselves allow this to occur. The same is true on a personal level in our individual lives. Security is what many would choose over freedom. We would rather live under paternalistic rule than take the scary risk of freedom and fend for ourselves. With the Egyptians closing in on them, many of the people must have felt, "Why did you rock the boat, Moses? We could have lived in comfortable slavery."

The inner psychological parallel is that when the ego is about to make good its "escape," superego closes in for the kill! It is terrifying to stand at the brink of the Red Sea with its raging waters ahead of you and the raging armies of the Pharaoh behind you. The terror of the Israelites must have been immense; it was paralyzing fear.

Moses did not fear, however, and through his sheer faith and will a great miracle happened that day. Jesus was later to say that if you had as much faith as a tiny grain of mustard seed, you could say to yonder mountain, "Be ye removed into the sea." Moses acted on just this kind of faith when he told his people to "Fear ye not, stand still, and see the salvation of the Lord. . . ." With his supreme faith, Moses "stretched out his hand over the sea; and the Lord caused the sea to go back by a strong east wind all night, and made the sea dry land, and the waters were divided." The children of Israel crossed over the Red Sea to the other side that morning, walking upon dry ground, but when the Egyptians tried to pursue them, the sea closed up over them, and they were drowned.

This episode has profound allegorical meaning and psychological significance. It is not whether it really happened or whether it is an allegory. Why can't both be true? It really happened and it is an allegory. Allegorically, we all have our Red Sea barriers that we are just too afraid to pass through. We are afraid to break free of mother and father; we would like to quit our job and try our hand at a whole new career, but we fear we would not make a go of it; we would like to move from where we live and go to a whole new place, but we feel too insecure to try, and so on. You know what your own personal Red Sea is. Generally, too, there is a Pharaoh on this side of your Red Sea. You feel that he or she keeps you there. You don't see how you freely give consent to your own enslavement. To be free, you must just walk out of whatever it is that enslaves you. Don't bother resisting, or self-justifying, *just leave*. But, even after we have left, we seem to come to a certain point, and we can't seem to go any farther. This is our Red Sea experience. To cross this "sea," we must exercise a rarely used power:

faith. Just what faith is, I do not know, but it can move mountains! Faith does involve a trust in a power greater than yourself, call him God, who hears and answers prayers. When you call on His Power, you can "stretch out your hand "over your own Red Sea and *it will part.* With faith, you can cross over to the other side to freedom. Faith is a real power, an enormous power, and it comes merely by believing that it will. It was faith that allowed the Israelites to cross the Red Sea, and faith that enabled David to challenge and defeat Goliath, and faith that gave Jesus the power to heal the sick and raise the dead. To cross your own personal Red Sea, you need only exercise a rarely used power: faith. This is the Fourth Way.

To summarize our discussion of the four ways: (1) *compliance,* or submission to the authority system in question, is the first way; (2) *rebellion* is the second way; (3) *self-justification* is the third way; and (4) *action through faith* is the fourth way. These four ways seem to involve different levels of consciousness and seem to come from different "places" within us. We will discuss this in greater detail in the last section of the book. Suffice it to say for now that action in the fourth way seems to involve consciousness of the Self. True prayer or true action of any sort comes from the "place" of the Self, and makes contact with the Supreme Being or God.

Moses led his people to the mountain called Sinai. God called out to Moses from the mountain and said this to him:

Thus shalt thou say to the house of Jacob, and tell the children of Israel. "Ye have seen what I did unto the Egyptians, and how I bore you on eagles' wings, and brought you unto Myself."

My friend, Pastor James Laughlin, used to speak about letting my spirit "soar upward like an eagle" above my problems. The eagle is a symbol of the Spirit. When the ego is lifted up by the Spirit, it transscends its isolation and limitations and becomes a servant of the Greater Life. In most extraordinary ways, things will fall into place, as it were, when the ego no longer tries to "lead" and "plan," but rather follows the voice that speaks deeply from within. Then one's life begins to make sense, and one's direction becomes quite clear.

When the Israelites crossed the Red Sea from bondage to freedom, they were by no means "home free" or in the "Promised Land." They found themselves in a barren wilderness, or desert. They spent forty years wandering in this desert. You will likewise have your "desert experience" after you have left your "Egypt." I had mine. It is not an unproductive time though, for it was in the desert that the Israelites received their Holy Law at Mount Sinai. It is during the "desert time" that you will receive your own "Holy Law" as well. It is a time of immense clarity.

God instructs the people gathered at Mount Sinai to consecrate themselves and wash their garments because on the third day the Lord will come down upon Sinai within the sight of all the people. The Lord tells Moses to set bounds around the mountain lest the people break through and gaze upon the Lord and die. Moses alone could ascend the holy mountain to commune with the Lord and receive his Law.

What does this mean in psychological terms? The "ascent of the holy mountain" is the rising to the level of consciousness of the Self and beyond to "contact with God." It is not something that everyone should do, for what is holy can also be very dangerous. Only a person of the stature of Moses, that is a mature person, has the psychological strength to endure a direct confrontation with the *Mysterium Tremendum*. Witness the psychological fatalities of the "psychedelic generation" of inexperienced youths who artificially, through chemical means, "ascended the holy mountain." Many of them did die, or lost their minds, or suffered long-term personality damage. The Journey is a sacred matter, and psychological maturity is a prerequisite. Moses was a psychologically mature man capable of withstanding the *numinosum* and returning to tell the story.

Moses communed with the Lord for forty days and forty nights upon Mount Sinai. The Lord gave Moses two tablets of stone upon which were written the Ten Commandments. The Bible says that they were written with the "finger of God." The Source of this message is what the Western tradition would call the "Holy Spirit." When he speaks, you will know, as Moses did, that you are being addressed. The "tablets of stone" upon which God "wrote" His commandments are to my mind symbols of the *reality* of the "messages" that one receives from the Unconscious Psyche. Carl Jung refers to these psychic events as "psychoid," which indicates that they are a reality every bit equal to that of "material objects," which in terms of modern physics we now conceive of as forms of "concentrated energy." Energy is still energy whether within or without; energy is the "stuff" of the Universe. The Holy Spirit, in the Jewish mystical tradition, is considered the "Breath of God" or the "Cosmic Breath." "He" is also considered to be the Voice through which God speaks. Where else does He speak if not from the innermost depths of the Self? In the soul of Moses did God write His Ten Commandments upon Mount Sinai, and upon your soul will He write His Word for you when you "ascend the holy mountain." The Law received by Moses is the underpinning of Judaism and Christianity. Let us now consider each of the Ten Commandments.

I. "I am the Lord they God, who brought thee out of the house of Egypt, out of the house of bondage." I AM is the Unitary One who sets one free from one's bondage. What is this bondage? It is the bondage to one's past, to one's family, to one's culture, to one's social conditioning, to one's neuroses. How can I AM set you free? "He" can do so by taking away any need whatsoever for contingencies to support one's sense of selfhood. I AM is the Absolute Self. When you come to know him, you will know that you are *a son or daughter of the Living God.* You will find your own *I am-ness.* This noncontingent Selfhood cannot be threatened in any way. It cannot be threatened by rejection, or loss of approval, or humiliation, or loss of possessions, or loss of security, or loss of one's accustomed style of life, or threat of loss of life, or even actual loss of life! Jesus was to later state this absolute sense of *I am-ness* when he said to those who questioned his authority, "Before Abraham even was, *I am.*"

God goes on to state that "Thou shalt have no other gods before me." The Hebrews beginning with Abraham and culminating with Moses were set free from the allegiance to the many gods of the cultures that surrounded them, be it Egypt or Mesopotamia. It is not that these "gods" were not true forces of nature or of personality. That is just what they were: archetypal representations in projection of the many forces that surround one without, and that inhabit one within. There was the sun god, and the moon god, and the earth god, and the sea god, and the god of the underworld, and so on. And there were the gods that represented interior forces of the personality such as gods of masculine aggression, gods of feminine charm, gods of wisdom, gods of love, and so on. These are all *real forces,* ones to be recognized and responded to. The Jungians have been very good at elucidating the inner nature of these ancient "gods" of the Sumerians, and Egyptians, and Greeks, etc., in terms of Jung's theory of the archetypes of the collective unconscious. Having been through this Journey, I fully verify their existence and their importance! The ancient Hebrew view, contrary to what they say in twentieth-century synagogues and churches, was not that the "other gods" were nonexistent. Not at all. The point is rather that they are all *created beings.* On the Kabbalistic scheme of the Tree of Life, these "other gods" would be the "sephiroth," or "spheres of divine activity." They are not *the Creator!* The Creator is One and His Name is One. To Him alone should worship be addressed.

Now, what does this mean on the psychological level? It means that there are many "part personalities" within us. Freud discovered three that he called "ego," "id," and "superego." Jung, and the Jungians, have greatly extended and enriched this overly narrow Freudian system, and they have introduced us to such parts of the psyche as the "persona," the "ego," the "shadow," the "anima," the "animus," the "wise man," the "wise woman," and so on. To really know these *beings within* is to make the Journey. They are not just "intellectual abstractions," but very real forces and personages that abide within us. But, though one must pay respect and heed to all of these archetypal forces within, the goal of the Journey is the Self. Like God, His Name is One, as well. One will be a divided and conflicted person whose name is "many" until one finds the center in oneself who speaks with One Voice.

II. The second commandment is the great injunction against idolatry: "Thou shalt not make onto thee any graven image. . . ." The injunction against idolatry refers not only to images of stone or metal, but just as surely to mind-created images. It means that God is absolutely undefinable, indescribable, and inconceivable. It means that God is *no thing.* The same can be said for the Self which was created "in the image of God." The illumined German mystic Jacob Boehme said, "Let the hands or the head be at labor, thy hearts ought to rest in God and God is a Spirit. Remember also thou art a spirit created in his image."[7]

The great religious truth is that when one has penetrated to the heart of the tabernacle and has entered the *holy of holies,* one finds that it is empty. The Divine cannot be represented. Neither can the Self be made into an image or a concept. To define God or the Self *is* idolatry. I once heard a Zen monk say, "To make the Self an object is the *worst sin.*" Moses and the Hebrew prophets would agree. But what is a "sin"? It is "missing the mark." In a sense, then, it is a lie, a falsehood, a form of ignorance. Idolatry, in the words of the Jewish prayer, "blinds the eye." The image or concept that one creates of God or the Self blocks one's spiritual vision. The idolater is spiritually blind. And idolatry is as prevalent today, if not far more so, as it ever was in Moses' time. Whether the idolatry of the God Mammon, or the God Moloch, or the Great God Science, etc., these idols blind us to the realms of human spiritual experience which they neither understand nor comprehend. These are mighty idols of our time, but they have "feet of clay," and they break. We will speak more about them later.

III. The third commandment instructs us "not to take the name of the Lord thy God in vain." Remember what is the Divine Name: I AM. It is also our name at the deepest level of our being. It is what it means to say that "we were created in the Divine image." When we take God's Name in vain, we also dishonor ourselves. As the Kabbalist mystic knows, *a name has power*. To invoke a name is to invoke the power behind that name. If you wish to call upon the goddess of war and wisdom, Athena, you can do so by calling upon her name. If you wish to invoke the archetypal Wise Man, you can address him too by his name. It is also possible to call upon the *Highest Power,* and that is exactly what we do in true prayer. You will notice that in all prayer, in whatever tradition, the Holy Name is invoked. One bows before the Holy Name. Jewish prayers speak of Him as "Adoshem," which means "Holy Name." It is a loss of Selfhood to take this name in vain.

IV. The fourth commandment deals with the remembrance and hallowing of the Sabbath day, or the seventh day of the week. In the Bible it says that God created the world in six days,

And on the seventh day God finished His work which He had made. And God blessed the seventh day, and hallowed it; because that in it He rested from all His work which God in creating had made.

Gurdjieff speaks of the esoteric tradition of the "law of the seven." Seven is a cycle of completion, as, for example, the "law of the octave": Do, Re, Mi, Fa, Sol, La, Ti, and Do begins a new cycle. "Ti" is the rest stop at the end of the seven steps before one reaches the "Do" of a whole new round. P. D. Ouspensky, the philosopher and student of Gurdjieff, says that "the law of octaves in all its manifestations was known to ancient knowledge."[8]

Ouspensky goes on to say that even our divisions of time into the days of the week, and Sundays, is a function of this general law. He states that "The Biblical myth of the creation of the world in six days and of the seventh day in which God rested from his labors is also an expression of the law of the octaves. . . ."[9] If Sunday, or "sun day," is the "day of creation," then Saturday, or "Saturn day" (Saturn is number seven counting outward from the sun), is the "day of rest." Like "Ti," it is a "rest stop" before the "Do" of a whole new cycle. I have found that when I observe the Sabbath "day of rest," I can sometimes "tune in," as it were, to the serenity of the created order. When I can do this, I feel "re-created," and I am ready to enter the cycle of a "brand new" week. "Recreation," by the way, is a derivative of the verb: "to re-create."

V. The fifth commandment is translated "Honor thy father and thy mother that thy days may be long upon the land which the Lord thy God giveth thee." In its short form, "Honor thy father and thy mother . . . ," it has become a cliché and a sentimental favorite. "They are your parents so you must honor them. . . ." "After all, he is your father. . . ." "I am your mother, and don't you ever forget it!" And so on. These banalities are misuses of the commandment which ignore its historical context. It was a warning against the pagan practice of abandoning the aged when they can no longer support or care for themselves. It looked to the reward of a stable society in which health and long life could be enjoyed. We may all be parents ourselves, and we will all be old one day too, so this commandment, as is true of the others, has an element of self-interest, as well as of social concern. Justice is concerned about both the individual and the culture as a whole.

The commandment about "honoring one's parents" has come full cycle in our age, and it has become in too many cases a "justification" for possessiveness and domination by parents over the lives of their children, even their full-grown "children." Emotional abuse of children by parents leaves wounds that can last a lifetime. These are the emotional wounds with which all psychotherapy deals. I once asked a Hasidic rabbi why there was no commandment about "honoring one's children." He replied that this was an "unwritten commandment" that should be self-evident to parents that their child was not "made" by them, but came through them via a *higher source*, whether you call it nature or God. No one expressed it better than Kahlil Gibran in *The Prophet:*

Your children are not your children. They are the sons and daughters of life's longing for itself. They come through you but not from you and though they are with you yet they belong not to you.[10]

Children are not "possessions," but "temporary wards" given by life to their parents' care for a limited period until it becomes time, and that should not be later than eighteen through twenty-one years, for "a man to leave his father and his mother. . . ." Where there has been such respect for children by parents, there will be natural respect and gratitude toward such parents on the part of the new generation. Respect or honor cannot be forced, "it must be earned," I was told by this same Hasidic rabbi. The greatest respect that parents can show their children is to recognize them as the totally unique and separate individuals they are. This includes allowing them to grow and develop along the lines that God intended for each individual child, and not as their parents intended! Parents must not confuse themselves with God. His Will is best known to each person from within his or her own heart and soul. Freedom is to follow God's will for ourselves. Parents must show their grown children the respect and love of *letting go*. Such parents deserve honor. Parents who treated their children as possessions, or as scapegoats for their own neuroses, or victimized them in other ways, cannot expect honor, even according to the Jewish Talmud. Honor must be earned to be real honor.

Jesus goes beyond the Talmud when he says: "If anyone comes to me and does not hate his own father and mother . . . he cannot be my disciple."[11] This would seem to contradict the Old Testament commandment to "Honor thy father and thy mother . . . ," but George Lamsa, a scholar of Aramaic origins, points out that the Aramaic word "hate" really means to "put aside."[12] In order to follow the Christ, or the true Self, you need to "put aside" parents, relatives, and even culture. To discover this, one needs to turn to *higher parents* than the merely biological. Carl Jung would say that you need to discover the "archetypal parents." These are Father Spirit and Mother Earth. The Spirit in traditional forms is the church and synagogue, Sabbath worship, holiday services, orthodox liturgies, and the like. Whereas this seemed satisfactory for traditional times, I do not think it is enough for our time which is beyond the "age of faith." We need *experience*. We need to go back to the origins of our religions to rediscover what the Great Ones, such as Moses and Jesus *knew directly*. Mysticism is the tradition of "direct knowing," and we can learn a lot from it of value. One can know through meditation, and one can know through paying attention to one's dreams and inner life. A dream of "fire" or "light" is the psychological equivalent of Moses' "burning bush" experience. The Spirit is there; we need only *look within*. In our present technocratic age, we need also to get away from our smoggy cities to the woods, the mountains, and the streams. We need to make contact with the "Earth Mother." After a year of writing in San Diego, I went up to the Sierra Nevadas to climb, and hike, and swim in cold mountain lakes and mineral hot springs. It was what I needed to restore my soul. Mother Earth will do that for you.

And so, "honor thy father and thy mother" refers on the interior level to honoring the *great archetypal parents*: Father Spirit and Mother Earth. One's parents on this earth should be "good representatives" of the archetypal parents until one has become an adult man or woman. Such a father would be masculine and "spirited," and he would pass along some of this spirit to his son; and to his daughter, caring masculinity. Such a mother would be a source of feminine warmth and nurturance to her children of both sexes, and a model of mature femininity to her daughter. Unfortuantely, not all (or even many) parents are such ideal models. Some severely distort these masculine and feminine archetypal qualities, and the children of such parents will suffer psychological damage to their inner parental imagoes. Psychotherapy in these cases would need to go beyond (but not neglect) "analysis" of the etiology of one's neurosis in childhood. It is necessary for the wounded individual to go deeper: to the *roots of parenting*. The neurotic needs to relive in his or her interior consciousness what he or she lacked in life. Forgiveness of one's actual parents will help too because they merely passed along what they received, and the chain must stop somewhere. Forgiveness will not change the past, but it will heal the present.

VI. The sixth commandment is translated "Thou shalt not murder" in the Jewish Masoretic text. Most English translations (King James, Revised Standard, etc.) translate this: "Thou shalt not kill." I believe the Masoretic text is closer to the intention of the Hebrew scriptures which do not imply any absolute pacifism. The Israelites fought many wars of national survival against enemies bent upon their destruction. There is no implication in the Hebrew scriptures that it is "wrong" to fight in self-defense. To be a pacifist in this century would mean the countenancing by inaction of the mass murders of Adolf Hitler, for example. To act in defense of oneself, one's family, one's neighbors, and even one's fellow human being, might be considered a moral duty. The murder of innocents is the act which the sixth commandment forbids. It is the deadliest of sins against the Creator to deny a fellow human being the right to live. According to the ancient Hebrews, each human person is the moral equivalent to the entire universe. To murder, therefore, is to end a universe. No commandment has been as flagrantly violated as the commandment against murder in this "civilized" twentieth century. This is the century of Auschwitz and Hiroshima. More human lives were senselessly destroyed in World War II than in all previous wars in history. Yet, our present "technology of death" is so awesome that more people would die in a single second of a World War III than died in the entire

Second World War. This is the god of science and technology gone berserk! International conflict aside, our American cities have become literal war zones themselves in this century.

But there are psychological and spiritual forms of murder, as well as physical murder. To treat another human being as a nonperson, as in slavery, is spiritual murder. Parents who treat their children as possessions and not persons, the boss who abuses the rights of his workers, the politician who deprives citizens of their human rights, the teacher who denies his students the freedom to think for themselves; all of these are examples of spiritual murder. Dr. Thomas Szasz, the psychiatrist and author, has spoken eloquently about the "psychiatric dehumanization of man." He calls involuntary mental hospitalization a "crime against humanity."[13] Psychiatry and pschotherapy can sometimes be guises for psychological and spiritual murder.

Jesus, more than a millennium after Moses, extended the prohibition against murder beyond the physical to the psychological and spiritual spheres. He said:

You have heard that it was said of the men of old, "You shall not kill . . ." But I say to you that every one who is angry with his brother shall be liable to judgment; whoever insults his brother shall be liable to the council, and whoever says, "You fool!" shall be liable to the hell of fire.[14]

In extending the prohibition against murder from the physical to the psychological and spiritual spheres, Jesus goes behind the behavioral manifestations of violence to the root causes: hate and anger. There is little hope of curing the plague of violence that has been with humanity since Cain and Abel without getting at the cause: the sickness of the soul.

VII. The seventh commandment is the prohibition against adultery. Moralistic Puritanism and Victorianism have taken this commandment to be a "divine edict" against sexuality. The Hebrew root of the word "adultery" has nothing to do with sex at all! It is made up of "ad," which means "to add," and "ulter," which means "other."[15] Adultery means to "add other." Our Food and Drug Administration has laws forbidding the adulterating of our food and drug products for the protection of our bodies. The Bible is speaking of the adulteration of our spiritual principles.

The commandment refers to sex only in respect to the abandonment it may involve of principles, as, for example, a wedding vow that we have freely entered into to "forsake all others." To have sexual relations outside of one's marriage is, then, the adulterating of a solemn vow. To treat a sexual partner merely as an object of one's lust, and to ignore the personhood of the other, is also committing a form of adultery. One may call it an adultery of "subtracting" rather than of "adding." In this case, one is subtracting the human dimension of one's partner. To add or subtract from the *wholeness* of something is the meaning of adultery.

The commandment against adultery applies to the adulterating of one's principles in other areas of life as well. The doctor who allows considerations of money and profit, rather than the health of the patient, to govern medical practice is surely guilty of adultery: The doctor is adulterating the Hippocratic Oath he or she swore to uphold with "other considerations." The politician who accepts bribery from special interest groups, and allows greed to influence decisions, is adulterating his oath of office. The psychiatrist who divulges confidences is an "adulterer" as well. Ergo: *be true to your principles.*

VIII. The eighth commandment, "Thou shalt not steal," seems clear in its meaning. We dread the plague of theft that menaces citizens today. But, there are also forms of "ideological disenfranchisement." In our Capitalist system, where life is reduced to *Private Profits,* material wealth tends to become concentrated in the hands of the very few. They use it in ways which care little about the welfare of people, the health of the environment, or the moral-aesthetics of life in general. In our present society, the poor are deprived of the little they have, and the rich grow richer. On the other hand, Communism, whose watchword is *Centralized Planning,* produced Stalin, the Gulags, and repressions in country after country. Equity and freedom are both rights of which we can be robbed. I was wondering, however, whether there is a more inward interpretation of the commandment against stealing? It occurred to me, while taking a class with a seventh degree Aikido master, that here was a man whom everybody (including me) wished to be like. But he was an imitation of nobody. He was just *himself.* Imitation of another can be viewed as "psychological stealing," just as taking another's property is "legal stealing." I have noticed, in observing some spiritual groups and cults, that the followers seem to strive (consciously or unconsciously) to be like their "guru." It seems to them that "enlightenment" will come through imitation. It does not work that way. There is artistic imitation, too, as well as artistic originality. The commandment "Thou shalt not steal" means, on this level: do not imitate others; your real treasure is to be *found within*.

IX. The ninth commandment says that we should not "bear false witness against our neighbor." The first level of meaning of this commandment applies most obviously to the judicial system, and to this very day the very basis of any system of justice depends upon truth telling: witnesses in any judiciary proceeding swear "to tell the truth, the whole truth, and nothing but the truth." One's testimony in court could have the effect of sentencing a person to a long prison term, or even to death, and all legal codes severely discourage perjury. The word "witness" is derived from the old English word "witan," which means "understanding."[16] What we would call "consciousness" is what is meant. To bear false witness is to be false to one's consciousness, or *conscience*. Even our bodies betray us when we lie, and the modern technology of lie detection is based upon this fact. To a person of conscience, lying about another cannot help but produce genuine guilt which can be alleviated only when one has confessed to one's dissimulation.

At a deeper level, the commandment about bearing false witness has to do with honesty about oneself. Most of us, in this age of complex social roles, don some "mask" every day in the course of our ordinary lives. We don the mask of "doctor," or "professor," or "police officer," or whatever. Even within the family we play various roles, e.g., "mother, " "father," etc. Roles, from the simple to the complex, are necessary in any society. Jung called this mask we put on in the course of our daily lives the "persona." To *identify with* the persona is to become the role you are playing, and to lose contact with the Self that you are. In Arthur Miller's play, *Death of a Salesman*, Willy Loman so identified with the role of salesman that when he lost his job, he also lost his will to go on living. He had become his persona, and when he lost that, he lost everything. The beginning of the Inner Path can correspond with the breakdown of the persona, and honesty with oneself is the first requirement of the Journey.

X. The tenth commandment adjures us against coveting. To "covet," to give the dictionary definition, means to "desire enviously." This is a very Buddhistic commandment, as the Buddha taught that it is *desire itself* which keeps one in Samsara, or Ignorance, and that the Way to Nirvana, or Enlightenment, is the cessation of desire. The teaching against coveting is quite common among the spiritual masters of humanity. It is covetousness or desire which keeps us enslaved within the boundaries of our little egos, and causes our neurotic suffering. What does the ego covet? It covets material things, power, the admiration of others, etc. What happens when the ego inevitably loses these things that it desires? It suffers. In the course of life even our bodies, and our egos themselves, are ineluctably extinguished. This is the greatest suffering of the ego, its knowledge that it is impermanent. It covets what it must inevitably lose. Moses in his tenth commandment, as the Buddha in his third noble truth, instructs people to "give up coveting." When you give up what the ego covets, and choose to accept what God freely gives, you will find what you never lost: the Self you are.

While Moses was upon the holy mountain communing with God, the people grew restless and impatient, and Moses' brother, Aaron, designed for them a golden calf to quiet them in their growing doubt. He did not intend that they worship this idol. But the people soon degenerated into idolatry, forgetting the Unseen God. They worshipped the golden calf, and offered sacrifices to it. When Moses returned to the camp, and saw the calf and the people dancing around it, he became enraged and smashed the Tablets of the Law that he had carried down with him. He severely punished the idolaters, and several thousand were put to death. He told the people: "You have sinned a great sin." The Bible says that God was greatly angered too, and He cut off the people from the Divine Presence for a time.

Why was this sin of idolatry so serious? The golden calf is the symbol of *all idolatry.* Idolatry is the greatest sin because it is the complete denial of the Source of being, and hence is a great lie about who we are, and what our world really is. It is the root of all other sins. In the days of the Israelites, they had their golden calf, and in our day we have our golden calves as well, or should we say our "golden pigs!" A visitor to this world of the 1980's would notice that the largest and greatest buildings are not the houses of the worship of God (as was the case in ancient times and in the Middle Ages), but banks! He would witness thousands of people coming in and out of countless banks each day, seemingly offering "sacrifices." This is the God Mammon. Likewise, such a visitor would notice that we put far more money into our vast weapons systems, e.g., nuclear missiles, huge bombers, great aircraft carriers, etc., than we put into the collection plates at the little buildings we call "churches" and "synagogues." Billions more. This is the God Moloch. And finally, the visitor would note that we devote a great deal of money, time, and effort to the enterprise we call "science." In it, we reduce God's creations to ever smaller and smaller units that we call "molecules," "atoms," and "subatomic parti-cles," in our disciplines of "physics" and "chemistry," in the search for the "nature of matter." The visitor would also note that we perform experiments upon, and sacrifice in the cause of "research," millions of God's little creatures in our attempt to understand "how life works," And so on. This is the Great God Science. These are the three chief idols of our age, and we worship at their shrines. There are other gods as well, such as the gods of hedonistic pleasure, and such a visitor from outer space would visit the zones where these gods are wor-shipped.

Why are these idols so pernicious? It is not that money, or power, or scientific knowledge, or pleasure in themselves are evil; they are per-fectly respectable parts of God's Creation. It is when any one of these, or others, is taken as the chief value, or *ultimate concern*, as Paul Tillich puts it, that the problem arises. One tends to subserviate everything else to one's ultimate concern, and where one's ultimate concern is a part, and not the whole, the actions which flow from it are unwhole, or unholy ones, if you will. For example, in the service of the god Mammon, practically every other commandment has been broken. For money, as ultimate concern, people have cheated, lied, robbed, and murdered. Every evil has been committed for this god. It is why Jesus said, "You cannot serve both God and mammon." It is not that money in itself is "bad," it is just a medium of exchange, and is morally neutral in itself. It is the "worship of money" that is the root of all evil, as St. Paul stated. It is not material possessions, but the idolatry thereof that is the problem. Human beings throughout history have been enslaved and corrupted by this idol.

In the service of the god Moloch, wars of aggression and destruc-tion have been waged since the beginning of humanity's sojourn on this planet. The ancient Babylonians were conquered by the Assyr-ians, and they by the Persians, and they in succession fell to the sword of Alexander's Macedonian army . . . , and this bloodshed has not ceased to this date. In this "enlightened" twentieth century, we have had two world wars. A third world war, if it were to occur, would annihilate most of the human race in a single afternoon! Need I say more about the evil of this idol? Yet, this is not to say that power in itself is bad; quite to the contrary, the aggressiveness needed to de-fend oneself and one's loved ones is absolutely necessary to survival. It is the setting up of power as the ultimate concern from which such evil as was perpetrated by such mass murderers as Hitler and Stalin (both of whom openly proclaimed power to be their god) has flowed.

The blood shed in the name of the god Moloch continues to flow to this day all over our world.

The third idol that I have spoken of has many worshippers in this "Age of Science." He is cherished in the universities, and the government spends many billions of dollars in his support. He does not seem so obviously "bad" as the gods Mammon and Moloch. In fact, many consider him to be the "hope" of mankind. "Salvation through science" is a popular theme of our time. Science is, after all, "objective," and it leads to "knowledge," and is not knowledge desirable? With all of its educated "defenders" with their white lab coats and Ph.D. degrees, the god Science is a pretty tough idol to crack. But he too is made of clay.

The rules of the god Science are: (1) public observability, (2) replicability, and (3) experimental verifiability. It deals with things that we can sense through our physical sense organs, our eyes, and ears, and sense of touch, and so on (at least in principle). It deals, then, with material things, and not with spiritual things. It deals with events that occur again and again; it doesn't deal too well with unique events. Finally, it deals with things which can be "proven" to some degree of probability through "experiment," i.e., it deals with things that we can control to some degree or at least measure. It does not deal very well with things that are beyond the realm of "measurement" and "control." As a method, science is fine and good in itself, and its practice has led to fantastic advances in our knowledge of the world in which we live and in our ability to predict and control events to some degree. The greatest advances have come in the last three hundred years or so, although they had some precursors, such as the Greeks, in "ancient civilizations." It has also led to really incredible applications of this knowledge, or "technology," and this has been beneficial to humanity, at least to some extent, and we all enjoy the benefits of modern medicine, communications, industry, agriculture, etc. However, there are harmful aspects of these things as well, as we are increasingly learning in terms of the damage we have done to the natural environment, to animal species, some of which have become extinct, or are in danger of becoming extinct, and to our own bodies through the artificiality of our foods, intoxicants, and other poisons we regularly ingest. Our minds and souls have been victims of environments that have become concrete wastelands and mechanical nightmares. There have been perhaps as many minuses as pluses to the Age of Science and Technology. Yet, it seems inevitable that science and technology will continue to evolve, and perhaps in time, in more and more humane ways. With science or technology itself, I have no serious quarrel; they are ways of knowing and applications of knowledge, among others, and useful ones to be sure. I do have serious quarrel with scientism or the worship of science. This is the claim that the methods and results of science are the *only* valid forms of knowing. It is the claim that scientific knowledge equals the Real. Such a claim is made by logical positivists, dialectical materialists, behaviorists, and the like. It is the modern idolatry that I call the Great God Science. Such people as these, and some of them are scientists and some are philosophers (although there are scientists and philosophers who by no means share their views), see science as the ultimate value, and they would argue that we should base our judgments and our decisions on the "findings of science." They also seem to feel that other values such as the aesthetic, the moral, and the spiritual, if they grant them any credence at all, should be subservient to the values of science. This is a very cruel god, and it is a god which distorts our perceptions of Reality. I will say a few words about why.

Since science can deal only with what is publically observable, replicable, and experimentally verifiable (or at least measurable), the claim that scientific knowledge is the only valid knowledge closes off from our serious consideration vast realms of human experience such as religion, mysticism, myth, and poetry. The idolator of science tends to regard such things as "mere superstition," "primitive belief," an 1 "emotion devoid of cognitive content." The idolator of science believes that only the functions of sensing and intellectual reasoning can lead to "real knowledge." Such a person discredits the human functions of feeling and intuition, sometimes quite contemptuously. He would scoff at the miracles associated with Moses and Jesus, or would attempt to explain them away with "naturalistic hypotheses." He has no use for the reports of Cosmic Consciousness, or the Kingdom, or the mystics of mankind. He has utter contempt for the ancient "occult sciences" of astrology, numerology, the *I Ching*, and the like. And the great myths, such as that of Osiris, or Gilgamesh, or Parcival, etc., are regarded as "children's stories" at best. The poetic truths of Dante Alighieri, Omar Khayam, or William Blake, are seen not at all, or if so, as merely "pretty." I do not know what the person would do with the great teachings of the spiritual masters, except to disregard them totally. If there are other valid sources of human knowledge beyond the sensory-intellectual, and if these are of great importance to living as human beings in this world, then we have very much indeed to lose by following lockstep the priests of the Great God Science.

What are some of the "benefits" that the worshippers of the Great God Science have proffered to humanity? In the "science" of psychiatry, we have the worshippers of this idol to thank for such "scientific innovations" as prefrontal lobotomy, electro-shock therapy, "modern drug therapies," and even the recent "experiments" into the implantation of electrodes into the brains of mental patients so as to render them "tractable." The first transforms human beings into vegetables, when it doesn't kill them, in order to "improve their behavior." The second violently obliterates the issues that are disturbing the patient by shocking the brain (destroying many cells in the process), and returns him or her to society as a blank. The third, which is considered "enlightened," paralyzes the patient's brain from within, as surely as the older straitjacket paralyzed his or her body from without. And this is called "treatment." The fourth "technique" rings of Aldous Huxley's *Brave New World* in which all human problems are reduced to technology. These four "modern therapies" have flowed directly from scientism, or the idolatry of science. What is wrong with them? They disregard the fact that the patient has a human soul. Since soul and consciousness are not observable (except by oneself), they are not considered at all in these applications of "psychiatric science." The soul, if it is considered at all, is regarded as a "mere epiphenomenon" of the physical brain, and the above four "therapies" are essentially interventions into the brain of the patient; in the first case, part of the patient's brain is surgically excised! If changing human beings into passive and compliant vegetables is a "cure," I suppose that these forms of psychiatry have some "success rate." It is not the kind of cure that the ancient physicians of the soul had in mind, though.

What about the modern psychotherapies? These extend from traditional Freudian psychoanalysis to behavior therapy to primal scream therapy; they run the gamut. There are about 250 extant psychotherapeutic schools today. Most of these "therapies" share a basically materialistic philosophy underlying their theory of human behavior and personality. Freud would certainly claim to be a materialist who believed that biology ultimately underlay psychology, although he admitted that he did not know just how at the time, and he dealt with psychological states, both conscious and unconscious, in his practice. The behaviorists are the extreme materialists of psychological schools, and they admit only "sensory stimuli" and "muscular responses" into their system. The primal therapists like to claim a "scientific basis" for their theory and techniques by relating them to the physical brain. Even "cognitive therapists," if you were to ask them, would say that psychology is ultimately reducible to biology, and biology to chemistry, and chemistry to physics. This explains the soul "away." These psychologists seem unaware of the fact that modern physicists such as the Nobel laureate Eugene Wigner are reintroducing consciousness into physics as an indispensable fact. To quote Wigner: "It was not possible to formulate the laws of quantum theory in a fully consistent way without reference to consciousness."[17] Among modern psychologists, Carl Jung affirmed the real existence of the soul, or psyche; he wrote a book on this subject called *Modern Man in Search of a Soul.*

What is wrong with most "scientific schools" of psychotherapy? For one thing, as we have discussed, most of them eliminate the soul from consideration. For a person whose wounds are of the soul, what good can soul-less psychotherapies do? Furthermore, most psychotherapies have a basically manipulative approach to the human being, from the "free association" method of psychoanalysis, these "free associations" paradoxically thought to be totally determined, to the "conditioning" methods of the behavior therapists. How is freedom to be learned from people who deny its existence? These psychotherapeutic schools also presuppose the status of "sickness" for the patient, and presumably "wellness" for the therapist. Can the already demoralized and wounded individual profit by being further demoralized and wounded by the "semantic blackjack" labels of the "mental health" profession? This assumption of "sick" patient and "healthy" therapist would portray the healing process as "flowing" from the latter to the former. This would presumably "justify" the outrageous fees, charged by "modern psychotherapists" totally contradict the teaching $100 an hour and ruling out all but the very rich as patients). The only healing that the spiritual masters acknowledge is the healing power of the Holy Spirit which flows between equal human beings who join together for the holy purpose of healing. The high fees charged by "modern psychotherapists" totally contradict the teaching of the masters: healing is free, you cannot buy it! Healing in the sacred traditions of mankind is a *holy profession* and it depends upon a *holy relationship* between the healer and the one who comes to him for healing. Healing is not "for sale," it cannot come about through "manipulation," and neither is it "comprehensible" according to man-made theories. It is not subsumable to any of the idolatrous gods of our time including the Great God Science. The healing of the soul is much holier than that.

In other sciences, the scientistic attitude has led to unfortunate results as well. Geologists can tell mining companies what is the potential for extracting oil from shale rock, for example, but they cannot tell them what the American Indian holy men could tell them, i.e., that such mining on a large scale would be a rape of the integrity of Mother Earth that could lead to serious consequences for the health of the planet as a whole. If the earth is a living being, as the ancient Greeks, the American Indians, and even a few enlightened scientists believe, then *how* we treat her will have to be informed by considerations other than those of merely materialistic science.

Chemists can tell a farmer how to make a pesticide that will kill certain varieties of insects, and make crop yields bigger, but they cannot tell the farmer how this intervention into nature will affect the ecological balance as a whole,[18] what species of birds will die out due to this pesticide, how these poisons will affect the streams that lead into rivers and lakes, what these will do to the various species of fish, and, ultimately, how these chemicals will affect the human body.[19] In this century, we seem to be finding out that substance after substance which science and technology has put into the hands of industry causes cancer and other deadly diseases (which were unknown to the American Indian). In recent publications, I have become aware of the lethal dangers of our nuclear energy industries that produce hundreds of tons of radioactive wastes per year. The most dangerous of these is plutonium (named after Pluto, the Greek god of the Underworld). One pound of this substance could kill every person on this earth. Its radioactive lifespan is 500,000 years. And there is no absolutely failsafe means of storage. This is the legacy we have left for our grandchildren!

The Wise Men of history knew that we must turn to faculties beyond those of sense and reason in dealing with questions of wholes and values. Feeling and intuition are as important faculties of the psyche as are sensation and intellect, if not more so. Based upon sheer intuition (or revelation), for example, Peter and Eileen Caddy planted a garden on the sandy, infertile soil of their trailer camp at Findhorn, Scotland, and grew gigantic vegetables that astounded botanists and other scientists who came to see them. They assert in their writings that they made contact with nature spirits which aided them in their remarkable agricultural experiment.[20] This sounded fantastic to me at first too, but the gardens are there for anybody to see, and they are growing larger all the time. An entire "New Age" community based upon a philosophy of cooperation has grown up around this remarkable garden which was started by a single middle-aged couple who were unemployed and practically destitute at the time and followed a voice of inner guidance which told them to "plant a garden." They claim, and I tend to believe them, that this project was given to them by God Himself. When we turn to Him, we can make deserts bloom, and cause gardens to burst forth from sandy soil. God gave man the first Garden of Eden, and man betrayed it, and went into exile. It may be man's task, under Divine Guidance, to plant a New Eden.

From science, we have received in this twentieth century the remarkable truth $E = MC^2$. This has led to the development of the atomic and hydrogen bombs. If we decide to use these weapons of mass destruction, it will not be a law of science, but a Law of God that we will be violating: "Thou shalt not murder."

Our healing guide, Moses, led the Israelites to the threshold of the Promised Land. He accomplished his mission of delivering the children of Israel from bondage and giving them their moral law. The Wise Man can only go so far in the Journey before he must "bow out." Among Moses' last words to his people before he died were: "I have set before thee life and death, the blessing and the curse; therefore choose life. . . ."

To Moses' successor, Joshua, the Warrior, the task of leading the Israelites across the River Jordan into the Promised Land was given. To him also was given the task of "bringing down the walls of Jericho." He accomplished this by encircling the walled city and having them shout and blow their trumpets. The walls "came tumbling down."

How are we to interpret the Joshua story? I doubt that it was literally true. The Canaanites lived in towns with thick stone walls surrounding them. What I think the story means on a socioreligious level is this: the spiritual message of the Israelites which they brought with them from their desert sojourn was to prove more powerful than any merely physical walls of the Canaanite cities. The radical monotheism of the Israelites supplanted the worship of the Baals, or fertility gods, of the Canaanites. Moral law replaced corruption.

On a psychological level, even after we have left the "Egyptian bondage" of our superegos and received the "Holy Law" of our true callings, we are still trapped within the "old walls of the old city"; the ego defenses of our neurotic selves. These "old walls" must come down, and the "old city" must be supplanted by the "radical monotheism" of the true Self who can say I AM.

NOTES

Primary Source:
The Holy Scriptures according to the Masoretic Text, The Jewish Publication Society of America, Philadelphia, 1955, Genesis, Chapter 2:1–3; Exodus, Chapters 1:14, 3:2–6, 3:11–12, 3:13, 5:22–23, 6:1, 14:12, 14:13, 14:21, 19:4–6, 20:1–14, 32:30; Deuteronomy, Chapter 30:19.

Secondary Sources:
1. Milton Meltzer, *Slavery: From the Rise of Western Civilization to the Renaissance,* Cowles Book Company, New York, 1971, p. 37.
2. C. B. Falls, *The First 3000 Years,* Viking Press, New York, 1960, p. 104.
3. Jean Houston, *Life-Force: The Psycho-Historical Recovery of the Self,* Delacorte Press, New York, 1980, p. 84; the exact quote is as follows: "In many years of observation I have never met a stupid child, but I have met many self-righteously stupid and debilitating—and yes, even brain damaging—systems of education."
4. In January, 1981, while I was writing this chapter, I read a newspaper article about a twenty-one-year-old black man who was talked out of suicide (he was standing on a ninth-floor fire escape) by Mohammed Ali. The young man said that even his parents said he was "no good."
5. Merril Unger, *Unger's Bible Dictionary,* Moody Press, Chicago, 1966, p. 760.
6. *The Freud/Jung Letters,* ed. William McGuire, trans. Ralph Manheim and R. F. C. Hull, Bollingen Series XCIV, Princeton, N.J., 1974, p. 540.
7. Jacob Boehme, *The Supersensual Life,* trans. William Law, Allenson, London, Dialogue II, p. 48.
8. P. D. Ouspensky, *In Search of the Miraculous,* Harcourt Brace Jovanovich, New York & London, 1977, p. 130.
9. *Ibid.,* p. 131.
10. Kahlil Gibran, *The Prophet,* Knopf, New York, 1980, p. 17.
11. *The Bible,* Revised Standard Version, New Testament, American Bible Society, New York, 1971, Luke 14:26.
12. Eric Butterworth, *How to Break the Ten Commandments,* Harper & Row, New York, 1977, pp. 53–54.
13. Thomas Szasz, M.D., *Ideology and Insanity,* Doubleday, Garden City, N.Y., 1970, p. 113.
14. *The Bible,* Revised Standard Version, Matthew 5:21–22.
15. Butterworth, p. 97.
16. Ibid.
17. Fritjof Capra, *The Tao of Physics,* Shambhala, Berkeley, Calif., 1975, p. 300.
18. Rachel Carson, in her book *The Silent Spring* (Houghton Mifflin, 1962), was the pioneer in the ecology movement.
19. In the August 17, 1981, issue of *Newsweek* magazine, there is an article entitled "Pesticides' Global Fallout." In this article, there is a table labelled "Killer Chemicals," which links the toxic chemicals used in pesticides to various diseases. The source of this information is the Toxicology branch of the Center for Environmental Health, U.S. Centers for Disease Control. Many of these pesticides are now tightly controlled for use in the United States, but are "freely sold" to third world nations.

Pesticide	Suspected Health Hazards	Approximate Lethal Dose
Aldrin	Cancer, damage to fetus, nervous disorders	Teaspoon
BHC	Cancer	Teaspoon
Chlordane	Cancer	Teaspoon to tablespoon
DBCP	Cancer, male sterility	Teaspoon to tablespoon
DDT	Cancer, nervous disorders	Teaspoon to tablespoon
Heptachlor	Cancer	Teaspoon to tablespoon
Kepone	Cancer, nervous disorders	Teaspoon to tablespoon
Parathion	Damage to fetus, nervous disorders	A few drops
Paraquat	Damage to fetus, nervous disorders	Teaspoon to tablespoon
Nitrofen	Cancer, birth defects, female sterility	One-half pint
Toxaphene	Cancer	Teaspoon
2,4,5-T	Cancer, birth defects	1 ounce

20. *The Findhorn Garden,* by the Findhorn Community, Harper & Row, New York, 1975.

Chapter Three

Jesus, the Christ

*J*ESUS, who came to be known as "the Christ," was born nearly 2,000 years ago in the days when Caesar Augustus was the emperor of Rome, and Herod the Great was the King of Judaea. Judaea was by then a province of the Roman Empire. The people of Judaea, i.e., the Jews, reacted to their loss of freedom in various ways: from the Sadducees, the aristocratic class, who made compromises with the Roman rulers, to the Zealots, the political revolutionaries of the time who waged a futile guerilla war to free Israel from her oppressors, to the Pharisees, who represented normative Judaism of the day with their strict concern for the observance of the Law, to the Essenes, who dealt with the harsh realities of the day by withdrawing from the world into monastic communities who practiced asceticism and rites of spiritual purification.[1] The common people of Judaea and the Galilee, the poor, the hungry, and the downtrodden, as well as the learned scribes and doctors of the Law spoke of the coming of an "anointed one," or Messiah, who would liberate Israel, and bring about the Kingdom of God on earth.

In the Gospel according to Matthew, which will be our primary source in this chapter, the story of the birth of Jesus is recounted. Mary was betrothed to Joseph, a carpenter, but before they came together, she was found to be with child. Joseph was a just man and he decided to divorce his young wife discreetly to spare her humiliation. But in a dream an angel of the Lord spoke to Joseph, and told him: "Joseph, son of David, do not fear to take Mary your wife, for that which is conceived in her is of the Holy Spirit; she will bear a son, and you shall call his name Jesus, for he will save his people from their sins."

Mary and Joseph went to Bethlehem from their home in Nazareth in obedience to a decree by Caesar Augustus that everybody was to be enrolled in a census, and the Jews were to return, each to the place of his tribal origin. Bethlehem, the "city of David," was the ancestral home of Jesus' parents. When they arrived in Bethlehem, Mary was in an advanced state of pregnancy, but they could find no room in an inn. So they spent the night in a stable, and Jesus was born in these most lowly circumstances.

What is the meaning for us of the birth of the Christ child in those days of the Roman domination of the land of the Jews in conditions so humble and obscure? Even after the Israelites had entered the physical "promised land," they fell away from God, and then fell to one foreign invader after another until finally they found themselves under the iron yoke of the Roman Empire. We too, even after we have freed ourselves from our parents, both outer and inner, and have established our lives in the world, can fall away from our connection to our real selves into a darkness and alienation that turns life into a joyless and barren "wasteland," in the words of the poet T. S. Eliot. The bills pile up, the company we work for becomes our prison, our marriage is in trouble, middle age approaches, and the hope of the soul is all but lost. Whether we "compromise" with the authorities of our lives (Sadducees), or we rebel violently against them (Zealots), or we try to be "good people" (Pharisees), or we escape into the inner worlds through drugs or the latest techniques on the "spiritual supermarket" (Essenes), nothing really seems to work for us, as nothing was working for the various sects of the Jews in the time of the birth of Jesus. At best, we have a hope, as the Jews had a hope of the Messiah. On the inward level, the "Messiah" is the Self. "He" tends to make his appearance when we least expect him, in a dream, or a vision, of a new-born child, a symbol of the nascent Self, or Christ-within. His birth is "virginal" because it seems to depend upon no external circumstances at all, but rather upon the spiritual reality which is within. Meister Eckhart called it the "birth of the Son in the castle of our soul."[2]

The Gospel speaks of the coming of three Wise Men from the East. They asked in Jerusalem, "Where is he who has been born King of the Jews?" They said that they had seen his star in the East, and that they had come to worship him. King Herod heard of this and he was disturbed. Herod inquired of the chief priests and scribes as to where the Christ child was to be born. They told him "in Bethlehem of Judaea." Herod sent for the Wise Men, and he sent them to Bethlehem, and told them to go and search for the child, and when they had found him, to bring word of him to Herod so that he too "may come and worship him." After they had heard the King, they went their way and followed the star they had seen in the East till it came to rest over the place where the child was. They went with great joy into the stable to see the child with his mother, and they fell down and worshipped him. They gave him gifts of gold, frankincense, and myrrh. Then they departed for their own country, having been warned in a dream not to return to Herod.

The story of the Wise men from the East, or the "Magi," is filled with archetypal symbolism. First the "East" is always the "place" of the Unconscious. I had a dream once about receiving spiritual wisdom from the East. The "Wise Man" is an archetype of the Collective Unconscious, and he is usually the first figure to be encountered in the Journey. It is fitting that there should be "three Wise Men" who should come to worship the Christ child. Three is a mystical number, as in the "Holy Trinity." Their gifts are symbolic too. Gold has always been a symbol of the Self, as in the alchemist's reference to "our gold." Frankincense is a sweet-smelling resin which is used as incense. Myrrh is a bitter-smelling substance derived from plant gum which is also used as an incense. This would indicate that the destiny of the Messiah, or Christ, was to be inexorably a mixture of sweetness and bitterness, joy and sorrow. Jesus surely knew them both from his baptism at the Jordan to his ordeal at Gethsemane; from his Crucifixion to his Resurrection. It is the Self's destiny to know and encompass both the dark and the light. This little episode of the Wise Men summarizes the Journey from the appearance of the Wise Man to the dawning of the Self, and a "heavenly star" leads the way. "Heaven" refers to a state of consciousness in mysticism, and the "star" is a symbol of the *inner light* which is at one and the same time that which we are seeking and that which leads the way.

We note that Herod tried to stop the Christ child in His tracks as Pharaoh before him had tried to destroy the prophesied liberator of the Jews whom we know as Moses. Herod failed in his attempt, as the Pharaoh had also failed in his efforts to prevent the inexorable course of God's plan. The Pharaoh had ordered the slaying of all the newborn Hebrew children, but Moses was placed in a basket by his mother, and picked up in the Nile River by Pharaoh's own daughter, who adopted Moses as her own, counteracting her father's evil design. Likewise, when Herod had realized that he had been tricked by the Wise Men, he became furiously enraged, and he ordered the slaying of all the male children in Bethlehem who were two years of age and under. Although the innocents were slaughtered, and there was inconsolable grief in Bethlehem, Jesus was saved through a dream of his earthly father, Joseph. The dream told Joseph to take the child and his mother down to Egypt and to remain there "until further notice."

What does it mean that the tyrants of the day, Herod and Pharaoh, were unable to destroy the prophesied Liberator or Messiah in terms of our individual psychology? It means that no matter what the repressive figures in your life do to hurt and demoralize you, there is *that within you* which they cannot touch, and it is this which will save you. We spoke of the archetype of the Wise Man who can lead you to the brink of the "Promised Land" in the last chapter. I am speaking of Moses. In this chapter, we will speak of the archetype of the Self, he who is within you who can save you from not only the harm that others can do to you, i.e., "victimization," but also from that harm which you do to yourself, i.e., "sin." It is "sin," or "missing the mark," which keeps you out of the Kingdom. The Kingdom, as Jesus himself said, *is within.* Jesus is the incarnation of the true Self. The true Self is the Christ, and so Jesus is *the Christ*.

When Herod died, an "angel" appeared once again in a dream of Joseph and told him to return to the land of Israel. Joseph settled with Mary and Jesus in Nazareth, a town in Galilee. Galilee was a verdant land of low mountains, fertile soil, fruit and palm trees, and a large lake known as "Gennesaret," or the "Sea of Galilee." Judaea, by comparison, was a barren place of rocky plateaus, deep gorges, the Jordan River Valley, and the Dead Sea. Judaea was the location of Jerusalem, the center of learning and culture, the home of the Scribes and the Pharisees and Sadducees. The Judaeans looked down upon the Galileans as "country bumpkins." The Judaism of Judaea produced the Talmud, but it was the Judaism of the Galilee which brought forth Jesus.

The Gospel according to Luke contains a brief account of Jesus at the age of twelve. As was the custom, his parents went to Jerusalem to observe the feast of the Passover. When they were on their way home, the boy Jesus stayed behind in Jerusalem without his parents' knowledge. They assumed he was with the caravan; it was only after a day's journey that they discovered that he was missing. They went back to Jerusalem to search for him, and three days later, they found him in the Temple sitting among the learned scribes and doctors of the Law, listening to them, and asking them questions. All of those who heard him were astonished at his intelligence and wisdom. When his mother saw him, she said, "Son, why have you treated us so?" The reply of Jesus was: "How is it that you sought me? Did you not know that I must be in my Father's house?"

This rather earthy tale about a parent's concern for a lost child contains a powerful message in it. The process of individuation, i.e., coming to Self, must supersede familial and tribal loyalties if it is to succeed. Jesus was later to speak of this in his sayings. With most people, we can hardly speak of a "process of individuation" before the age of thirty, or even forty, if we mean by individuation the Journey to Self. The historical Jesus was certainly precocious!

About the years of Jesus' growing up, nothing is known with any certainty. We may presume that he became Bar Mitzvah, a son of the Law, at the age of thirteen, as was and is the Jewish tradition. He no doubt became a skilled carpenter under the tutelage of his father, Joseph, and in that way he learned to earn his living. He also surely became a master of the Hebrew scriptures, both in their outer and inner interpretations, as is evident in his sayings. We may presume that he received his religious training in the local synagogue. Some speculate that he spent time with the masters of the Essene brotherhoods, and this is possible, but by no means certain, as his teachings were by no means the same. The Essenes believed in withdrawal from the world, whereas Jesus preached redemption in, and through, and in spite of, the world. Others have speculated that Jesus travelled to the East to lands as far as India and Tibet to study with the masters of Eastern wisdom. Again, this is possible, but we just do not know anything of these years with certitude. It is possible that he grew up, and spent his entire youth, as a "local boy" of Nazareth. Spiritual enlightenment does not depend upon either time or place. The biblical record begins again with Jesus at the age of thirty going down to the River Jordan to be baptized by John.

John the Baptist preached in the wilderness of Judaea the message of repentance. He was a rather "wild" man who wore a garment of camel hair with a leather belt around his waist. His food consisted of locusts and wild honey. People from all over Judaea came to be baptized by him and to confess their sins. He spoke the words of Isaiah the prophet when he said: "The voice of one crying in the wilderness: Prepare the way of the Lord, make his paths straight."

When a number of the Pharisees and Sadducees came to John to be baptized, he rebuked them as a "brood of vipers," and he warned them of the wrath to come. He questioned the sincerity of their repentance. John then goes on to speak of one mightier than he who is to come: "I baptize you with water for repentance, but he who is coming after me is mightier than I, whose sandals I am not worthy to carry; he will baptize you with the Holy Spirit and with fire."

What is the difference between these two "baptisms," the one "of water" and the one "of fire"? On the symbolic level, what is "water"? It is the Unconscious. To be baptized with water is to return to the Unconscious Depths, to the "Maternal Womb," for the purpose of being reborn. But the "water" alone is not sufficient. What is needed is the "fire" of the Spirit. It is found only after one has made the regression back to the Maternal Depths. It was of this "fire" that Jesus spoke with the learned Pharisee Nicodemus (as recorded in the Gospel according to John), when he said, "You must be born anew." It was this "fire" which came upon the disciples on the Day of Pentecost as "cloven tongues like as of fire." This is the *light* of enlightenment.

No sooner did John make this statement about the two forms of baptism, that of "water" and that of "fire," than Jesus stepped forth to be baptized. John objected that he needed to be baptized by Jesus; why does Jesus come to him? Jesus answered him: "Let it be so now; for thus it is fitting for us to fulfill all righteousness." John consented to Jesus' request: "And behold, the heavens were opened and he saw the Spirit of God descending like a dove, and alighting on him; and lo, a voice from heaven, saying, 'This is my beloved Son, with whom I am well pleased.' "

This experience of the enlightenment of Jesus is, in certain ways, analogous to Moses' experience at the Burning Bush. In both cases, there is the consciousness of Light and the Voice for God, which is to say, the Holy Spirit. Moses received from the Holy Spirit the commission of a Prophet. Jesus received the commission of the Messiah. The Messiah is, in the Jewish mystical tradition as well as in the Christian tradition, "the Son of God." In the Kabbala, this is the place of "Tifereth," or Self.

Following his experience of Divine Illumination, it seems inevitable that Jesus should experience its opposite, or Satan, the Adversary. Mystics who have experienced illumination throughout history have reported this movement to its opposite, the encounter with the forces of darkness. Jesus was no exception to this Law of Opposites. He confronts Satan in the wilderness of Judaea during forty days of fasting. Satan came and put Jesus through three temptations. First he challenged Jesus as the Son of God to change stones into loaves of bread. Jesus rejected this temptation to magic and said: "It is written,

Man shall not live by bread alone, but by every word that proceeds from the mouth of God."

Next, Satan took Jesus to the Holy City and placed him on the parapet of the Temple and challenged him to throw himself down. He said that if he was the Son of God, angels would protect him. Jesus rejected this temptation to egotism, replying:

Again it is written, "You shall not tempt the Lord your God."

Finally, Satan took Jesus to a very high mountain and he showed him all of the kingdoms of the world, and he said that he would give all of these to Jesus if he would fall down and worship him. This was the temptation to worldly power, and Jesus had this to say to Satan: "Begone, Satan! for it is written, 'You shall worship the Lord your God and him only shall you serve.' "

Following this, Satan departed. Jesus did not have to go through all of the "four stages" of which we have spoken in conjunction with Moses and his reactions to Pharaoh. The devil tempted Jesus to magic, to egotism, and to power, but in each case Jesus successfully countered him. He did not submit (first way), or use forceful resistance (second way), or self-justification (third way), but in each case he spoke in complete faith (fourth way) the Word of God. Each of his statements, incidentally, is a direct quotation from the Book of Deuteronomy.

What does it mean that the Christ acts with perfect faith (or what I have called the fourth way)? It means that the Christ within us, or "the Self," acts with perfection. What is it to "act with perfection"? It is to act in harmony with God. As Jesus, the Christ, was in complete harmony with the Father whom he called "Abba," the Self is in direct relation to God, the "All in All." This is not so mysterious as it sounds, as we have all had some experience of the Self, or the Holy Grail, as it was spoken of by the medieval Christian mystics. "Modern" psychologists might refer to this as a "peak experience," since they like to take it out of a religious context. I think they err, for the experience of the Self is what religious experience really is. From the position of the Self, one can know God.

My most holy experience of this kind took place on a summer day in August of 1962 when I was twenty years old and deeply in love with a girl named Margaret. Margaret and I were walking along a beach at a lake in New York State, holding hands, and feeling a great love and communion between us. We were "I and Thou," each for the other. This love was apparently all that was needed to "open the door" for us, as it were, to the Kingdom. We rapidly passed through all levels of consciousness (neither of us had ever experimented with any drug, practiced meditation, or any other spiritual discipline in our lives at that time). We entered what the mystics call "Cosmic Consciousness." We felt that we had become "invisible" to others around us, and others seemed to be virtually unconscious, or "asleep" to us. We walked from the beach into the nearby woods and we literally "entered the Unity of all Things." We walked around the nearby woods for about a half hour in this consciousness. Everything was *absolutely perfect*. All things fit together into One Vast Unity. The character of this Unity was most definitely Love. We saw a fisherman fishing, and he seemed absolutely perfect. And then a deer approached us and we had a moment of communion with him. We perceived somehow that what was really the Self was eternal and would never die. Although I had not been a "believer" before this experience, I knew now what Jesus meant when he said: "He that believes in me, though he were dead, yet shall he live."

Margaret and I walked back to the beach and the bathhouse. A flag was being lowered. It was "closing time" at the beach. We knew somehow that when the flag came down, we too would "come down" to normal ego consciousness. This was my "baptism" experience. I also "moved to the opposite," a month or two after this experience of the Kingdom, and had an encounter with a Satanic figure. I was not rooted in myself, as Jesus was so completely, and the "seed of the Kingdom" was taken from me by this Satanic one. I fell into such terrible despair having received the "Fisher wound." Robert Johnson talks about this in his book *HE:*

Many psychic wounds in a man come because he touches his Christ nature, that is, his individuation process, prematurely, can't handle it, doesn't see it through and is wounded by this.[3]

The next nineteen years of my life (to now) have been almost entirely a "Quest for the Holy Grail." The Holy Grail is the only healing to such a wound.

Jesus, the Holy Grail in person, following his temptation in the wilderness and his vanquishing of Satan, returned to Galilee and the town of Capernaum by the sea. Jesus learned that John the Baptist had been arrested by Herod Antipas, the tetrarch of Galilee. From this time forth, Jesus took up where John had left off preaching the Good News of the Kingdom of Heaven. Walking by the Sea of Galilee, Jesus called his first disciples. They were all fishermen: Simon called

Peter, Andrew, his brother, James, the son of Zebedee, and John, his brother. Jesus said to them: "Follow me and I will make you fishers of men." They left their nets and followed him.

When you have an encounter with someone who incarnates this Christlike quality, the experience is overwhelming. You may even "leave your nets," and follow him. My experience with Pierre, whom I have spoken of in a previous chapter, was like this. Pierre had the numinous quality of a Self-realized man. When one experiences the symbols of the Self in a dream, or inner vision, it is equally compelling.

One may wonder why Jesus, the God-realized man, chose such simple men as these Galilean fishermen as his first disciples. Why didn't he choose learned men and doctors of the Law? Perhaps because these simple hearty fishermen were not burdened down in their minds by excessive scholarship and intellectualism. You recall the story about the scholar and the Zen master? The scholar was too full of his own pre-existing opinions for the Zen master to teach him anything. Fishermen, farmers, people of nature are often much closer to their essential selves than are intellectuals and inhabitants of the city. They are more "fertile ground" in which to sow the "seed of the Kingdom." The choice of fishermen *per se* is interesting in light of the fact that the fish was the earliest Christian symbol. I had a dream once about the baptism of Christ in which he came up from the water covered by three fish. The fish is the dweller in the waters. The "waters" are a symbol of the Unconscious. The Christ, as the fish, is the treasure found only in *the depths*.

Jesus went all over Galilee teaching in the synagogues and preaching his gospel of the Kingdom. "Gospel" means "good news." Jesus also healed the sick among the people, and his reputation as a teacher and healer spread all over. Those afflicted by every manner of disease—demoniacs, epileptics, paralytics—came, and he healed them all. Seeing the crowds, Jesus went up on a mountain and preached what has come to be known as the Sermon on the Mount. The first nine statements are known as the Beatitudes. It has been said that they reveal the secret of happiness.

Blessed are the poor in spirit, for theirs is the kingdom of heaven.

Blessed are those who mourn, for they shall be comforted.

Blessed are the meek, for they shall inherit the earth.

Blessed are those who hunger and thirst for righteousness, for they shall be satisfied.

Blessed are the merciful, for they shall obtain mercy.

Blessed are the pure in heart, for they shall see God.

Blessed are the peacemakers, for they shall be called the sons of God.

Blessed are those who are persecuted for righteousness' sake, for theirs is the kingdom of heaven.

Blessed are you when men revile you and persecute you and utter all kinds of evil against you falsely on my account. Rejoice and be glad, for your reward is great in heaven, for so men persecuted the prophets who were before you.

The Master spoke these sublime words to the poor multitudes gathered around him that day, the hungry, the sick, the ill-clad, the dejected, and the hopeless. He did not speak that day to the rich, the satisfied, the worldly, or the educated. Yet he seemed to be saying that it was just those people to whom he spoke, the "poor in spirit," who would inherit the Kingdom of God. This is strikingly contradictory to the world's standards. In the Greek culture of the time, the word *ptochos* meant a "poor man," and this was a term of derision and shame.[4] Even in Plato's ideal "Republic," the poor and beggars would be shunned and ostracized. In our world today, the poor are little better treated. Yet, Jesus called them "blessed," which is a term generally reserved for God in the Jewish tradition! The holiness of the poor, or *ani* in Hebrew, is not entirely novel with Rabbi Jesus, but has a long Old Testament tradition.[5] David, in his Psalms, speaks of the poor, the down-trodden, and oppressed, who are without help on earth, but faithful and wholly committed to God, and God does not ignore them, but rather lifts them up from their troubles. He bears them up on "eagle's wings," as it were. When one is without the props of the world, e.g., wealth, social status, and position, but one's reliance is upon God (because you have nothing else), one is not very far from the Kingdom. When St. Francis stripped himself of everything, even the clothes on his back, he entered the Path which leads to the Kingdom. The Kingdom involves a total transmutation of values. it is not worldly possessions or arrogance or power which brings it, but rather humility and poverty of spirit. When you live in the world of "things," you live in the consciousness of "I - it," in Martin Buber's language. We cannot live without this world either, without the "I - it," but if this is all we know, we will die without knowing the soul or God. What a poverty that will be! What a spiritual poverty we live in in our "modern," materialistic world of the West. We have television sets, fancy cars, expensive homes, luxury hotels, skyscrapers, great airports, giant industries, and all the other "things" we so "treasure" and wish to "protect." These things are as nothing, Master Jesus would tell us. Rather, he would point us to the *state of our soul*. Do we experience the sacredness of existence, the "I - Thou"? Do we apprehend the Christ in ourselves and in other people? Is our "home" in Heaven or is it in Hell? To those around him that day on the mountain, even to the persecuted and reviled, Jesus said: "Rejoice and be glad, for your reward is great in heaven . . . ." By "heaven," he was not referring to the "hereafter," as "heaven" is most often misconstrued, but rather the reward of a "heavenly" or "illumined" soul. Then, even if you have no material possessions, you have *everything*!

To the multitudes gathered around him on the mountain that day, Jesus also had this to say: "You are the salt of the earth . . ." and "You are the light of the world." What does he mean by these metaphors? In the days of Jesus, salt was a greatly valued commodity, both as a preservative and as a spice to flavor food. The thing about salt is that a little goes a long way. It is also invisible when dissolved in food, but you know that it is there! The "salt" is the soul within the human being that gives life its savor. Jesus goes on to say ". . . but if the salt has lost its taste, how shall its saltiness be restored?" If your soul has lost its joy, it can no longer season your life either. When Jesus speaks of the "light of the world," he is speaking of the Self which is the *light of God* in us. Jesus advises us not to hide our light, but he says "let your light so shine before men, that they may see your good works and give glory to your Father who is in heaven."

In his sermon that day, Jesus sets down the most stringent code of ethics ever proposed by any spiritual teacher. In comparison to the commandment forbidding murder, Jesus says that everyone who is angry with his or her brother or sister shall be liable to the judgment, and whoever says "You fool" shall be liable to the hell of fire. He states that anyone who looks at a woman lustfully has already committed adultery with her in his heart. In comparison to the Old Testament teaching about "an eye for an eye and a tooth for a tooth," Jesus says this:

Do not resist one who is evil. But if any one strikes you on the right cheek, turn to him the other also; and if any one would sue you and take your coat, let him have your cloak as well; and if any one forces you to go one mile, go with him two miles.

In comparison with the old ethic of loving your neighbor, but hating your enemy, Jesus says this; "Love your enemies, and pray for those who persecute you so that you may be the sons of your Father who is in heaven; for he makes his sun to rise on the evil and on the good, and sends rain on the just and on the unjust."

To his audience of poor Galilean Jews, most of whom were at least to some extent aware of the Law of Moses with its 613 prescriptions and proscriptions of behavior, Jesus has this to say: "You, therefore, must be perfect, as your heavenly Father is perfect."

What person can live up to such an ethic? The one who is angry at his or her brother or sister is in danger of the Judgment. A man who looks at a woman lustfully has committed adultery with her in his heart. Turn the other cheek. Love your enemies. Pray for those who persecute you. Jesus actually asks us to *be perfect*! Is a human being, as ego-self, capable of such perfection? Not likely. Look at the history of our world. Is not Jesus saying that we must all inevitably fail by our own (ego's) effort to be "righteous"? Is he not pointing to the inadequacy of "abiding by the Law" as a way to salvation? In the Law, at least in Jesus' Law of Perfection, we are all "sinners," i.e., we all "miss the mark." The Law deals with the outward behavior of a person, but Jesus looks at his inward consciousness, at the state of his soul. By these standards, we all fail. We are wholly incapable (modern utopians notwithstanding) of saving ourselves through our own (ego's) efforts. So what can we do? Is our situation so hopeless as our modern pessimistic thinkers such as Freud, Nietzsche, Kierkegaard, Sartre, and others would have us believe? Not according to Jesus in his reply to Nicodemus, "You must be born anew."

So Jesus is saying this: it is not your ego's efforts which will save you or permit you to live up to his standard of perfection. Rather, it is the Christ in you, or the true Self as we have phrased it, which *saves*. There is nothing you can do to "earn" this Christ-Self, nor can you attain it by "trying"; it cannot be won in this way. The Christ is a gift of God's Grace which can only be accepted, and ego needs step down from its position of pride in order to do this. When the ego takes the "second place," *you* will gain the "first place."[6]

In regard to praying, Jesus says that you do not need to "heap up empty phrases as the Gentiles do; for they think that they will be heard for their many words." Jesus teaches us to pray like this:

Our Father who art in heaven
Hallowed be thy name.

Thy kingdom come,
Thy will be done,
On earth as it is in heaven.
Give us this day our daily bread;
And forgive us our debts,
As we also have forgiven our debtors;
And lead us not into temptation,
But deliver us from evil.

Jesus goes on to say: "For if you forgive men their trespasses, your heavenly Father also will forgive you; but if you do not forgive men their trespasses, neither will your Father forgive your trespasses."

The Lord's Prayer, as it has come to be known, is the chief prayer of the Christian disciple. It can have great healing power, i.e., the power to make whole. It begins by proclaiming the holiness, or in Hebrew the *kadosh*, of God's name. As we have said, holiness and wholeness have one root. The prayer then asks us to reconcile our will to God's will. On the psychological level, this can be viewed as the reconciliation of ego's will with the will of the Self, or what Christian mystics would call the Christ-within. On a practical level, how can we distinguish between ego's will and the will of the higher Self? Our ego is the conscious self which we usually call "I." It is the center of the conscious side of ourselves. Most people, even most psychologists and psychiatrists, consider this "the self." Those who have made the Inward Journey, everyone from Dante Alighieri to Carl Jung, discover within themselves a deeper center which we have called "the Self." St. Paul discovered this within himself when he said, "not I, but Christ in me." In the Buddhist tradition, the masters speak of the "Buddha nature." The Hindus speak of the "Atman." How can we discover the Self's voice as opposed to the voice of the ego? The ego's voice is not too hard to ascertain; it is the constant "chatter" that goes on in our heads. The ego has its "rationality" too, and when we make "great plans," it is usually ego doing so. Since our culture has so thoroughly confounded the meanings of ego and Self, when you ask yourself, "Self, what do you want me to do?" it is usually ego who will respond. It is better if you address Self as "Christ," for this is truly what he is, the Christ-within. If you are a Christian, this should be no problem. Suppose you wish to know what the higher Self, or Christ, wants for you in a given issue, e.g., whether you should embark on a new career, say, as a writer or artist, and give up your old job. You can engage in what is called "active imagination" (in Jungian circles) with Christ, however you perceive him. You might sit in a quiet place with your eyes closed, and ask him, for example, "Christ," or "Jesus," "should I leave my career as a banker to pursue a career in art? Christ may speak against the course your ego wishes to follow, however. For instance, if a professional mercenary soldier were to have the inner intuition to ask Christ what he should do, I suspect he would give up this way of life, for the Master said, "Those who live by the sword will die by the sword."

Active imagination is a very direct approach to the Unconscious and is sometimes very difficult to do—in emotionally charged areas particularly. Our dreams which recur every night are a very sure guide to the Unconscious Self. In the Bible, "angels" often speak to people in dreams, as in the dreams of Joseph we have mentioned in this chapter. Jung would call these "archetypes." Whether angels or archetypes, the dream is often a vehicle for the higher Self. Sometimes, advice is very directly offered, and sometimes it is given in a highly symbolic way which requires interpretation. Interpreting a dream is a way of becoming more conscious of yourself. You might say that it is a way of becoming aware of "the will of God" for yourself.

Prayer is another, and very ancient, way of attuning to the will of God, or higher Self. There are a number of different forms of prayer. There is the prayer of "petition" for something that we (ego) want. For example, "God, please make me a millionaire!" This is almost the reverse of the teaching of the "Lord's Prayer" (unless this is God's will for you!), and is an attempt of ego to make God, or the Higher Self, comply with its wishes. Surprisingly, this can and does work, but when it does, we must live with the consequences. King Midas wished that everything he touched would turn to gold. His request was granted, but when he found that his food, and even his wife, also turned to gold, Midas lived to regret having made this prayer. A second form of prayer is "intercessory prayer." It is the prayer of a person for beneficial or healing things for another. It, too, can and does work, when one is sincere. I have prayed in this way, at times, for the healing of others and have seen the power of this form of prayer. Thirdly, there is the prayer of the disciple who asks God or Christ for *His Will*. This is what the Lord's Prayer is speaking about. Fourthly, there is a form of prayer which is the prayer of "communion with God." It is similar, if not identical, to true meditation. It is what Jesus did all the time!

The Lord's Prayer goes on to the apparently very ordinary request for our "daily bread." This can be viewed as the food we need for physical survival. Sometimes this can be received in a very miraculous way, as in the "manna from heaven" which the Israelites were given in the desert. Nor do I think that the wheat and grain that farmers grow to provide the bread we need is any the less miraculous! On a deeper level, Jesus referred to the bread he took and broke at the Last Supper as "my body." This kind of bread is the "bread of life."

We pray, in the Lord's Prayer, for God's forgiveness, and we are also asked to forgive those who have wronged us. We are told that if we forgive others their trespasses, then God will forgive us, but if we do not forgive others their trespasses, then neither will God forgive us our trespasses. When we forgive, we let go of inner hate and resentment. This "letting go" is the healing in itself of forgiveness, and is what it means, perhaps, to say that "God will forgive us." When we cannot forgive, neither can we "let go" of inner hatreds and resentments, and therefore we continue to carry them by our own choice, despite the fact that these inner grievances and grudges, some of which we carry for many years, are tearing us up inside. The effects of our unforgiveness is inner hurt, fear, anger, depression, and seemingly endless misery. This is perhaps what it means to say "if you do not forgive men their trespasses, neither will your Father forgive your trespasses." In the nature of the case, unforgiveness produces its own punishment, and forgiveness its own release. And what is "the nature of the case" is God.

Now, it is difficult and maybe impossible for ego to forgive wrongs that it perceives have been done against itself. This despite the fact that unforgiveness, or not letting go of hate, is a very unpleasant state to be in. Rather than forgiving, despite the pain, we often go on hating for a lifetime. Why would Jesus include something that is so difficult, if not impossible, in his Lord's Prayer? He includes it for the same reason that he requires an ethic of perfection: while it may not be possible for ego, it is perfectly possible for the Christ-Self within you, and to this higher Self you are required to turn. It is possible to look at your "enemies" through the eyes of Christ. If you see them in *this light*, your enemies will be transformed into your saviors.[7] Meditation and prayer are helpful in this. If you have difficulty in forgiveness, and we all do find it difficult to forgive those who have hurt us, pray for help in your problems of unforgiveness. If ego cannot forgive, Christ surely can. His light burns away impossibilities!

The prayer ends with the request not to be led into temptation but to be "delivered from evil." We cannot resolve the mystery of evil here; it has involved the greatest minds of history in religion, ethics, philosophy, and, more recently, psychology, and we can be very sure that despite the vast literature on the subject nobody understands it!

Why God allows evil to exist in the world has never been resolved, and probably never will be. Is evil a real force, is it the absence of God, is it the result of free will, is it the rejected half of the Self, or is it chaos itself? These are all probably part-truths about evil. One thing we do know, however, is that the man who is thought by Christians to be the "Son of God" said that we should "resist not evil." And he also advises us in his Lord's Prayer to pray to God the Father to "deliver us from evil." This may be the best advice that has ever been given to human beings. When we turn to God, who is the Whole One, to deliver us from evil, rather than struggle against it with the ego (which often results in greater evil), then Jesus is saying, there is nothing that the world, or even the devil himself, can do against us. Or as St. Paul said, "All things work for good for those who love God."

To illustrate this mystery of the transformation of evil by turning it over to God, let me speak of some examples from the Bible. The fact that Joseph was sold into slavery by his brothers seems "evil," indeed. But, if it were not for this fact, Joseph would not have interpreted the dream of Pharaoh that saved Egypt from a famine, nor would he have risen to regent over Egypt, nor would Joseph's brothers and his families have been saved thereby from starvation. Remember that he and his brothers constituted the original twelve tribes of Israel. One might say that if Joseph had not been sold into slavery, there might never have been a future history of Israel! Again, it would seem to have been an evil, and it surely was, that the descendants of Joseph and his brethren, the Israelites, were enslaved by a later Pharaoh in Egypt. Yet, if they had not been enslaved, and had lived "happily ever after" in Egypt, there never would have arisen the need for a liberator, Moses, nor would they have received the revelation on Mount Sinai, nor would there have been any real future for the Hebrew religion, nor for its descendants, Christianity and Islam. The world would have been denied the revelation of the One God.

Finally, everyone would agree that the crucifixion of Jesus was an evil thing, and it was; but without the crucifixion, how could there have been a resurrection? And without this mighty act of redemption, how could the message of Christ have spread throughout the world? In each case I have cited, and in many others in the Bible, a person of faith was involved, Joseph, Moses, and Jesus, and somehow through mysterious Providence, an apparent evil was transformed into a greater good, and a higher purpose was achieved. In each case, it happened through a synchronicity of events far beyond the ken of any individual ego to comprehend, predict, or control.

Jesus goes on to speak of the treasures of God's Kingdom versus the treasures of an earthly nature. Material treasures are subject to moth, rust, and decay, and thieves can steal what you have. But heavenly treasures, that is to say, treasures of your soul, are impervious to any material forces of corruption. When you are a happy person, the whole world becomes a happy place to you. On the other hand, you may have all the possessions in the world, and still be an unhappy and miserable person. Happiness is not found in things, but in the heart.

This same point about spiritual treasure is made again by Master Jesus when he compares the eye of the body and the eye of the soul. If your bodily eyes are sound, you will see the world's light; if your eyes are unsound, you will live in darkness. By analogy, if there is light in your soul, you will live in a world of light, but, as Jesus puts it, "If the light in you is darkness, how great is the darkness!"

The Rabbi from Galilee says that "No one can serve two masters. . . ." This is a teaching that seems to be almost totally ignored in the Christian world of the West today. We seem to think that we can serve the corporation and the "profit system" between Monday and Friday, and pay our tribute to God on Sunday. This is not possible according to Jesus who said this about serving two masters: "For either he will hate the one and love the other, or he will be devoted to the one and despise the other. . . . You cannot serve God and mammon."

With regard to our "Puritan work ethic," Jesus would hardly seem to agree, for he has this to say about our cares and worries about food, clothing, and other material needs:

Do not be anxious for your life, what you shall eat or what you shall drink, nor about your body, what you shall put on. Is not life more than food, and the body more than clothing? Look at the birds of the air; they neither sow nor reap nor gather into barns, and yet your heavenly Father feeds them. Are you not of more value than they?

I think of our smoke-belching factories, and our day shifts and night shifts of mass production and joyless labor. What is all this for? For a world of "things"? A world of gadgets, appliances, department stores, supermarkets, crowded airline terminals, noisy superhighways jammed with commuters, steel-skeletoned glass-walled buildings filled with white collar "employees" working their lives away in their cubicles, and computerized everything! Is this what life is about? It reminds me of the line in the song "St. Peter, don't you call me for I can't come, I owe my soul to the company store." I am not sure that this is what the Son of Man had in mind for us. Rather, he says we should "seek first the Kingdom of Heaven," and when we do, all the things we need will be ours as well. I have heard that the American Indian placed prayer and communion with the Great Spirit as their highest value. They lived in perfect harmony with nature with the simplest technology for at least 25,000 years before the white man came from Europe. I heard a Chumash chief say that his people still lived in Eden. He said that the white man's cities resembled his tribe's conception of hell! We have much to learn from the Native American who actually *lived* more closely to the way of life that the sayings of Jesus imply than we in the "Christian West" do.

Jesus summarizes the Law in a way that has come to be known as the "Golden Rule." It has been stated by spiritual masters in every tradition. Confucius taught a version of it, and so did Rabbi Hillel, a contemporary of Jesus, who said: "Do not unto others what you would not have others do to you." Jesus restated this in a positive form: "So whatever you wish that men would do to you, do so to them; for this is the law and the prophets."

If this simple rule of all spiritual traditions were followed and ap-plied, this would be a different world indeed in which to live. It simply asks you to put yourself in the place of the other person; it is a rule of *empathy.* It would ask the boss of a company to put himself in his employee's place, a teacher to put himself in his student's place, a husband to put himself in his wife's place (and vice versa), a parent to put himself or herself in his or her child's place, and so on. If this simple rule were followed, what need would we have of police, or courts, or jails, or armies?

Continuing in his Sermon, Rabbi Jesus speaks of the "narrow gate" which leads to life, and the "wide gate" which leads to destruction. He says that there would be *few* who would find the narrow gate leading to life. This contradicts the Christian "universalist" assumption that Jesus saved us all by "paying for our sins." It's not that simple. The true way of Christ is not a "mass way" or a "collective way." It is a highly personal path of consciousness and awakening, not a way of collectivism and conformity. The "gate" that leads to the Kingdom is a "narrow way," the "eye of a needle," an "anxious passage," a "har-rowing journey." It requires the highest degree of consciousness and vigilance. It is what Jesus meant by, "And what I say to you I say to all: Watch." "Watch" implies "be awake." John A. Sanford writes in his book *The Kingdom Within:* "The wide road is the way through life which we travel unconsciously, the road of least resistance and mass

identity."[8] He goes on to say that "The narrow road requires consciousness, close attention, lest we wander off the path, only the few
take it . . . because it entails the hardship of becoming conscious."[9]

The road is narrow in the sense that it is found in the *here and now,*
not in the past or the future. It is narrow in the sense that only the
guidance of the true Self will lead you rightly. No other "pilot" will
guide you on this course, not parents, churches, or schools, or any
other social institution upon which we usually depend for instruction.
It would take a truly enlightened parent, member of the clergy,
or teacher to offer this advice that a father gave to his son in
Shakespeare's *Hamlet:* "This above all: to thine own self be
true. . . ."[10]

Jesus concludes his Sermon on the Mount by saying that those who
hear his words and do them will be like someone who built his house
on rock. It will endure storm and flood. But as for those who hear his
words and do not do them, he compares them with someone who has
built his house on sand. Such a house will not endure the storms and
floods of life. The "rock" is a metaphor for the Self, or Christ-within.
The "house" is a metaphor for the ego. When you let the Christ be the
builder of your ego's house, it will endure because it is built upon
indestructible rock. To build the ego's house on any other basis, e.g., the
philosophies and ideologies of our time from materialism to existentialism to humanism, or whatever "ism," is to build upon sand. The
"storms and floods," i.e., the emotional upheavals of life, will wash this
house away. The rock of the Christ is no "ism" or abstraction; it is the
very heart of the Universe.

When Jesus concluded his Sermon, and came down from the
mountain, he began his healing ministry with the healing of a leper.
The leper said, "Lord if you will, you can make me clean." Jesus
stretched out his hand to him and said, "I will; be clean." Immediately, his leprosy was cleansed. In Jesus' day, lepers were totally
shunned for fear of contagion. The Torah itself instructed against
contact with lepers. Jesus broke a cultural and religious barrier by
reaching out his hand to the leper. This touch by the Son of Man was
sufficient to heal the leper of his dreadful disease. Taking the story in
its allegorical sense, we realize that the touch of the Christ, or the true
Self, in a dream, or a vision, or even a feeling, is often all that is
needed to heal the wounds of the soul. Whether we are speaking of
the leprosy of the body or of the soul, a "touch of the Christ" is all that
is needed to heal us.

Following the healing of the leper, Jesus and his disciples entered the city of Capernaum. A Roman soldier came up to Jesus and pleaded with him to heal his servant who was lying at home paralyzed and in great pain. Jesus said that he would come, but the centurion said that he was unworthy to have Jesus come under his roof. He said: "Only say the word and my servant will be healed." Jesus was astonished at the centurion's faith for nowhere in Israel had he found faith comparable to this. Jesus replied: "Go; be it done for you as you have believed." The centurion's servant was healed at that very moment.

It would seem that spiritual healing can occur even in the absence of any direct contact between healer and "healee." This is the basis of all "intercessory prayer" for the healing of another in either mind or body. During a certain period of my life, I experienced "successful healings" of people for whom I prayed. These were healings of physical illnesses including a person with a form of cancer and another with critically low red-blood cell count. In each case, I *imaged* the "problem" in question, and spontaneously I perceived in my inner vision Christ "doing something," in some cases highly symbolic. Much to my astonishment, the persons in question, with whom I did not have direct physical contact, got well. They were not "expected" to get well by their doctors either. This "healing at a distance" implies the interconnection of minds at a level beneath the conscious one. The concept of the "Collective Unconscious" would seem to imply this. But what is *the power* that permits healing to take place at all? Jesus would call it "faith." It is more a matter of the heart than the head. It is not "intellectual belief" that will move mountains, or part the Red Sea, or heal the sick, or raise the dead. It is rather *a trust* in the power of the Unseen God. Faith is the bridge between "two worlds," between the Creator and the Creation, the "two" who are "not two."

The power of the Christ extends not merely over the human mind and body but over Nature Herself, as when Jesus calmed the sea. Jesus and his disciples were in a boat in the Sea of Galilee during a storm. Jesus, who was sleeping, was awakened by his disciples, who said, "Save us, Lord; we are perishing." Jesus replied, "Why are you afraid, O men of little faith?" Jesus arose and rebuked the wind and sea and there was a great calm. You can imagine the astonishment of his disciples! What sort of man was this that even the winds and sea obey him?

Did this really happen? I believe it did. But the same story is also a profound allegory of the fact that the Christ-in-us can calm the emotional storms of our lives. Relying upon the ego, we are like the disciples in the small boat, tossed about by the "huge waves" and "violent winds" of life. But, if we can rely upon the power of the Christ-within, which is the true Self, we have mastery over life's storms. Recently, with personal events upsetting me, I meditated upon a saying of Christ for a few minutes, and entered into a spiritual peace which calmed the "inner storm." It made the external world look like a much more peaceful place as well.

Jesus crossed to the other side of the Sea of Galilee and he continued to heal the sick. He healed men possessed by demons, a paralytic, and a woman suffering from a hemorrhage of twelve years, who was cured by merely touching the fringe of Jesus' garment. He healed a little girl who was thought to be dead and a dumb demoniac. Jesus went all about the cities and villages preaching the gospel of the Kingdom and healing the sick. He also sat and ate with tax collectors and sinners. When the Pharisees heard of this, they rebuked him, but Jesus said, "Those who are well have no need of the physician, but those who are sick. . . . I came not to call the righteous, but sinners."

Jesus called together his twelve disciples and gave them authority to heal the sick and cast out unclean spirits. He told them that he was sending them as sheep among wolves, so therefore they should be "wise as serpents and innocent as doves."

The truest disciple of Christ whom I have ever met was Pierre whom I have spoken about in a previous chapter. I don't know whether he could "cast out unclean spirits," but I saw him bring joy to the heart of an old French farmer who had not smiled in all the years since he had been a prisoner of the Nazis during World War II. And I saw Pierre deal with two French policemen who angrily stormed over to where Pierre and I, and others, were eating dinner outdoors. We had "broken the rules" in crossing the border between Switzerland and France. Pierre arose when the two policemen arrived and he was "as wise as a serpent, and as innocent as a dove!" His smile totally "disarmed" the gendarmes, and they joined us for dinner rather than putting us in jail. Pierre had that union of wisdom and innocence that one sees only in Christ-realized ones.

To his disciples gathered around him that day, Jesus gives a "hard teaching." He says that he has "not come to bring peace but a sword," and that he has come to "set a man against his father, and a daughter against her mother, and a daughter-in-law against her mother-in-law," and that "a man's foes will be those of his own household." Jesus is saying that his Path transcends all biological and tribal considerations. He is also saying that those ties that we call "family" can be the worst enemies of the Kingdom. We have seen in the chapter on Moses that it is necessary to break free of "Pharaoh" and "Pharaohess" in order to become free men and women. Jesus reiterates this point even more strongly. He wants us to become the *persons* we were created by God to be, and this is sometimes a very different matter from what our parents or culture programmed us to be.

Jesus makes another "hard" statement, and a paradoxical one, to his twelve disciples when he says, "He who finds his life will lose it, and he who loses his life for my sake will find it."

What does this mean? Jesus is saying that even when we "find" the "self" we "think we are," i.e., the ego, we will lose the true Self, or Christ. But when we give up the "life" of the "little self" or ego, for the sake of the higher Self, or Christ, we will find the Self we truly are. We need to "die" to little self in order to be reborn to the God-created Self we are. This "dying" has nothing to do with physical death, but everything to do with the process of spiritual transformation in this life. If this sounds "mysterious," it is because we are speaking of *inward realities* which must be experienced within oneself. What do we mean by "ego" and "Self"? The "ego" is little you, separate, suffering, fearful, and in a state of exile. The "Self" is the greater you who is no longer separate from, but reunited with, God. This "Self" lives in an ineffable peace and joy. This Self is the I AM who will always be and not the "Sam Smith," or "Mary Jones," or "Richard Roe" who lives in fear of sickness, old age, and death (the three "great woes" that the Buddha discovered). The horrible suffering of conscious unwholeness will have ended; conscious wholeness will have come in its stead.

Jesus has made these "hard" statements about "a man's worst foes" and "losing your life." Now he makes an "easy" statement: "Take my yoke upon you, and learn from me; for I am gentle and lowly in heart, and you will find rest for your souls. For my yoke is easy, and my burden light."

The Sanskrit word for "Yoga" means "yoke." Jesus, although he is a Jew and not a Hindu, is saying that his "Yoga is easy." Easy in what sense? It does not require you to learn the many complicated "techniques" of Eastern Yogas; it requires only one thing of you: surrender to the Christ-Self. To "surrender" yourself seems fearful, but there is no reason to be afraid, for the One you are asked to surrender to is the Self you really are. When you "take his yoke upon you," you will discover this Mystery within yourself. The ego is, of course, defensive and alarmed about any "threat" to its autonomy, and the "battle" is, at first, ego versus Self until the ego learns this of the true Self, or Christ: "My yoke is easy and my burden is light."

When Jesus was asked by certain Scribes and Pharisees for a "sign" from him, he told them that their faithless generation would be given only one sign: "the sign of the prophet Jonah." Jonah spent three days in the "belly of a whale." The Son of Man will spend three days in the heart of the earth! This is a very powerful allegory of the second phase of the Inner Journey when the seeker encounters the Archetype of the "Great Mother" in his Deep Unconscious, and he is "swallowed up" by her. Both the "whale" and the "earth" are symbols of the Great Mother. Before the coming of Rebirth, the hero must return to the symbolic womb, there to spend a period of gestation in the "Place of the Mothers." The "three days" may, in reality, symbolize three years in the Inner Journey. I experienced this very thing when I had come to the experience of the *inward light,* and I thought that I had "made it." Not long thereafter, I had a dream that I was a monk in a brown robe who had walked out into the Nile River, and there I was "swallowed up" by a giant Nile crocodile. This began what was to be a "three-year stay" in the "belly of the dragon." It was a "return" or "regression" to the Unconscious Source, the "Place of the Mothers." From this place, one may be lost forever, or one may be "born anew."

That same day that Jesus commissioned his disciples, great crowds gathered around him on the shore of the Sea of Galilee. Jesus spoke to the crowds in parables. These were the parables of the Kingdom of Heaven. They are somewhat analogous in function to the teaching tales of the Hasids or Sufis and even the "Koans" of the Zen Buddhists. However, there has never been a master of the parable the equal of Master Jesus of Nazareth. The following parables are exemplary.

Parable of the Sower

A sower went out to sow. And as he sowed, some of the seeds fell along the path, and the birds came and devoured them. Other seeds fell on the rocky ground, where they had not much soil, but when the sun rose they were scorched; and since they had no root they withered away. Other seeds fell upon thorns, and the thorns grew up and choked them. Other seeds fell on good soil and brought forth grain, some a hundredfold, some sixty, some thirty. He who has ears, let him hear.

Jesus explains the parable of the sower to his disciples. The "seed" is the Word of the Kingdom. When one hears it without understanding, the evil one comes and snatches it away. These were the seeds which fell "along the path." As for the "rocky ground," this is an allegory of one who hears the word, and receives it with joy, yet has no root in himself, so it endures for a little while, but when persecution or tribulation comes, he immediately falls away. As for that which was sown "among thorns," this refers to the person who hears the word, but the cares of the world and its riches choke the word and it proves unfruitful. Finally, as for what was sown in "good soil," it refers to someone who is receptive to the word and has root in himself, but is not mired in the cares of the world. Here the seed of the Kingdom bears much fruit.

To reinterpret on a psychological level, in order for the "seed of the Kingdom to bear fruit," there must first be "good ground." This implies a person of strong and healthy ego who is also open to the spiritual values of the Kingdom. A certain psychological maturity and strength have always been a prerequisite for admission to the spiritual schools of various traditions from Kabbala to Zen. What of someone who is neurotic or sick? In this case, having despaired of receiving healing from "ego repair" therapies, the person may be impelled to take the perilous Journey to Self for the purpose of ego rebirth and rebuilding, this time on a sounder level. The person has found a *higher architect* than his primary agents of socialization (parents and culture): this time Christ will be his "carpenter." Then he too will bear much fruit.

Parable of the Mustard Seed

The kingdom of heaven is like a grain of mustard seed which a man took and sowed in his field; it is the smallest of all seeds, but when it has grown it is the greatest of shrubs and becomes a tree, so that the birds of the air come and make nests in its branches.

The Self, in its latent stage, is like a "tiny seed" because it is an invisible potentiality that is overlooked by most people. This was so in Jesus' time, and it is as true in our "modern world," including the twentieth-century Pharisees and Sadducees we call "psychiatrists" and "psychologists," who, strangely enough, are the most likely ones to deny the Self. They will usually say it is an "unscientific concept," in the words of one psychiatrist to me. Saint Paul said somewhere, "Beware of such sciences, so-called!" C. G. Jung, virtually alone among psychologists and psychiatrists of the modern West, affirms the reality of the Self and gives it a central place in his psychotherapeutic theory and method. Jung considered the Self to be the "central archetype" of the Collective Unconscious. The Self is signalled in dreams and visions by what the Eastern systems call a "mandala." Most religious systems, both East and West, have mandalas, as, for example, the Star of David, the Cross, the Buddhist Wheel of Life, and the Taoist Tai Chi symbol. When mandalas appear in dreams, it is a powerful experience adumbrating the coming to Self. Two dreams of this sort in my experience were: (1) a dream of a three-sided cross which was joined by a "fourth side" arising from the Deep Unconscious forming a "four-sided" cross of light, and (2) a dream of an "enlightened artist" who painted a "circle" and then filled it with every color under the sun! Dreams of this kind signal a major change in your life. They are what the American Indians call "big dreams."

Parable of the Pearl

Again, the kingdom of heaven is like a merchant in search of fine pearls, who, on finding one pearl of great value, went and sold all that he had and bought it.

Jesus refers to the Kingdom within as the "pearl of great value." This is a metaphor and more than a metaphor as the enlightened ones know. Many spiritual traditions, for example, Christian, Buddhist, Hindu, Taoist, etc., refer to the Self as a "pearl," the "jewel within the lotus," the "diamond body," etc. This is a mystery. The medieval alchemists spoke of this mystery as the "philosopher's stone." The only way to discover its meaning is within yourself.

Jesus returned home to Nazareth, and he preached there, but he was not accepted by his own. He was known as "Mary and Joseph's son." Sound familiar? Jesus said, "A prophet is not without honor except in his own country and in his own house."

When Jesus heard that John the Baptist had been beheaded by Herod Antipas, he was saddened, and he withdrew to the privacy of a lonely place by the Sea of Galilee in a boat. But people heard of this, and when Jesus had come ashore, a crowd had gathered. Jesus took compassion on them and healed their sick. That evening, when there was insufficient food, his disciples told him that he should send the people away to villages to buy food for themselves. Jesus said that there was no need to do so. He requested that they bring what food they had to him; that amounted to two fishes and five loaves of bread. Jesus looked up to heaven and said a blessing, and a miracle happened. There was enough food to feed five thousand men, as well as women and children.

Later that day, Jesus again seemed to transcend the laws of nature when he walked on water out to his disciples who were on a boat at sea. At these times (the miracle of the loaves and fishes, and walking on water), Jesus seems to be the master of nature herself! In the Jewish mysticism tradition known as the "Kabbala," what we view as "nature" is considered to be the very "embodiment of God." This is what is called "Malkuth," which is translated "the Kingdom." The Creator-God is known as "Kether," or "Crown." The Messiah-Self is called "Tifereth"; it is the *mediator* between "Kether" and "Malkuth," Creator and Creation. The Messiah-Self, or Christ, is "at command" over the laws of the natural world; he can even suspend them. When he does so, it is called a "miracle." In his name, we are told that we can perform miracles ourselves. Jesus says that we can do what he did and "greater." All we need is a little faith. When Peter, the Apostle, tried to walk on water, he was able to do so for a short time. Then he lost his faith, and he began to sink. Jesus said to him, "O man of little faith, why did you doubt?" Miracles require *miracle consciousness*. This is a state of faith in which you are "connected with" God.

I had a dream not long ago in which Christ worked a miracle. There was a young man who was captive in a castle run by "wicked bandits." He was tied up and tortured. Christ came into the castle and surrendered himself in order to free the young man. Christ smiled because he was not really "captive," but allowed the wicked men who ran the castle no more power over him than he chose. Christ was sent to the same room where the young man was tied up and a captive. He said to the young man, "the Christ transcends the laws of time and space." At that instant, the young man was no longer a captive inside the castle, but found himself outside. When he realized that he had been freed by Christ, he ran away to his freedom. He returned later (months or years) to that same castle, totally transformed, and no one recognized him. He went downstairs to a "bar and restaurant" of the castle in the basement. No one knew him, neither the bandits nor even his parents who had come to the restaurant for dinner. He had a drink at the bar with Christ, who was clean-shaven and dressed in ordinary clothes. No one recognized him either. The young man was myself, and he is probably you too. Only the Christ can set us free from our bondage. Only he can so totally transform us that no one (but God) will recognize our transformed inner being, not our former captives, nor our parents, nor anyone. Spiritual transformation is a "secret" between the soul and God.

Jesus went with his disciples to Caesarea Philippi, and there he asked his disciples who men "said that he was." They answered that some said "John the Baptist," others said "Elijah," and some said

"Jeremiah," or "one of the prophets." Jesus said, "But who do you say that I am?" Simon Peter said "You are the Christ." Jesus told him "flesh and blood" had not revealed this to him, but "my Father who is in heaven." Jesus said, "You are Peter, and on this rock I will build my church." What does Jesus mean by this statement to Simon Peter? "Peter" is the English word for the Greek name "Petros" and the Aramaic name "Cephas." They both mean "rock." Jesus has spoken of himself at various times as the "rock." The term "rock" is a metaphor for "the Christ." Peter has perceived the Christ in Jesus, not through his bodily eyes, but through his inward spiritual perception. It is not upon Peter, the man, but upon the Christ, the "rock of salvation," upon which Jesus will build his church. Peter very soon loses his insight when Jesus speaks of the fact that the Son of Man must go to Jerusalem to suffer many things, be killed, and on the third day be raised. In his shock, Peter says, "God forbid, Lord!" Jesus rebukes him, "Get thee behind me, Satan! You are a hindrance to me; for you are not on the side of God, but of men." "Satan" means "adversary," and refers to whatever blocks the will of God (or tries to). This inter-play of inner-Satan versus inner-Self takes place in everyone. The Self is the stronger will for it is *all-including* and it is *whole*.

Jesus took Peter, James, and John to a "high mountain." It was there that Jesus was utterly transfigured before them and shone with light. The disciples saw Moses and Elijah appear and speak with Jesus. From a bright cloud overshadowing them, they heard a voice say: "This is my beloved son, with whom I am well pleased; listen to him." The disciples fell down in awe. Jesus touched them saying "rise." When they arose, they saw no one but Jesus. The Transfiguration was the second illumination of Jesus, the first being the Baptism. In each case the "Shekhina," or the Immanence of God, is present. Jesus was so utterly transfigured by this spiritual light that others could see this light as well. The same thing was true of Moses when he came down from Mount Sinai the second time. Medieval painters portrayed saints with a "halo." This is the *spiritual light* which shone so brilliantly from Master Jesus on the Mount of Transfiguration that his disciples fell down in awe and hid their faces. Following his first illumination, Jesus met the Adversary, Satan, in the wilderness. Following his second illumination (or "Transfiguration"), Jesus was to meet the Adversary again, this time in the form of the events which were to ensue in Jerusalem: his rejection by the scribes and elders, his betrayal by Judas, his sorrow at Gethsemane, his trial and humiliation, and his Passion.

Mystics speak of the Christ story as symbolizing five great initiations of the Path: the birth of the Christ child, the baptism, the transfiguration, the crucifixion, and the resurrection. I found this sequence of inner events to be true in my own experience. I have spoken of the "birth" experience, and the "baptism" experience, and I experienced the "transfiguration," as well as an inward "initiation." I was walking around the reservoir in New York's Central Park and I experienced the Christ in all things, no matter how small, and a tremendous sense of Love. I felt that this was my "transfiguration."

Jesus and his disciples moved on from the "Mount of Transfiguration" inexorably toward Jerusalem, "the city of peace," where the final events of his earthly life were to take place. They travelled by foot from Galilee to Capernaum to Jericho and finally to Jerusalem. Along the way, Jesus taught and healed and spoke of the tribulation to come.

On the roadside between Jericho and Jerusalem sat two blind men. They heard that it was Jesus who was passing by and they cried out to him, "Lord, have mercy upon us, Son of David!" Jesus stopped and asked what they wanted of him. They said, "Lord, let our eyes be opened." Jesus took pity on them and touched their eyes. Their sight was restored.

I had a dream about a year ago of Christ restoring the sight of the blind Sigmund Freud. Obviously, Freud was not blind in a physical sense, but in a spiritual sense. Christ can open the eyes of both the physically and the spiritually blind.

Jesus came into Jerusalem, the holy city, seated upon a donkey. The multitudes waved palm branches and shouted "Hosanna to the Son of David! Hosanna in the highest!" Jesus was a new kind of king, not like Saul or David or Solomon, for he was meek and he rode on a lowly ass! He was greeted not with the shouts of soldiers, but with the songs of children. The whole city was stirred saying, "Who is this?"

When you come to the Christ-within-you, it will not be like the experience of a "great king" who leads armies either; it is, rather, the coming of something very different, something very subtle, and very beautiful. Gentle though it is, it is paradoxically the most powerful force in the world!

In the Temple of God, Jesus drove out those who bought and sold, and he overturned the tables of the moneychangers. He said that they made God's house into a den of thieves. In the Temple, Jesus also healed the blind and lame. Children gathered around him and shouted words of praise. The priests and scribes were indignant, but Jesus asked them if they had read: "Out of the mouth of babes and sucklings thou hast brought forth perfect praise."

It seems paradoxical that the qualities of the Self, or the Christ, of which Jesus was the Incarnation, are immediately perceived by children and innocents, but the learned and worldly wise are often blind to the presence of the Spirit. I remember a painting that I saw in a museum in New York City called "The Blindness of Scholars." It is as true today as it was in Jesus' time.

Jesus was questioned again and again by the Scribes and Pharisees who attempted to "trip him up," but he answered them most deftly. For example, they asked him whether it was lawful to pay taxes to Caesar. Jesus asked them to take out a coin and look at it. He asked them whose image they saw on the coin. They replied, "Caesar's." Jesus answered them, "Render therefore to Caesar the things that are Caesar's, and to God the things that are God's." In all his answers, they were astonished at his teachings.

When asked by what authority he did the things he did, Jesus asked them, "The baptism of John, whence was it? From heaven or from men?" They were unable to answer because if they replied "from heaven," they reasoned Jesus would say, "Why then did you not believe in him?" And if they said, "from men," they feared the multitudes who believed John was a prophet. So they replied, "We do not know." Jesus said, "Neither will I tell you by what authority I do these things."

When you act by the inward authority of the Christ, or true Self, you need not "justify" your actions any more than Jesus did. You need not submit, nor rebel, nor self-justify, but you need simply *act in freedom* (I have called this the "fourth way").

No one was able to answer Jesus a word. Not from that day till his trial by the Sanhedrin did anyone dare ask him any more questions. But Jesus has some very strong words to say about the hypocrisy of the Scribes and Pharisees. He says that they "shut up the kingdom of heaven against men." He calls them "blind guides. . . ." He says that they "cleanse the outside of the cup and of the plate, but inside they are full of extortion and rapacity." Jesus sums up his indictment of the Scribes and Pharisees thusly:

Woe to you, scribes and Pharisees, hypocrites! for you are like whitewashed tombs, which outwardly appear beautiful, but within are full of dead men's bones and all uncleanness. So you also outwardly appear righteous to men, but within you are full of hypocrisy and iniquity.

John A. Sanford, in his book *The Kingdom Within*, refers to the "Pharisee in each of us." He speaks of the necessity of shedding our

Pharisaic mask. "The mask is the person we pretend to be—the false outer personality which we turn to the world, but which is contradicted from within."[11] Jung calls this mask the "persona." In society, we cannot do without a persona, or social self, but the danger of the mask is our tendency to identify with it, "to think we *are* the person we pretend to be, and thereby remain unconscious of our real self."[12] The first step on the Journey is the uncovering of the "Pharisaic mask," or persona, so that we may see beyond to the neglected side of ourselves. "Unmasking" is the beginning of the Path.

During my last year of full-time college teaching before I resigned to "enter the Path," I had a dream of horseback riders who were wearing the iron masks of the horses they were riding. The dream was telling me that I was identifying with my social role as "college professor." I was far from my real Self. I think we are more a "people of the mask" today in twentieth-century America than the old Pharisees and Saduccees was in actuality a service to them, but one for tives, "white-coated" doctors, "white-collared" priests, "hard-hat" construction workers, "horn-rimmed glasses' wearing, pipe-smoking" university professors, etc. What lies "beneath the mask"? It must be faced if we are to ever *know ourselves*. Jesus' unmasking of the Pharisees and Saduccees was in acutality a service to them, but one for which they never forgave him!

When he left the Temple, Jesus spoke to his disciples about "time's end"; he speaks of wars, famines, earthquakes, and this is only the beginning of birthpangs. He may be speaking of the "apocalypse," but what he says is equally true of the individual journey. Jesus says that there will be many false rumors of the Messiah's coming, but when the Son of Man truly comes, it will be like "lightning striking." It was this way for Saul of Tarsus, also known as St. Paul, on the road to Damascus when he was suddenly illumined by brilliant light. It was the most unexpected thing.

Jesus admonishes his disciples to "stay awake." He is speaking of the necessity of consciousness on the Path. The Buddha called this "mindfulness." G. I. Gurdjieff spoke of "self-remembering." Moses was the "Great Liberator." Jesus, as I see him, is the "Great Awakener."

There are moral requirements of the Kingdom. Jesus says that when the Son of Man comes in his glory, he will separate "the sheep" from "the goats." The former will inherit the Kingdom because: "I was hungry and you gave me food, I was thirsty and you gave me drink, I was a stranger and you welcomed me, I was naked and you clothed me, I was sick and you visited me, I was in prison and you came to see me." Jesus says that "when you do these things unto the least of my brethren, you do it to me." To the latter, those who do not feed the hungry, or give drink to the thirsty, or welcome the stranger, or clothe the naked, or visit the sick, or see the prisoner in prison, Jesus says, "as you did it not to one of the least of these, you did it not to me." The morality of the Kingdom transcends what the Jungians call "individuation"!

Jesus and his disciples celebrated the Passover at the home of one of his disciples. He said that one of the twelve would betray him. While they were eating, Jesus took bread, and he blessed it, and said: "Take, eat; this is my body." Then he took a cup of wine, and he said: "Drink of it all of you; for this is my blood of the covenant which is poured out for many for the forgiveness of sins." Thus, Jesus instituted the sacrament of Holy Communion, an outward sign of inward and invisible Grace. The bread and the wine are concrete symbols of the Christ Reality inherent in all things.

When I first took Holy Communion as a Jewish-Christian disciple at the age of thirty-three, I was literally awestruck to partake of the "body" and "blood" of Christ in the form of bread and wine. Strangely, and I don't know the "why" of it, I "invented" the Holy Communion service as a Jewish child at the age of three. I used to "say prayers" over grape juice and bread wearing the maid's white dress as a kind of "priestly robe." It was a most precious memory of my early childhood. It gave me a "sacred feeling"; which I felt once again when I partook of the Holy Communion, as an adult, at the Cathedral of St. John the Divine in New York City in the winter of 1976. This "holy feeling" is an experience of the Self, or the "indwelling Christ."

Following the Passover Seder, Jesus and several of his disciples retired to a small garden called Gethsemane. It was here that Jesus became most sorrowful and profoundly troubled, for it was here that he consciously and painfully faced the immanence of his death in the prime of his young manhood. Jesus fell on the ground, and prayed, "My Father, if it be possible, let this cup pass from me; nevertheless, not as I will, but as thou wilt." Jesus at this time, as in all others, went with the Will of God for himself, or we could say, the Voice of the Higher Self. In doing so, he provides the supreme example for humanity.

While Jesus and his disciples were still in the garden, Judas appeared with several armed men sent by the high priests. Judas Iscariot had "sold out" his Master for thirty pieces of silver. Judas went straight to Jesus, saying, "Hail, Master," and he kissed him. This was a prearranged sign. The armed men seized Jesus. His disciple, Peter, drew his sword and struck off the ear of one of the high priest's men, but Jesus told him to put back his sword, "for all who take the sword will perish by the sword." Jesus was taken into captivity, and his disciples fled for their lives. Fear overtook them.

Jesus was taken before Caiaphas and the chief priests. They sought witnesses against him. Two came forward and said that Jesus claimed to have the power to destroy the Temple and raise it up again in three days. When Jesus was asked to reply to the charge, he kept his silence. Then Caiaphas, the high priest, asked him, "I adjure you, by the Living God, tell us if you are the Christ, the Son of God." Jesus replied, "You have said so." He added, "But I tell you, hereafter you will see the Son of Man seated at the right hand of Power." The high priest tore his robes and said, "You have heard his blasphemy." The Sanhedrin decreed the death sentence for Jesus.

The Jewish court lacked authority to carry out death sentences so the priests and elders took Jesus before Pontius Pilate, the Roman governor of Judaea. When Pilate asked Jesus whether he was the "King of the Jews," Jesus replied that it was he (Pilate) who said it. To the accusations of the priests and elders, Jesus remained silent. Pilate was greatly puzzled by Jesus' behavior. A Zen master, Seung Sahn, whom I asked, "How should we deal with evil?" replied, "Multiply it by zero." $0 \times Evil = 0$.

Pilate, in attempting to absolve himself of responsibility, followed an ancient custom at the Passover of releasing one prisoner. He gave the people the choice between Barabbas, a Zealot charged with murder, and Jesus. The people shouted for the release of Barabbas. When Pilate asked, "What shall I do with Jesus who is called the Christ?" the crowd shouted, "Let him be crucified." Pilate, after symbolically "absolving himself" of Jesus' death by washing his hands and saying, "I am innocent of this man's blood," handed Jesus over to the Roman soldiers to be scourged and then crucified.

I have spoken of the five great initiations of the Christian mystical path: birth, baptism, transfiguration, crucifixion, and resurrection. In the winter of 1979, I experienced "the crucifixion" within my soul. I beheld the image of Christ within myself "bleeding to death" and "suffocating" for lack of oxygen. I literally experienced myself "choking to death," and I understood what Jesus meant when he said "Eli, Eli, lama sabachthani?" or "My God, my God, why hast thou forsaken me?" This ordeal ended only when I "let go," on some level, and "surrendered myself to God." Following the agony of this "psychic crucifixion," my mind was flooded with thoughts on the meaning of this. I share some of these thoughts from my diary with you:

The Crucifixion is the extreme of the war of opposites begun when Adam and Eve ate of the Tree of Knowledge of Good and Evil and were expelled from the Unity of Eden into the warring opposites of the world we know, the ego-world. The Crucifixion is the extreme of the warring opposites of this world. Now I see that the war between good and evil cannot be "won" by "trying to be good." Evil is repressed and projected as Shadow. Nor is "fighting evil" the answer, for you become the evil you fight. Rather one needs to yield or surrender to the Greater Whole, to the Tao, to God, to the Father, who includes, transcends, and unifies the opposites. So Jesus dies to the ego-world of opposites, commending himself to the Father, and enters the Resurrection-world of Unity and Everlasting Life.

This is what happened to the historical Jesus of Nazareth who was crucified and bled to death upon that cross at Calvary. Before he died, when his great agony was over, he said, "Father, into thy hands I commend my spirit." When he died, the curtain of the Temple was torn in two, there were earthquakes, and the graves of saints were opened. The awestruck centurion said, "Truly this was the Son of God."

Joseph of Arimathea, a rich man who had been Jesus' disciple, requested Jesus' body from Pontius Pilate. He wrapped the body in a shroud, and placed it in a new tomb hewn in rock. He rolled a great stone in front of the entrance to the tomb. The Pharisees asked Pilate to secure the sepulchre and place guards around the tomb (fearing that Jesus' disciples might steal the body). Pilate agreed to this request.

After the Sabbath, toward the morning of the first day of the week, Mary Magdalene, and Mary, the mother of James, went to visit the tomb. There was a great earthquake, and they beheld an angel who "descended from heaven," and rolled back the stone. His appearance was "like lightning." The guards fainted dead away. The angel said to the women, Do not be afraid; for I know that you seek Jesus who was crucified. He is not here; for he has risen, as he said.

An empty tomb and an angel who proclaims "he is risen—these are the true symbols of Christianity, and not the cross upon which the Master died so horribly. It was not the Crucifixion, but the Resurrection which Jesus had come to preach. Before the birth of the New Being, however, there must be a Crucifixion, or a dying of the old self. The "crucified one" is the ego who finally "lets go" in the face of the overwhelming opposites within the psyche and the world. The

"Resurrected One" is the true Self, or Christ. The monk and author Thomas Merton wrote, "To be born again is not to become somebody else, but to become oneself . . . yet at the same time, in order to become oneself, one must die. That is to say in order to become one's true self, the false self must die.[13]

"In the language of the mystics," he continues, "there is no more ego-self, there is *only Christ*."[14] At this point, Jesus, the human ego, in his case an ego in so complete a harmony with the Self, is gone, and there is only the Christ-Self. God, through Christ, has closed the gap begun by Adam when he ate of the Tree of Knowledge of Good and Evil. Christ turned the cross of death into a *Tree of Life*. It is *he* who says to his disciples: "Lo, *I am* with you always even unto the end of the world."[15]

NOTES

Primary Source:
   The Bible, Revised Standard Version, The New Testament, American Bible Society, New York, 1971, Matthew, Chapters 1:20–21, 3:3, 3:11, 3:16–17, 4:4, 4:7, 4:10, 4:19, 5:3–11, 5:13–14, 5:16, 5:39–41, 5:44–45, 5:48, 6:9–14, 6:23, 6:24, 6:25–26, 6:34, 7:6, 7:7–8, 7:12, 8:2–3, 8:8–9, 8:25–27, 9:12, 10:16, 10:34–36, 10:39, 11:29–30, 13:3–9, 13:31–32, 13:33, 13:45–46, 13:57, 14:31, 16:15–17, 16:22–23, 17:5, 17:31, 17:33, 21:9, 21:16, 21:25, 21:27, 22:21, 22:42–45, 23:13, 23:24, 23:25–26, 23:27, 25:35–36, 25:40, 25:45, 26:26–27, 26:42, 26:52, 26:63–65, 27:22, 27:24, 28:5–6, 28:20; Mark, Chapter 13:37; Luke, Chapters 23:46 and 23:47

Secondary Sources
   1. Charles Guignebert, *The Jewish World in the Time of Jesus*, University Books, New York, 1959, pp. 162–187.
   2. Meister Ekhardt, *Meister Eckhardt, A Modern Translation*, trans. Raymond B. Blakney, Harper & Row, New York, 1941, Sermon 24.
   3. Robert Johnson, *HE*, Perennial Library, Harper & Row, New York, 1977, p. 9.
   4. William Barclay, *The Beatitudes and the Lord's Prayer for Everyman*, Harper & Row, New York, 1964, p. 23.
   5. Ibid.
   6. *A Course in Miracles*, Copyright by the Foundation for Inner Peace, Coleman Graphics, Huntington Station, N.Y., 1975, Volume Two: Workbook, p. 455.
   7. Ibid., pp. 210–212.
   8. John A. Sanford, *The Kingdom Within*, Paulist Press, New York, 1980, p.65
   9. Ibid.
   10. William Shakespeare, *Hamlet*, Pocket Books, New York, 1958, Act I, SC. III, line 82 (p. 20).
   11. Sanford, p. 95.
   12. Ibid.
   13. Thomas Merton, *Love and Living*, Bantam Books, New York, 1979, p. 176.
   14. Ibid., p. 177.
   15. Holy Bible, King James Version, New Testament, World Publishing Company, Cleveland & New York, 1611 edition, Matthew, Chapter 28:20

Chapter Four

Gotama, the Buddha

THE word "Buddha" means "enlightened one." It was the name given to an Indian prince, Siddhattha Gotama, who was born in 563 B.C. in Lumbini Garden close to the northern border of India in the foothills of the Himalayas.[1] His father's name was Suddhodana and he was a ruler of the "Sakya" clan.[2] His mother's name was Mayadevi. He grew up amid great luxury and married his cousin, Yasodhara, in his sixteenth year. Thirteen years later, when Siddhattha was twenty-nine, a son who was named Rahula was born. It was just after the birth of his son that Siddhattha left his wife and son and his hereditary riches to become a "sannyasin," or spiritual seeker.

There is a legend as to why Siddhattha Gotama left home and family on his quest for enlightenment. It goes like this. Siddhattha's father, Suddhodana, had kept his son protected from even the vision of suffering. He was not to know that there was evil in the world. But the young prince was eager to see the world, and he pleaded with his father for permission to do so. Thus Siddhattha rode with Channa, his charioteer, through the streets of the city and through the countryside. It was on this journey that he encountered the "three woes."

By the wayside, they encountered a withered old man. His hair was white, his eyes were dimmed, and his body was so weak that he could barely support himself with his staff. The prince asked the charioteer, "Who is this?"

These are the symptoms of old age. This same man was once a suckling child, and as a youth full of sportive life; but now, as years have passed away, his beauty is gone and the strength of his life is wasted.

113

While they were passing on, they came upon a sick man who was gasping for breath, convulsing, and groaning with pain. The prince asked the charioteer: "What kind of man is this?"

This man is sick. The four elements of his body are confused and out of order. We are all subject to such conditions: the poor and the rich, the ignorant and the wise, all creatures that have bodies, are liable to the same calamity.

Siddhattha was moved by these two sights. The pleasures of his royal life seemed empty to him. The charioteer sped on, but they were stopped in their course by four persons passing by who were carrying a corpse, and the prince, shocked by the sight of a lifeless body, asked the charioteer: "What is this they carry?"

This is a dead man: his body is stark; his life is gone; his thoughts are still; his family and the friends who loved him now carry the corpse to the grave.

Siddhattha was stricken with terror, and he asked the charioteer whether this was the only dead man, or whether there are other instances. The charioteer replied that it is the same all over the world: "He who begins life must end it. There is no escape from death."

When he returned to his palace, the prince was greeted by his wife, but she saw that he was heavy of heart. She asked him to tell her the cause of his grief. He answered that he saw that men grow old, sicken, and die. That was the cause of his sorrow.

It is remarkable how our culture covers the facts of life, the truth of suffering, of sickness, old age, and death, all of which are inevitable, with our worldly pleasures, our scientific-technological veneer, our preoccupation with things and possessions, our social escapes, our psychotherapies, etc. In modern middle-class America, the old are hidden away in rest homes, the sick in hospitals, and death, the last great taboo, is antiseptically concealed from our daily lives in "safe" and "clean" mortuaries. Youth, beauty, and vigor are the new idols constantly paraded before our eyes in television, movies, and magazines. We assume that "science" will soon cure the uncomfortable facts of old age, sickness, and death. It may happen in Bombay, India, sickness, starvation, and dying in the streets, but these "unpleasantries" are largely hidden from our sight in our "modern world." But it strikes, nonetheless: cancer, heart attack, alcoholism, mental illness, sudden death of loved ones, and the coming to our own thirtieth and fortieth birthdays, and the realization that we too are mortal. We have dreams, and they are like flowers, they are beautiful, but they inevitably pass away. It was this "darker" side of life that Siddhattha realized now. Beneath the surface persona of worldly pleasures was the reality of universal human suffering, "fear and trembling and sickness unto death," in the words of the existentialist philosopher, Sören Kierkegaard. No "philosophy," no matter how idealistic, can cover the raw suffering of existence; physical, mental, and spiritual *angst*.

Prince Siddhattha could no longer find rest on his soft pillow, and he arose and went out into his garden. He cried out, "Alas! All the world is full of darkness and ignorance; there is no one who knows how to cure the ills of existence." He groaned in pain. While pondering the problems of suffering, he beheld in his mind's eye a lofty figure endowed with dignity and calm. Siddhattha asked the visionary figure "who mayest thou be?" The vision replied:

I am a samana. Troubled at the thought of old age, disease, and death I have left my home to seek the path of salvation. All things hasten to decay; only the truth abideth forever. Everything changes, and there is no permanency; yet the words of the Buddhas are immutable. I long for the happiness that does not decay; the treasure that will never perish; the life that knows of no beginning and no end. Therefore, I have destroyed all worldly thought. I have retired into an unfrequented dell to live in solitude; and, begging for food, I devote myself to the one thing needful.

Siddhattha asked the vision whether peace can be gained in this world of unrest. He said that he was struck with the emptiness of worldly pleasure and lust. "All oppresses me, and existence itself seems intolerable." The vision answered:

Where heat is, there is also a possibility of cold; creatures subject to pain possess the faculty of pleasure; the origin of evil indicates that good can be developed. For these things are correlatives. Thus where there is much suffering, there will be much bliss, if thou but open thine eyes to behold it. Just as a man who has fallen into a heap of filth ought to seek a great pond of water covered with lotuses, which is nearby: even so seek thou for the great deathless lake of Nirvana to wash off the defilement of wrong. If the lake is not sought, it is not the fault of the lake. Even so when there is a blessed road leading the man held fast by wrong to the salvation of Nirvana, if the road is not walked upon, it is not the fault of the road, but of the person. And when a man who is oppressed by sickness, there being a physician who can heal him, does not avail himself of the physician's help, that is not the fault of the physician. Even so when a man oppressed by the malady of wrongdoing does not seek the spiritual guide of enlightenment, that is not the fault of the evil-destroying guide.

Siddhattha experienced what we might call an "encounter" between his ego and his true Self which appeared to him in the form of a vision. Such an encounter, whether in a dream or a vision, sets out one's destiny. It was at this point that Siddhattha decided that now was the time to sever all worldly ties that would prevent him from following the path of enlightenment.

Many mystics of history from El Ghazzali to St. Francis of Assisi have felt the need to sever ties with the world, at least for a time, in order to "enter the path." I felt this call myself at age twenty-nine, and quit my academic teaching job in order to pursue the spiritual path. The last year of my teaching career I felt as if "two roads diverged in a wood, and I—I took the one less travelled by . . . ," as in the poem "The Road Not Taken" by Robert Frost[3]. There seems always to be a "call" when one leaves the securities of the world for the uncertainties of the Path. Yet, though one forsakes outward certainties, there is an inward certainty about the Path, as when Siddhattha said: "Verily I shall become a Buddha."

Prince Siddhattha returned to the bedroom of his wife and child to take a farewell glance at his loved ones. His pain in parting was great, but he was determined that nothing, be it good or evil, would shake his resolution to follow his destiny. He cut his long hair and he exchanged his royal robe for the ochre robe of the sannyasin. He left his great palace, his family, and his riches, with only a beggar's bowl in his hand. In this, he was similar to the disciples of Jesus who took "neither scrip nor haversack" with them on their journeys.

One of the first persons whom Siddhattha met on his journey was a king named Bimbisara who had heard that Siddhattha was from a royal family, although he was dressed as a beggar. The king offered Siddhattha a place of wealth and power in his government. But the great Sakyamuni (sage of the Sakya clan) said:

I have severed all ties because I seek deliverance. How is it possible for me to return to the world? He who seeks religious truth, which is the highest treasure of all, must leave behind all that can concern him or draw away his attention, and must be bent upon that one goal alone. He must free his soul from covetousness and lust, and also from the desire for power.

Jesus meant something very similar when he said, "You cannot serve both God and mammon."[4] The spiritual path seems to impose, whether you wish it or not, the conditions of poverty, obedience, and chastity. It is difficult to be less than wholly committed to this Path. A

normal job may occupy your attention eight hours a day; the spiritual
path occupies your attention twenty-four hours a day! I speak in all
earnestness that this path is the most all-consuming and demanding
work that one can ever engage in. But it is work upon one's self.

Siddhattha sought teachers of the path and found them among the
Brahmans who were unsurpassed in learning and philosophical
knowledge. His first teacher was Alara who taught Siddhattha the
traditional Hindu philosophy of the soul. He taught him that the "I"
is the one who feels the touch of the body, the "I" is the one who
smells the smells of the nose, the "I" is the one who tastes the tastes of
the tongue, and the "I" is the seer of sights of the eye, and the hearer
of the sounds of the ear, and the thinker of the thoughts of the mind.
"The I is the soul."

The Bodhisatta (Buddha to be) found no satisfaction in these philosophical teachings. He said that the ego was the cause of bondage, and
that those who have not yet removed the idea of ego were enslaved by
it. Siddhattha denied the real existence of an ego behind touch,
smells, tastes, sights, sounds, and thoughts. This ego, according to
Siddhattha, was an illusion. There is a similarity between this teaching
of the Buddha, and that of Jesus, who said: "He who finds his life will
lose it, and he who loses his life for my sake will find it."[5] I take the
word "life" there to mean "self."

The Bodhisatta goes on to say that "Rituals have no efficacy; prayers
are vain repetitions; and incantations have no saving power." Siddhattha is speaking in the context of the Hinduism of his time, as
Jesus said very similar things, as you will recall, about the Judaism of
his time. Jesus said that "vain repetitions" have no efficacy, but only
true prayer. The Buddha said that to abandon covetousness, lust, evil
passions, hatred, and ill-will is "the true worship." I would think that
the one who taught "Love your enemies and pray for those who
persecute you"[6] would agree with this assessment.

The Brahman sage Uddaka also upheld the existence of the ego.
He said that all of the parts of the body, as well as our mental experiences, are not the ego, but the ego possesses these parts. He compared this with the river Ganges. Is the Ganges the sand, or the water,
or the banks? No, according to Uddaka; rather, the Ganges is a
mighty river which possesses these various qualities. Exactly so, he
said, is our ego.

The Bodhisatta replied: "Not so, sir!" "If we except the water, the
sand, the hither bank and the farther bank, where can we find any
Ganges?" It is the same for what we call our "ego."

Siddhattha, in these stories of his meetings with the Brahman sages, has gone through a stage which I will call "the philosophical." It is really prior to the true spiritual path, yet it is a stage in the journey of consciousness which can neither be skipped over nor bypassed. The future Buddha, Siddhattha, dealt with it admirably!

The Bodhisatta went on in his search for enlightenment after he left the Brahman wise men. He came to a settlement in the jungle of Uruvela where five bhikkus, or ascetic renunciates, lived and practiced their austere self-disciplines. Siddhattha gave himself up to their program of mortification and asceticism. Where the five bhikkhus were severe, Siddhattha was severer still. The Bodhisatta went on like was their junior in years, as their master. The Bodhisatta went on like this for six years suppressing the wants of nature, and exercising his body and mind in the ascetic life.

Following the period of philosophical inquiry (which may be a long one), one enters deeper levels of the Path which are almost inevitably experienced as profound suffering. The great mystic and saint, St. John of the Cross, has described very well these "dark nights of the soul." This suffering passes through the despair that the existentialists such as Sartre and Camus speak about, into a "despair unto death." Let me quote you from my diary during this period of my Journey when I was living in a spartan and tiny YMCA room in New York City in the winter of 1974 (I lived there for two years):

I don't care if I die in my sleep tonight. My life has been a horrible mess and a hell. I can't go on like this; must either go on or die. Please stop the pain, God. Please stop the pain. . . . Better if I were never born. My life has been a hell—an unbearable hell.

The Bodhisatta was shrunken and attenuated. He had sought for enlightenment in this way, but he did not find it. He came to the conclusion that mortification would not extinguish desire, nor could he attain Nirvana by continuing in this ascetic way, any more than he could by pursuing his former way of indulgence, as a rich prince. He bathed himself in a river, and fainted after he had pulled himself out of the stream. Nanda, the daughter of a herdsman, came upon the Bodhisatta, and gave him rice-milk to drink. He took food for several days and regained his strength of body and mind. His former disciples left him, thinking he had abandoned the spiritual path.

The Bodhisatta, who had discovered the *middle way* between the extremes of asceticism and indulgence, directed himself to a Bodhi-tree

beneath whose shade he sat for forty days in quest for enlightenment.
All the heavens rejoiced, except for Mara, the evil one. As Jesus was
tempted by Satan, the Buddha was tempted by Mara, and his three
daughters, Tanha, Raga, and Arati. They, and a host of demons, went
to the place where the Bodhisatta sat, but he heeded them not, main-
taining his clear state of meditation. Mara, the evil one, ordered all
the evil spirits at his command to attack and to overwhelm the Bodhisatta, but: "the Blessed One watched them as one would watch the
harmless games of children. All the fierce hatred of the evil spirits was
of no avail."

This episode of the Buddha confronting the evil demons while
sitting calmly beneath the Bodhi tree is symbolic of a very long phase
of the Journey. It is the period past the "despair unto death" when
one faces the "raw Karma" of one's personal and collective unconscious. This phase of the Journey can either drive one mad (the "in-
sane" in hospitals are stuck at this point), or one can endure the
coming to consciousness of one's complexes and of the archetypes,
and one can acquire wisdom. *To observe* "as one would watch the
harmless games of children" is the secret transforming of one's
Karma into wisdom. In this state of conscious mediation, "the flames
of hell became wholesome breezes of perfume, and the angry thun-
derbolts were changed into lotus-blossoms."

In my own Journey, I discovered Buddhist meditation during the
period mentioned above, my first Dark Night of the Soul, at a Tibetan
Buddhist meditation center located a few blocks away from my
YMCA room (my "monastic" cell). To quote my diary of February,
1974:

In state of terrible pain and anger. Did meditation from 8 to 9 P.M. in my
room. Felt at peace. It is a workable situation. The Buddha knew what he was
talking about. Such a simple meditation. We must *face the truth*—that's all.

It is the light of consciousness that will transform Karma into wisdom, or as the Buddha stated it:

As the rays of the sun drown the darkness of the world, so he who perse-
veres in his search will find the truth and the truth will enlighten him.

Or as Jesus put it, "You shall know the truth and the truth shall set
you free."[7] Perseverance on the Path is a most important quality. The
universe of the psyche is as great as the physical universe, and the

journey of healing is a very long one. Both the Buddha and Jesus speak of the importance of perseverance, or endurance. In the Book of Revelation, Jesus says, "I know you are enduring patiently and bearing up for my name's sake, and you have not grown weary."[8] To those who endure, Jesus says, "I will give to eat of the tree of life that is in the midst of the paradise of God."[9] Where Jesus spoke of the "Kingdom," the Buddha referred to the goal as "Nirvana."

The Bodhisatta, having overcome Mara, gave himself up tő meditation. All the evils of the world passed before his mind's eye. He thought:

Surely if living creatures saw the results of all their evil deeds, they would turn away from them in disgust. But selfhood blinds them, and they cling to their obnoxious desires.

What the Buddha did under the Bodhi tree was to assimilate and transform, within himself, the evils of the world. It was a kind of "alchemy." Five hundred years later, Jesus did the same thing in an even far more drastic way while crucified upon a "tree."

After his enlightenment, the Buddha began to expound upon his teaching, or Dharma. He first spoke of what he called the "twelve nidanas," which are the links which bind us to the wheel of birth, death, and rebirth, and the never-ending cycle of suffering. It begins in ignorance and ends in the illusion of ego which is the cause of suffering, old age, sickness, and death, and an endless cycle of renewed births. Ignorance is the root of lamentation, anxiety, and despair.

In the beginning there is existence blind and without knowledge; and in this sea of ignorance there are strivings formative and organizing. From stirrings, formative and organizing, rises awareness or feelings. Feelings beget organisms that live as individual beings. These organisms develop the six fields, that is, the five senses and the mind. The six fields come into contact with things. Contact begets sensation. Sensation creates the thirst of individualized being. The thirst of being creates a cleaving to things. The cleaving produces the growth and continuation of selfhood. Selfhood continues in renewed births. The renewed births of selfhood are the cause of suffering, old age, sickness and death.

The cause of suffering, according to the Buddha, lies at the very beginning: "It is hidden in the ignorance from which life grows." The Buddha says that if you remove that ignorance, you will break the chain of "Samsara." If you do this, you will be above birth, old age, disease, and death. You will escape suffering. This is what the Buddha calls "Nirvana."

It is interesting to compare this with the Judeo-Christian tradition, for there are parallels and also differences. What the Buddha calls ignorance is, I believe, identical to what Moses or Jesus would call "sin." "Sin" has accrued to itself certain associations due to Puritanism which are not contained in its original meaning. In the Biblical Hebrew it originally had the meaning of "missing the mark," a term borrowed from archery. In this sense, sin and ignorance are practically the same in meaning. The Buddha without any contact with the Mosaic tradition also formulated "ten commandments" which are remarkably similar and support the idea that the concepts of sin and ignorance lead to very similar conclusions. The Buddhist ten commandments, or "precepts," are as follows:

I. Kill not, but have regard for life.

II. Steal not, neither do ye rob; but help everybody to be master of the fruits of his labor.

III. Abstain from impurity, and lead a life of chastity.

IV. Lie not, but be truthful. Speak the truth with discretion, fearlessly and in a loving heart.

V. Invent not evil reports, neither do ye repeat them. Carp not, but look for the good sides of your fellow-beings, so that ye may with sincerity defend them against their enemies.

VI. Swear not, but speak decently and with dignity.

VII. Waste not the time with gossip, but speak to the purpose or keep silence.

VIII. Covet not, nor envy, but rejoice at the fortunes of other people.

IX. Cleanse your heart of malice and cherish no hatred, not even against your enemies; but embrace all living beings with kindness.

X. Free your mind of ignorance and be anxious to learn the truth, especially in the one thing that is needful, lest you fall a prey either to scepticism or to errors. Scepticism will make you indifferent and errors will lead you astray, so that you shall not find the noble path that leads to life eternal.

The Buddha's ten commandments encompass aspects of both Moses and Jesus. The commandments exhorting us to "kill not" and "steal not" and "lie not" are very Mosaic in force and content. Commandment nine which says "Cleanse your heart of malice and cherish no hatred, not even against your enemies . . ." is very close to the teaching of Jesus who said "Love your enemies. . . ."

The difference between the Buddhist and the Judeo-Christian tradition is as obvious as the similarity. The Buddha says that "in the beginning there is existence blind and without knowledge . . . ," and the Judeo-Christian scriptures say "In the beginning God created the heavens and the earth." This is a difference that cannot be "explained away." For the Buddhist, ignorance was inherent in the nature of existence from the beginning. For the Jew or Christian, "the beginning" is the God-created world which is proclaimed "good." It is man's act of rebellion, or "sin," as symbolized in the Garden of Eden story, which results in the state of exile in which man finds himself. I personally prefer the latter myth, but this is in no way to take away from the profound psychospiritual insights of the Buddha into the nature of human suffering and its cure. Moses gave humanity the Torah, Jesus preached the Gospel of the Kingdom, and the Buddha proclaimed his Dharma which begins with the "Four Noble Truths," which point out the path which leads to Nirvana:

The first noble truth is the existence of suffering.

The second noble truth is the cause of suffering.

The third noble truth is the cessation of suffering.

The fourth noble truth is the eightfold path that leads to the cessation of suffering.

To expound upon each of these, we note that the first noble truth to which the Buddha awakened on that night of May under the full moon was the truth of suffering. There is physical suffering, mental sickness, pain, grief, sorrow, loss of loved ones; there is the inevitability of one's own death; there is the not getting of what one wants in life; there is the being tied to what one hates; and there is anger, fear, loneliness, and despair. Millennia before modern physics discovered the equivalence of matter and energy, the Buddha realized the fundamental impermanence of all phenomena which he called "Anicca." This includes what we call our egos, our bodies, our minds, our sensations, our perceptions, our thoughts, and our feelings. The impermanence of all phenomena, or "Anicca," leads to the inescapability of suffering, or "Dukka." to put it more simply, that we inevitably lose the things we have, that we often never even attain what we want and that we often must live with what we don't want, this is the ultimate "unsatisfactoriness" of existence, or "Dukka."

The second noble truth is the truth of the cause of suffering. It is through the failure to realize the truth of impermanence, or "Anicca," that people grasp at the constant flux as though it were something stable. We grasp at youth, and it passes into old age. We grasp at health and it passes into sickness. We grasp at love, and it passes away too. This is profoundest suffering. We, in our materialistic culture, are in a lifelong game of grasping for what we consider to be the "goodies" of life, i.e., wealth, position, power, glamor, and the like. We may never attain these things, or if we do, we will inevitably lose them. Old age, sickness, and death are the great equalizers. Millionaire and pauper are the same in the grave. "World conquerors" suh as Genghis Khan, Alexander the Great, and Juliuis Caesar vanquished nations, but they could not defeat death. The greatest Hollywood beauty eventually becomes a grayhaired and wrinkled old woman. The greatest athlete, even the Olympic champion Jim Thorpe, eventually succumbs to sickness, old age, and death. The things we value and crave pass away. It is the *craving itself*, or "Tanha," which is the cause of suffering according to the Buddha's teaching. The Buddha noted that it is this "fellow" we call our "self" that we crave most. We would like him or her to go on forever, but somewhere, deep down, we know that this will not be. This cleaving to the ego is perhaps the greatest suffering of all for we all know that it will be ultimately frustrated. The Buddha called the impermanence of ego "Anatta," and the craving for the continuation of ego (and all other things we crave) "Tanha." You will recall that "Tanha" is one of the three daughters of "Mara," the Evil One.

The third noble truth is the truth that there is the possibility of the cessation of suffering. This state of the nonarising of suffering, or "Dukka," is called "Nirvana," which means "extinction." It is the giving up of "Tanha," or craving, which is the "way out" of suffering. Buddhism is a religion which requires sacrifice, not the sacrifice of animals, or of other living things, but the sacrifice of one's craving or desiring or "Tanha." It is not entirely a "negative way," as it seems at first sight, because the renunciation of craving results in the highest reward: Nirvana. The Buddha never speaks directly of what Nirvana is like, but neither, for that matter, does Jesus speak directly of the nature of the Kingdom, except by analogy in his parables. (The Buddha was a parable teller as well, and some of his parables are remarkably similar to those of Jesus.)

The fourth noble truth is the truth of the eightfold path that leads to the cessation of suffering. It is the "Way" of the Buddha. It is the "how to" in terms of how to give up "Tanha," or craving. The eightfold noble path consists of the following: right views, right aspirations, right speech, right behavior, right livelihood, right effort, right mindfulness, and right meditation. Each of these deserves some commentary.

Right views, or right understanding, means that one must see life as it really is. According to the Buddha, life has three aspects: (1) Anicca—impermanence, (2) Dukka—dissatisfactoriness, or suffering, and (3) Anatta-egolessness, or no self.[10] These three components make up the world of Samsara. Right views also entail knowledge of the four noble truths, and the eightfold noble path, which can lead one from Samsara to Nirvana.

Right aspirations or motives imply the weeding out of unwholesome or evil motives such as the motive to hurt others, or the motive to steal, or to tell untruth, and so one, and their replacement by wholesome motives such as those of kindness, generosity, the desire to acquire wisdom, and so on.

Right speech involves not indulging in lying, or harsh talk, or backbiting, or idle gossip. It implies a change in the use of language to truth telling, calmness in speech, and the forgoing of speaking ill of others.

Right behavior, or right action, implies actions that proceed from a clear and unobstructed mind, and abstaining from actions which proceed from a disturbed mind. Wholesome actions lead, in the Buddhist view, to good Karma, and unwholesome actions lead to bad Karma. In the Jewish view, one's act, or "mitzvah," is of the essence; it is the basis of the Torah. Jesus went even farther, and asks us to "be perfect," as our heavenly Father is perfect. As I discussed in the chapter on Jesus (3) I believe that Jesus was implying that to behave as he would have us would require a spiritual revolution within oneself.

Right livelihood in the Buddhist sense implies that one makes one's living in a way that breaks none of the ten commandments, or precepts of behavior. The Buddhists interpret "kill not" as referring to all sentient beings, so one could not be a butcher who slaughters animals, for instance, and follow the teaching of right livelihood. Neither could one, in the strict sense, be a soldier or military person, although many of the most violent Samurai of feudal Japan claimed also to be Buddhists. But then this is equally true of Christians, and the Crusaders who slaughtered Moslems and Jews also claimed to be "good Christians." Right livelihood in a positive sense would imply we seek out an occupation that is conducive to our growth and development as the persons we are.

Right effort involves the development of one's will power. It is not something that we see very much of in our modern Western culture. Sure, people can be seen to work very hard, but this is quite another thing than right effort, or will power. Will power would imply the exercising of freedom. What we are usually doing when we are going about our daily activities is the acting out of our long-established behavior patterns that have not changed much, if we really knew the truth, from how we behaved as children and adolescents. We behave according to the conditioning of our family and culture groups and conformity is the rule of our world. People conform so much to the role expectations of their particular social role that it is a wonder to behold! You see business people wearing almost the same kind of suits, carrying their attaché cases, and talking about the very same kind of things, usually financial things, day in and day out. Students in their blue jeans with notebooks in hand, or back pack, ambling from class to class, talking about this course, or that professor, or such and such a test, or the weekend football game, also present a stereotypic pattern. You can observe remarkable conformity of dress, style, and behavior in almost any group whatsoever from doctors to construction workers. Right effort is the exercise of will power or free will and one must *really try hard* to do this. The "mere" giving up of simple habits like smoking or overeating take all kinds of "clinics" and "therapies," and usually without much success! Can you imagine the effort or will power necessary to change lifelong patterns of neurotic and self-defeating behavior? To overcome obsessions, and compulsions, and phobias, and fears, and cycles of depression, and so one, requires years and years of "psychotherapy," often with a very limited rate of "cure." The Buddhist disciple is asked to exercise the effort required to change the universal and age-old human failing of "Tanha," or craving, in order to break out of the Samsaric cycle of birth, death, and rebirth. To overcome Samsara and suffering, what an effort that must require! But rather than try to "do it all at once," I think that the Buddha would advise you to make the journey one single step at a time.

Right mindfulness, for the Buddhist, is the pivotal factor on the Path. This is what Gurdjieff would call "self remembering" or "self observation." It has many levels. The first level could be called "body mindfulness." We have become so unconscious of our bodies in the twentieth-century West that it is surprising that they function at all. Many Eastern spiritual disciplines have a body training component from the Chinese Taoist discipline of Tai Chi Chuan to the ancient

Hindu practice of Hatha Yoga. All of these venerable disciplines involve body movement *with awareness*. This is quite another thing from "calisthenics," or "bodybuilding," and the like. It is almost the reverse of these, in fact. To become conscious of one's body, and its capabilities, is a revelation to most of us. A second level of right mindfulness is the mindfulness of, or attention to, one's emotions and feelings. Many forms of psychotherapies deal with this, and some do it pretty well. Right mindfulness would involve what Freud called "making conscious the unconscious." On the level of emotions, this would involve becoming aware, for example, of all of the anger that we have kept repressed for years. It would involve the de-repressing of sexual feelings as well. The "Freudian revolution" has involved, for the most part, the lifting of the sexual and aggressive repressions of the Victorian era. There are more subtle areas of feeling and emotion as well, and the development of sensitivity to the realm of one's feelings is neglected education for most of us. The third level of mindfulness is mindfulness of our thoughts, both conscious and unconscious. Unconscious thoughts, or "programming," is particularly important in the psychotherapeutic process of overcoming lifelong neurotic patterns. Some of us have an unconscious program which prevents us from succeeding at anything no matter how talented we may happen to be. It may go like this: "If I succeed I will be able to be independent of Mommy, and Mommy won't like it if I am independent of her." The making conscious of the unconscious, on the levels of body, emotion, and thought, is what "right mindfulness" is all about. You might say that the Buddha anticipated psychoanalysis and psychotherapy by about 2,500 years.

Right meditation is the great subject of Buddhism. It is the spiritual dimension and the last and highest of the eightfold noble path which culminates in the breaking free of the Samsaric world, and entering Nirvana. Be aware, or course, that Samsara and Nirvana are the same thing, although viewed differently. Meditation is more highly refined in Buddhism than in any other great religion and it is the way to "transform" one's consciousness from "Samsaric consciousness" to "Nirvanic consciousness." Samsaric consciousness sees the world through the lenses and filters of ego; it sees a world of hate and fear and danger that is filled with all of its projections. If there is a nightmare within, we will "see" a nightmare without. Nirvanic consciousness is a perception of the world *as it really is* without the distorting lenses, and filters, and defenses of the ego. The meditation way of the Buddha is a method of gradually gaining *in-sight* into self and world until one attains "satori," which is to say clear seeing. Let me quote the Japanese Zen master Kosho Uchiyama Roshi on the nature of "zazen," or Zen Buddhist meditation, and its relationship to "satori" or awakening:

The aim of doing zazen is to do zazen. It's never doing zazen for some purpose . . . . Zazen is itself *satori* . . . . Doing zazen is to practice, put into effect, and actualize this satori here and now.[11]

The process of Buddhist meditation, or insight meditation, ia analogous to the unpeeling of an onion. You see through level after level of mind-created delusion until you come to *that* which has never been described, but which has been called "the truth." This is what the historical Buddha had to say about his experience of enlightenment at the end of his forty days of meditations under the Bodhi tree:

There is self and there is truth. Where self is, the truth is not. Where truth is, self is not. Self is the fleeting error of samsara; it is individual separateness and that egotism which begets envy and hatred. Self is the yearning for pleasure and the lust after vanity. Truth is the correct comprehension of things; it is the permanent and everlasting, the real in all existence, the bliss of righteousness.

I believe that the distinction that the Buddha makes between self and truth is the same as the one that I have made between ego and true Self. Ego is the self that feels itself to be separate, that identifies itself with the mortal body and hence lives in fear of death, that experiences hatred and envy, and which yearns after temporary pleasures and vanities. True Self, in the sense in which I have used it, is your identity in God or the Tao. This is not a sense of separation or existential anxiety, but one of unity with all things and joy which is indescribable. You can receive a glimpse of this in your very first meditation session, and the method of Buddhist meditation is very simple. In the words of one Zen Buddhist master, it is "just sitting, and doing nothing." Usually one sits upon a cushion with legs crossed in full or half-lotus posture, keeping one's back straight, with eyes slightly open. It is good for the novice to attend to his or her breathing in the beginning. And then simply: Observe! Don't try to stop thoughts. Don't try to stop emotions. Don't try to "do" anything. To "be" is enough. In Zen practice, one usually sits for forty minutes. I would suggest that this is much too long for the beginner. Ten or fifteen minutes, twice per day, will be quite sufficient at first. Surprisingly, this regular discipline of meditation will make a difference in your life. You will see that right away. But the spiritual path is not a matter of weeks or months, but of years and years. But that should not discourage you for you are in truth always right where you are in the present moment, and it is in the present moment that one finds the true Self. This is what Gotama, the Buddha, says about the true Self:

. . . verily, ye should learn to distinguish between the false self and the true self. The ego with all its egotism is the false self. It is an unreal illusion and a perishable combination. He only who identifies his self with the truth will attain Nirvana; and he who has entered Nirvana has attained Buddhahood; he has acquired the highest good; he has become eternal and immortal.

The goal, then, of the Buddha's path is the attainment of Nirvana, which is to say Buddhahood, which is to say one's true Self. It will be interesting to compare Gotama, the Buddha's, statement with the sayings of some of the historical Buddhist masters who followed him. This is what Bodhidarma, the Indian Buddhist sage who brought Buddhism to China in the sixth century A.D., had to say about the Buddha nature:

If you wish to seek the Buddha, you ought to see into your own Nature [hsing] for this Nature is the Buddha himself.[12]

Bodhidarma goes on to say:

If, instead of seeing into your own Nature, you turn away to seek the Buddha in external things, you will never get at him.[13]

What Bodhidarma says about the Buddha nature, or true Self, reminds me about what Jesus said about the Kingdom of Heaven, namely, "the Kingdom of Heaven is within." In our materialistic culture, we are always looking outside of ourselves for our identity, e.g., "I am a Harvard professor," or "I am an engineer with I.B.M.," or "I am a doctor," etc. No matter how "prestigious" the external institution or thing with which we identify ourself, it is not the Self. And it is something that can be taken away from you. In the Great Depression of 1929, when the "bottom" fell out of the stock market, many a former millionaire committed suicide. Your "own Nature" of which Bodhidarma is speaking is the Self which can never be taken away!

Hui Neng, the Chinese Buddhist master who was to become the

sixth patriarch of Ch'an Buddhism, was born in 638 A.D. He was a simple farmer who received his commission from the fifth patriarch based upon a simple poem he had written which impressed the master very much. He had a quiet and unassuming air about him, but his master recognized in him the highest spiritual attainment. About one's true Nature, Hui Neng said:

All the Buddhas of the past, present, and future, and all the Sutras belonging to the twelve divisions are in the self-nature of each individual, where they were from the first. . . . There is within oneself that which knows, and thereby one has a *satori*.[14]

"Satori" is the Chinese Ch'an (and the Japanese Zen) Buddhist term for enlightenment. In Christian terms, this would be to say that each individual has within himself or herself the Christ; it is a matter of recognizing it. This saying of Hui Neng's made me think of when I was a Jewish child in Sunday school. I used to wonder why people used to talk with God in "biblical times," and not now. The answer to this is that we have forgotten how. We have also forgotten where to look!

Chih, a Chinese Buddhist monk of the eighth century A.D., had this to say with regard to one's Self-nature:

This Nature is from the first pure and undefiled, serene and undisturbed. It belongs to no categories of duality such as being and non-being, pure and defiled, long and short, taking in and giving up; the Body remains in its suchness. To have a clear insight into this is to see one's Self-nature. Therefore, seeing into one's Self-nature is becoming the Buddha.[15]

Chih reminds me of Lao Tzu's saying about knowing others versus knowing yourself: "He who knows others is wise; he who knows himself is enlightened." Enlightenment is not just the realm of saints and sages; it is the potentiality of everybody. It can happen to the most unlikely people as when Saul of Tarsus experienced the blinding light of the Christ on the road to Damascus. He was one of the chief persecutors of the fledgling group of followers of Jesus. Jacob Boehme, a humble German shoemaker, experienced an enlightenment while looking at the physical light reflected from a pewter dish. Without education, he went on to write great works of Christian mysticism. His first book was entitled *The Aurora*. These two examples from the Christian tradition would seem to confirm the "sudden illumination" school of Zen. There are many other saints and sages, however, such as St. John of the Cross, and St. Theresa of Avila, and so on, whose experience would tend to confirm the "gradual path to enlightenment" school of Zen. It is different for different individuals whether one reaches one's Self-nature in a "flash," or whether it is the most prolonged and arduous journey imaginable. Rapidity is not the issue really, but whether or not one is "climbing up the ladder," as in the vision of the Hebrew patriarch, Jacob, of the ladder "between heaven and earth."

Huang Po was a ninth-century Ch'an Buddhist master who speaks of the Mind which is the Buddha, outside of which there is no way to attain enlightenment. He is the originator of the "Mind Only" school, and this is what he had to say about the "Buddha nature":

There is just this One Mind, which constitutes Buddhahood, and in it are the Buddhas and all sentient beings, showing no distinction, only that the latter are attached to form and seek (the Mind) outside themselves. Thus the more they seek, the farther it is lost. Let the Buddha seek himself outside himself, let the Mind seek itself outside itself, and to the end of time there wil be no finding. Stop your thoughts, forget your hankerings, and the Buddha reveals himself right before your eyes.[16]

Huang Po reinforces the point that seeking oneself in external things, in "titles," in "possessions," in "position," or in "fame," etc., is to place the Self beyond the finding. Huang Po says that "to the end of time there will be no finding." How to find it? "Stop your thoughts, forget your hankerings, and the Buddha reveals himself right before your eyes."

In the "Buddhist period" of my Journey, I met, or had some contact with, a number of Buddhist masters in the Zen and Tibetan Buddhist traditions who are teaching in the United States, although they are from places as diverse as Japan, Korea, and Tibet. I practiced meditation for about one year at the New York "Dharmadhatu," the Tibetan Buddhist Meditation Center under the direction of the Ven. Chogyam Trungpa. I spoke with him only once, and rather briefly. Trungpa, Rimpoche was primarily based at their central headquarters in Boulder, Colorado. Yet, he became "my teacher" for a while, and I even occasionally dreamed about him. In one such dream, his eyes were luminous with light, and he said to me: "You are close to enlightenment, follow me." The Jungians would say that he was a figure who (for a while at least) represented the true Self to me.

Chogyam Trungpa's school of Buddhism, which is sometimes called "Tantric Buddhism," involves more a "cutting through" the illusions of the ego than affirming the reality of the Self. Trungpa compares the ego with a "huge bubble" in this quotation from his book *Meditation in Action:*

So this huge bubble prevents any fresh air from coming in, and that is "I"—the Ego. So in that sense there is the existence of Ego, but it is in fact illusory. Having established that, one generally wants to create some external idol or refuge. Subconsciously one knows that this "I" is only a bubble and it could burst at any moment, so one tries to protect it as much as one can—either consciously or subconsciously. In fact we have achieved such skill at protecting this Ego that we have managed to preserve it for hundreds of years.[17]

This denial of the *reality* of the ego is not unique to the Buddhist tradition. After his experience of the blinding spiritual light, Paul said it was no longer "I" but "Christ in me." The Buddhist teacher Trungpa speaks in this way of what one experiences beyond the barriers of the ego:

And when that barrier is removed one can expand and swim through straight away. But this can only be achieved through the practice of meditation, which must be approached in a very practical and simple way. Then the mystical experience of joy or Grace, or whatever it might be, can be found in every object.[18]

Walt Whitman wrote a poem called "Unseen Buds," which is about the buds of spring flowers that lie unseen beneath the winter snow. Ego's barriers can be seen as the winter snows, meditation as the warm sunshine, and the mystical experience as the beautiful flowers that bloom in spring! One term that Trungpa frequently used was "spaciousness." When one breaks through the "bubble" that is one's ego concept, one "expands" into the realm of "pure space." This is a realm in which one can "breathe freely."

Another contemporary Buddhist master who impressed me very much in the one lecture of his that I attended (he spoke one evening at New York Dharmadhatu) was the Japanese Zen master, Joshu Sasaki, Roshi. "Roshi" means Zen master, incidentally. He is one of the funniest men I've ever heard, even though he spoke in Japanese, and was immediately translated into English by his interpreter. Humor is a very large part of the Zen tradition, and one can literally laugh one's way into "satori." Laughter is one of the greatest "natural therapies." Sasaki, Roshi has written a marvellous little book on Zen called *Buddha Is the Center of Gravity.* On the back of the book Sasaki, Roshi writes "Buddha is not the Center of Gravity." This is indicative of his humor.

I want to quote one short passage from his book which goes as follows:

If you can hold this world in your hand, that must be the most magnificent thing. There are many wonderful things in this world, but the best of all is to hold the whole world together in your hand, beautiful ladies, handsome men, good and evil people, everything.[19]

Joshu Sasaki, Roshi was obviously on the same "wave length" as the poet, William Blake, who said: "Hold Infinity in the palm of your hand and Eternity in an hour."[20] Blake and Sasaki, Roshi are both speaking of the Wholeness aspect of the Self which can encompass both what the ego considers to be pleasant and unpleasant, beautiful and ugly, good and bad. All these "pairs of opposites" are constituents of the Totality. That which can embrace both ego and Shadow is *the Self*. This is what Sasaki, Roshi calls "the center of gravity."

A third modern Buddhist master with whom I have had some contact through his lectures in New York City is the Korean Zen master, Seung Sahn. He is also a very humorous fellow, and a luminous fellow as well, and I learned a lot of value from his lectures. He speaks of the reality which the Buddha discovered 2,500 years ago as the "don't know mind." He says this about it:

Always keep this don't know mind. When this don't know mind becomes clear, then you will understand. So if you keep don't know mind when you are driving, this is driving Zen. If you keep it when you are watching television, this is television Zen. You must keep don't know mind always and everywhere. This is the true practice of Zen.[21]

This statement of Seung Sahn's makes me think of what the great sage Lao Tzu said about "not knowing:" "Not knowing that one knows is best." The Taoists and Zennists have a lot in common. We Westerners have a great penchant for "knowledge." Our universities are "knowledge factories." Ever more "knowledge" about the less and less important. One of the doctoral dissertations of new Ph.D.'s at New York University in the year that I received my B.A. degree was entitled: "A Pressure-Temperature Study of the Tympanic Membrane of a Sea Urchin Egg." While the moral basis of our society disintegrates before our eyes, our learned "savants" are busy "dissecting the brain of a leech." They "stare at a gnat and swallow a camel," in the words of Master Jesus. The scholarly journals multiply, and the library shelves are more and more crowded with new tomes. But do we *see* more clearly? I don't think so. We need a little more of Seung Sahn's "don't know mind!"

The Zen Buddhists say that when you have been through all stages of the Journey, through heaven, hell, and purgatory, you attain to "emptiness." But even this emptiness is not enough. The very final stage of the Journey is the "Return to the Marketplace." Then you have "made it." But the Buddhists would say that there was nothing "to make" anyway! Your true Self was there all the time. It takes a shedding of the opaque layers of the ego to see it, though: your "Original Face before your parents were born." Seung Sahn compares the true Self to the full moon in the sky in the following passage which speaks about how the ego can block our perception:

Clear mind is like the full moon in the sky. Sometimes clouds come and cover it, but the moon is always behind them. Don't worry about this clear mind; it is always there. When thinking comes, behind it is clear mind. When thinking goes, there is always clear mind. . . .[22]

A Buddhist master whom I spoke with a couple of times, and knew as Rato, Rimpoche, was so absolutely ordinary that I thought he was the janitor. I learned that he was a very high-ranking Tibetan Buddhist master, and the author of an autobiographical book entitled *My Life and Lives*. He didn't say very much really, and was quite self-effacing in a humorous way. One hippie follower he introduced as "my teacher," and to a girl who came up to him and said, "I'd like to study with you," he replied, "I have nothing to teach you." This man, Rato, Rimpoche, taught by the very unpretentiousness and ordinariness that he manifested. I have heard that ordinary mind is the Tao, and he had that. We all had it at one time. Little children are with the Tao. They are perfect little Buddha masters. But we lose it in our mad world where technology has become our god, and the human heart has been relegated to thirtieth place in our hierarchy of values. Despite the "sophistication" of scholarly academic books on Buddhism, and all their Sanskrit words, what the Buddha discovered was a very simple thing. It is so simple that it defies verbalization, and is the reason for the use of the Zen Koan. What he found was the "Original Face before one's parents were born."

I searched through my own diaries of this period during which I was practicing Buddhist meditation, and studying with Buddhist teachers, and I would like to share certain passages with you in a personal, historical sequence of development. It was part of my search for true Self in which I sought, I think, what the Buddha sought, and learned something of his distinction "between the false self and the true self."

January, 1974—Was I born just to suffer and to die? It can't be. The Universe does not produce a human being just to suffer and to die. There is a reason that I was born. I was not sent here for nothing.

January, 1974—I am the Universe becoming conscious of itself.

January, 1974—Reality, Christ, Hitler, Walt Disney, Buddha, John Wayne, Richard Nixon, squirrels, cockroaches, dog dung, lightning, Cheerios, love, hate, trees, clouds, urine, coal, uranium, ping pong, Mr. Ranier, Lone Ranger, Mozart. . . .

January, 1974—There is no end—There was never a beginning. There is no death—There is no life. All distinctions, strange as it seems, we create. . . .

January, 1974—Observe, let be, see what is. You will not see an individual ego. You will not see consciousness. You will not see the cessation of consciousness.

January 1974—Observe, Only God is. Who is there to observe that God is? No one. Only no one is. How do you know? MU!

January, 1974—I AM, YOU ARE, THE SITUATION IS.

January, 1974—We are the eyes and ears of God.

January 1974—Buddha's Way is the Way of Mindfulness. "Be ye a lamp unto yourselves."

January, 1974—Let go of suffering. Let go of the past. Let go of the false ego. Let what is be. As it is, so be it.

February, 1974—I saw the truth of Buddha's teaching on February 27, 1974. When my agony (dukka) was unbearable, I practiced right meditation and my suffering disappeared. The meditation is so fine, I will do it the rest of my life. It turned unbearable pain into voidness.

February, 1974—Not a matter of words or concepts or thinking at all, but of seeing, of piercing the fog of Maya to the Clear Void (Shunyata).

March, 1974—The Real reveals itself when we are open and receptive, not filled with thought and opinions. Be empty and you will be filled.

March, 1974—I met Chogyam Trungpa in a dream. His eyes were luminous. He said that I was close to enlightenment; follow him.

March, 1974—How to be your true Self? Don't try. You already are. Just observe.

March, 1974—The manifestations of your true Self are everywhere, inside, outside, everywhere.

April, 1974—The only sin is to make the Self an object, to worship false gods.

April, 1974—I dreamed of meeting Chogyam Trungpa and driving somewhere.

April, 1974—You are yourself. There is nothing special to do.

April, 1974—In truth, ego and its idols and the external world are mind creations.

April, 1974—Say yes to life.

April, 1974—Accepting here and now. Trusting in living because, hell, I am here and now.

May, 1974—Our mind is the slayer of Reality. The Mystic Way is to slay the slayer.

May, 1974—Our limited egos that create the delusion of limitation, finitude, and separation—this is Satan. This is the adversary. How to slay the slayer? Knowing there is a slayer is the first step. The second step is the creating of gaps—such as love, letting be, meditation, and ecstasy.

May, 1974—Get to know the slayer and observe him. Trust in Reality which will eventually slay the slayer.

May, 1974—Take it easy—trying too hard is egotistical. Let be, let go. The ego needs to develop to the utmost and then it will eventually wear itself out through use. To overcome the ego, just attend to it, or forget about it.

May, 1974—When you are struggling to be free—this is unfreedom. Surrender to your prison, then, strangely enough you are free.

May, 1974—What is the secret? To fully accept what is, and be nonattached. Let what comes come, then let it go. It is the glorious dance of God.

May, 1974—Buddha's Way is the only solution to suffering. Suffering is disappointed hopes or wishes. Give up your wishes and you will not suffer.

May, 1974—You lose your center by taking on what you think is the other's view of you; hence your center of gravity is projected outside of yourself, and you are "off-balance."

December, 1974—All efforts to name it, to define it, to analyze it, to describe it, to contain it, evade it!

December, 1974—The true way is lived, it cannot be spoken. It is the Reality of our lives as lived and experienced: the Sacred Reality, the Being and the Becoming, the Nameless, the Formless, the Unthinkable.

The Buddha preached his Dharma in terms of the abstract teachings of the Four Noble Truths and the Eightfold Nobel Path to his disciples. But to simple folks (like you and me), he simply told parables and stories. He said, "If they cannot grasp the truth in the abstract arguments by which I have reached it, they may nevertheless come to understand it, if it is illustrated in parables." Many of the

Buddha's parables bear a remarkable similarity to those of Jesus of Nazareth who lived and taught a half millennia later in another part of the world.

THE LOST SON

There was a householder's son who went away into a distant country, and while the father accumulated immeasurable riches, the son became miserably poor. And the son while searching for food and clothing happened to come to the country in which his father lived. And the father saw him in his wretchedness, for he was ragged and brutalized by poverty, and ordered some of his servants to call him.

When the son saw the place to which he was conducted, he thought, "I must have evoked the suspicion of a powerful man, and he will throw me into prison." Full of apprehension he made his escape before he had seen his father.

Then the father sent messengers out after his son, who was caught and brought back in spite of his cries and lamentations. Thereupon the father ordered his servants to deal tenderly with his son, and he appointed a laborer of his son's rank and education to employ the lad as a helpmate on the estate. And the son was pleased with his new situation.

From the window of the palace the father watched the boy, and when he saw that he was honest and industrious, he promoted him higher and higher.

After some time, he summoned his son and called together all his servants, and made the secret known to them. Then the poor man was exceedingly glad and he was full of joy at meeting his father.

Little by little must the minds of men be trained for higher truths.

The parable of the "lost son" bears remarkable resemblance to the parable of the "prodigal son" which was taught by Jesus to tax collectors and sinners. In the parable of Jesus, the prodigal son squandered his money in loose living, and he found himself in uttermost poverty in a great famine which arose in his country. He returned to his father's estate and was welcomed with great rejoicing. In the Bible, it says that he "was dead, and is alive; he was lost, and is found."[23] Its meaning has been interpreted theologically as an allegory of the return of the sinner to the Father, i.e., to God, and the great joy that is attendant upon that reunion. In the Buddha's tale, there is also a "lost," or "prodigal," son who is separated from his father, and who has fallen into dreadful poverty. I would interpret the "father" in this case to be the Truth that the Buddha had discovered in his enlightenment, and the "lost son" to be the soul who is lost in the world of samsara, or illusion. In this story, the point is made that most people have to be introduced gradually, little by little, to the Truth.

THE LIGHT OF THE WORLD

There was a certain Brahman in Kosambi, a wrangler and well versed in the Vedas. As he found no one whom he regarded his equal in debate he used to carry a lighted torch in his hand, and when asked for the reason of his strange conduct, he replied: "The world is so dark that I carry this torch to light it up, as far as I can."

A samana sitting in the market-place heard these words and said: "My friend, if thine eyes are blind to the sight of the omnipresent light of the day, do not call the world dark. Thy torch adds nothing to the glory of the sun and thy intention to illumine the minds of others is as futile as it is arrogant."

Whereupon the Brahman asked: "Where is the sun of which thou speakest?" And the samana replied: "The wisdom of the Tathagata is the sun of the mind. His radiancy is glorious by day and night, and he whose faith is strong will not lack light on the path to Nirvana where he will inherit bliss everlasting."

One cannot help but think of the statement of Jesus to the people gathered around him in his "Sermon on the Mount," in which he says: "You are the light of the world."[24] He goes on to say, "Let your light so shine before men, that they may see your good works and give glory to your Father, who is in heaven."[25] The samana is saying very much the same thing to the Brahman, in Buddhist terms, when he says that "The wisdom of the Tathagata is the sun of the mind." Spiritual light is spiritual light in whatever culture or religious tradition. Whether we speak of the Kingdom or we speak of Nirvana, the view from the top of the mountain is the same, and it is "bliss everlasting."

THE SOWER

Bharadvaja, a wealthy Brahman farmer, was celebrating his harvest-thanksgiving when the Blessed One came with his alms-bowl, begging for food.

Some of the people paid him reverence, but the Brahman was angry and said: "O samana, it would be more fitting for thee to go to work than to beg. I plough and sow, and having ploughed and sown, I eat. If thou didst likewise, thou, too, wouldst have something to eat."

The Tathagata answered him and said: "O Brahman, I, too, plough and sow, and having ploughed and sown, I eat."

"Dost thou profess to be a husbandman?" replied the Brahman. "Where, then, are thy bullocks? Where is the seed and the plough?"

The Blessed One said: "Faith is the seed I sow: good works are the rain that fertilizes it; wisdom and modesty are the plough; my mind is the guiding rein; I lay hold of the handle of the law; earnestness is the goad I use, and exertion is my draught-ox. The ploughing is ploughed to destroy the weeds of illusion. The harvest it yields is the immortal fruit of Nirvana, and thus all sorrow ends."

Then the Brahman poured rice-milk in a golden bowl and offered it to the Blessed One, saying: "Let the teacher of mankind partake of the rice-milk, for the venerable Gotama ploughs a ploughing that bears the fruit of immortality."

Jesus came from an agricultural country, as did Gotama, and they both allegorize the sowing of the seed in their respective parables of "the sower." In Jesus' parable, the point is that the seed of the Kingdom will bear fruit only when it is sown in good soil. The good soil, he explains, is a man "who hears the word and understands it. . . ."[26] The Buddha says that the seed he sows is faith. Jesus says the same thing in his parable of the "mustard seed." He says that: "If you had as much faith as a grain of mustard seed, you will say to this mountain, 'Move from here to there,' and it will move; and nothing will be impossible for you."[27] Faith is a commonality of both Christianity and Buddhism. Faith in the Buddha Dharma is certainly a prerequisite for the Buddhist seeker. The Buddha says that "good works are the rain" that fertilizes the seed of faith. Jesus would agree, and he spoke of the good works that one need do unto "the least of these my brethren,"[28] if one is to enter the Kingdom. The Buddha calls wisdom and modesty his "plough." Jesus told his disciples to be as "wise as serpents, and innocent as doves."[29] He also displayed remarkable modesty when he refused even to be called "good," when he was addressed as "good master."[30] The Buddha says that "mind is the guiding-rein." Jesus frequently admonished his disciples to "watch," as in his statement to his disciples: "And what I say to you I say to all: Watch."[31] "Watch" has the connotation: "Be awake." The Buddha certainly emphasized the importance of "mindfulness" in his teachings. The Buddha says that he lays hold of "the handle of the law." The "law," or "Dharma," for Jesus would be his "Gospel," or "Good News," of the Kingdom of God. The "Dharma" for the Buddha is his "four noble truths," and "eightfold noble path" which leads the seeker from Samsara to Nirvana. The Buddha says that "earnestness is the goad I use, and exertion is my draught-ox." Jesus exemplified earnestness, or sincerity, and he also spoke of the hard work or exertion that his followers would have to endure, as when he said: "No one who puts his hand to the plow and looks back is fit for the kingdom of God."[32] The Buddha says that "this ploughing is ploughed to destroy the weeds of illusion." Jesus preached the baptism for the repentance from sin. "Sin" means "to miss the mark," which is very similar in connotation to the Buddha's term "illusion." Finally, the Buddha speaks of the "harvest," which is "the immortal fruit of Nirvana." Nirvana ends all sorrow. Jesus repeatedly spoke of the "harvest" as the "Kingdom of God." The Kingdom ends man's state of exile (or sorrow). "Nirvana," the "Kingdom of God," the "Tao," etc., are semantic terms in different cultures for a universal spiritual experience, and I would say *spiritual reality*. The Buddha said, "All the Buddhas teach the same truth."

THE WOMAN AT THE WELL

Ananda, the favorite disciple of the Buddha, having been sent by the Lord on a mission, passed by a well near a village, and seeing Pakati, a girl of the Matanga caste, he asked her for water to drink.

Pakati said: "O Brahman, I am too humble and mean to give thee water to drink, do not ask any service of me lest thy holiness be contaminated, for I am of low caste."

And Ananda replied: "I ask not for caste but for water"; and the Matanga girl's heart leaped joyfully and she gave Ananda to drink.

Ananda thanked her and went away; but she followed him at a distance.

Having heard that Ananda was a disciple of Gotama Sakyamuni, the girl repaired to the Blessed One and cried: "O Lord, help me, and let me live in the place where Ananda thy disciple dwells, so that I may see him and minister unto him, for I love Ananda."

And the Blessed One understood the emotions of her heart and he said: "Pakati, thy heart is full of love, but thou understandeth not thine own sentiments. It is not Ananda that thou lovest, but his kindness. Accept, then, the kindness thou hast seen him practice unto thee, and in the humility of thy station practice it unto others.

"Verily there is great merit in the generosity of a king when he is kind to a slave; but there is a greater merit in the slave when he ignores the wrongs which he suffers and cherishes kindness and good-will to all mankind. He will cease to hate his oppressors, and even when powerless to resist their usurpation will with compassion pity their arrogance and supercilious demeanor.

"Blessed art thou, Pakati, for though thou art a Matanga thou wilt be a model for noblemen and noblewomen. Thou art of low caste, but Brahmans may

learn a lesson from thee. Swerve not from the path of justice and righteousness and thou wilt outshine the royal glory of queens on the throne."

There is a parallel in the Gospels when a woman of Samaria came to
draw water at a well, and Jesus asked her to give him a drink, just as
Ananda, a Brahman. Both cultures, the Jews of Jesus' time, and the
tan woman asked Jesus, "How is that you, a Jew, ask a drink of me, a
woman of Samaria? For Jews have no dealings with Samaritans."[33]
Likewise, Pakati thought herself of too low caste to render a service to
Ananda, a Brahman. Both cultures, the Jews of Jesus's time, and the
Brahmans of the Buddha's time, had their forms of "caste system."
Both the Buddha and Jesus abrogated the systems of bias and preju-
dice of their times and cultures. Both of them taught of a love and
kindness that knows no racial or cultural or class barriers, or any
barriers whatsoever. Jesus spoke of the love which he had to give as
"living water," and "whoever drinks of the water I shall give him will
never thirst. . . ."[34] The Buddha taught of the "waters of kindness"
as well, and one who has this outshines "the royal glory of queens on a
throne."

THE PEACEMAKER

It is reported that two kingdoms were on the verge of war for the possessions
of a certain embankment which was disputed by them.

And the Buddha seeing the kings and their armies ready to fight, requested
them to tell him the cause of their quarrels. Having heard the complaints on
both sides, he said:

"I understand that the embankment has value for some of your people; has it
any intrinsic value aside from its service to your men?"

"It has no intrinsic value whatsoever," was the reply. The Tathagata continued: "Now when you go to battle is it not sure that many of your men will be
slain and that you yourselves, O kings, are liable to lose your lives?"

And they said: "Verily, it is sure that many will be slain and our own lives be
jeopardized."

"The blood of men, however," said Buddha, "has it less intrinsic value than a
mound of earth?"

"No," the kings said, "the lives of men and above all the lives of kings, are
priceless."

Then the Tathagata concluded: "Are you going to stake that which is priceless against that which has no intrinsic value whatsoever?"

The wrath of the two monarchs abated, and they came to a peaceable agree-
ment.

Jesus said, "Blessed are the peacemakers, for they shall be called sons of God."[35] The Buddha would qualify for this designation because he brought peace between the two warring kings by making them aware of what they really valued more, human life above a "mound of earth." We live in a time of potential nuclear annihilation with two superpowers armed to the teeth with nuclear arsenals capable of destroying life on this planet as we know it. What are their differences? Basically, they differ on ideology, one capitalist and the other communist. The Buddha might ask them, which is of higher value, the life of every man, woman, and child on the planet earth, or your capitalist or communist ideologies? If the leaders of our two superpowers had at least the sense of those two Brahman kings, we might have a chance for a future on this planet!

THE MARRIAGE-FEAST IN JAMBUNADA

There was a man in Jambunada who was to be married the next day, and he thought, "Would that the Buddha, the Blessed One, might be present at the wedding."

And the Blessed One passed by his house and met him, and when he read the silent wish in the heart of the bridegroom, he consented to enter.

When the Holy One appeared with the retinue of his many bhikkhus, the host whose means were limited received them as best he could, saying: "Eat, my Lord, and all thy congregation, according to your desire."

While the holy men ate, the meats and drinks remained undiminished, and the host thought to himself: "How wondrous is this! I should have had plenty for all my relatives and friends. Would that I had invited them all."

When this thought was in the host's mind, all his relatives and friends entered the house; and although the hall in the house was small there was room in it for all of them. They sat down at the table and ate, and there was more than enough for all of them.

The Blessed One was pleased to see so many guests full of good cheer and he quickened them and gladdened them with words of truth, proclaiming the bliss of righteousness

"The greatest happiness which a mortal man can imagine is the bond of marriage that ties together two loving hearts. But there is a greater happiness still: it is the embrace of truth. Death will separate husband and wife, but death will never affect him who has espoused the truth.

"Therefore be married unto the truth and live with the truth in holy wedlock. The husband who loves his wife and desires for a union that shall be everlasting must be faithful to her so as to be like truth itself, and she will rely upon him and revere him and minister unto him. And the wife who loves her husband and desires a union that shall be everlasting must be faithful to him so as to be like truth itself; and he will place his trust in her, he will provide for her. Verily, I say unto you, their children will become like unto their parents and will bear witness to their happiness.

"Let no man be single, let every one be wedded in holy love to the truth. And when Mara, the destroyer, comes to separate the visible forms of your being, you will continue to live in the truth, and you will partake of the life everlasting, for the truth is immortal."

There was no one among the guests but was strengthened in his spiritual life, and recognized the sweetness of a life of righteousness; and they took refuge in the Buddha, the Dharma, and the Sangha.

I chose this parable because it is remarkably similar in concept to the Christian mystical idea of the marriage of the soul to God. The Buddha speaks of being "wedded in holy love to the truth." St. John of the Cross says "I found Him Whom my heart and soul love; I held Him and I will not let Him go."[36] St. John speaks of God in the personal sense of the Judeo-Christian tradition, and the Buddha speaks of the impersonal truth. But, know this, one of the highest names of God is "Truth."

The Buddha's parable of the "marriage feast" finds its parallel in Jesus' parable of the marriage feast found in the Gospel according to Matthew. In this parable, a king gave a marriage feast for his son, and he sent out his servants to call upon those who were to be invited to the feast: but they would not come. So the king had his servants go out into the streets, and invite anyone they could find. So the servants went all over gathering guests, and brought them to the marriage feast. The "marriage feast" is the marriage between the soul and God, or the soul and Truth, and not everyone who is invited will come to this feast. But to those who do come, in the words of Gotama, the Buddha, "you will partake of the life everlasting."

A Party in Search of a Thief

Having sent out his disciples, the Blessed One himself wandered from place to place until he reached Uruvela.

On his way he sat down in a grove to rest, and it happened that in that same grove there was a party of thirty friends who were enjoying themselves with their wives; and while they were sporting, some of their goods were stolen.

Then the whole party went in search of the thief and, meeting the Blessed One sitting under a tree, saluted him and said: "Pray, Lord, didst thou see the thief pass by with our goods?"

And the Blessed One said: "Which is better for you, that you go in search for the thief or for yourselves?" And the youths cried: "In search for ourselves!"

"Well, then," said the Blessed One, "sit down and I will preach the truth to you."

And the whole party sat down and they listened eagerly to the words of the Blessed One. Having grasped the truth, they praised the doctrine and took refuge in the Buddha.

In this case, I think the "thief" symbolizes that which robs us of our true Selves, be that parental or cultural conditioning, and the Blessed One, the Buddha, is advising us to search rather for our lost Selves than for the "thieves" who robbed us in the first place. Psychoanalytic therapies undoubtedly contribute to the uncovering and identification of the "thieves," i.e., the etiology of our neuroses in the foggy distant past of our childhoods, but it is questionable whether they contribute all that much, if at all, to the rediscovery of our true Selves. In this higher task, we need turn to higher teachers, and strangely, they are found millennia ago in such masters as Gotama, the Buddha. Gotama's way is what I have called in previous chapters a "fourth way" psychology. This is the level of the true Self, and it takes a certain faith to operate at this level as both the Buddha and Jesus have said. When you find your true Self, the "thieves" will no longer bother you. Jesus indicated this when he said: "Do not lay up for yourselves treasures on earth, where moth and rust consume and where thieves break in and steal, but lay up for yourselves treasures in heaven, where neither moth nor rust consumes and where thieves do not break in and steal."[37] The Buddha's parable makes precisely the same point.

The Buddha continued to preach his Dharma until he was eighty years old. During the rainy season at Beluva, near Vesali, the Blessed One fell gravely ill, but he remained mindful and self-possessed to the end. He chose Ananda, his disciple of many years, to be his successor. His last teachings to Ananda were these: "Therefore, O Ananda, be ye lamps unto yourselves. Rely on yourselves, and do not rely on external help."

This is in keeping with the Buddhist teaching that the source of salvation is within oneself. If this seems "contradictory" to Christianity, it is a superficial Christianity that we have in mind. Jesus of Nazareth said: ". . . behold, the kingdom of God is within you."[38] In the recently discovered Nag Hamadi manuscripts, there is a document which is called *The Gospel According to Thomas*. Translated literally from the original Coptic, Jesus has these words to say to Didymos Judas Thomas:

Jesus said: if those who lead you say to you: "See, the Kingdom is in Heaven," then the birds of the heaven will precede you. If they say to you: "It is in the sea," then the fish will precede you. If you will know yourselves, then you will be known and you will know that you are the sons of the Living Father.[39]

The difference between the Buddha and Jesus is perhaps that Jesus related to the *sacred reality* in the most personal way as the "Living Father," whereas the Buddha referred to it as "the Truth." The Buddha said, "Hold fast to the truth as a lamp. Seek salvation alone in the truth." This "difference," however, might tend to evaporate when we remember that Jesus referred to himself as "the truth," as in his statement: "I am the way, and the truth, and the life."[40] Nevertheless, one cannot deny that despite their many similarities, Buddhism and Christianity lie on opposite ends of the spectrum from impersonal to personal in their conceptions of the Ultimate Truth. Yet, before we choose one, and exclude the other, let us consider the possibility that this entire spectrum, as in the rainbow with its many colors, is *the reality*, and that the different religions which we consider in this book (and other religions) represent different places along this spectrum, different "colors," if you will.

The last words of the Buddha before he died were these: "Seek ye for that which is permanent, and work out your salvation with diligence."

Jesus said something very similar in his discourse on the "end of days": "In your patience possess ye your souls."[41] Both of these great physicians of the soul seem to be referring to the need for patience and endurance in the spiritual quest. The goal of the quest for both is that which is *most precious* within ourselves. It cannot be spoken of, but it can be experienced. The highest step of the Buddha's Way is "right meditation." It is the *way through* the "cloud of Maya," or ignorance, to the "truth of Nirvana," or enlightenment. I do not think it is incorrect to say that the neurotic self is "Maya" and the true Self is "Nirvana." The neurotic self produces the most intense suffering, and it seems very real indeed. The goal of the historic Buddha was to find the "cure" of this pervasive human suffering.

The Korean Zen master, Seung Sahn, whom I have spoken of, showed me something about the mind-created nature of suffering a couple of years ago. I asked, "How can I overcome my suffering?" Seung Sahn replied "Give me your suffering." Not sure what to do, I placed my hands in his. Looking at me with a Buddha smile, Seung Sahn asked, "Where is your suffering now?" I smiled.

When we look at the "demons" and "evil spirits" within ourselves as the Buddha did when he sat for forty days under the Bodhi tree, i.e., "as one would watch the harmless games of children," they are no more. This is the meditation way of the Buddha and his answer to the perennial problem of human suffering.

NOTES

Primary Source:
Paul Carus, *The Gospel of the Buddha*, Open Court Publishing Company, Chicago & London, 1915, Chapters II:18, VI:7,10,14,16, VII:1,5,7, VIII:13, IX:3,11,23, XI:10, XII:2, 8, 17, XLVI, LXV, LXIX, LXXIV, LXXVI, LXXVII, LXXXI, LXXXII, XCIII:13, XCIV:20., C:2.

Secondary Sources:
1. H. Saddhatissa, *The Buddha's Way*, George Braziller, New York, 1971, p. 19.
2. "Sakya" means "lion clan." The Buddha is referred to as "Sakyamuni," the "Sage of the lion clan." It is interesting to note that Jesus was a member of the tribe of "Judah" whose symbol is the lion.
3. *The Mentor Book of Major American Poets*, eds. Oscar Williams & Edwin Honig, Mentor Book from New American Library, New York & Scarborough, Ontario, 1962, "The Road Not Taken," p. 250.
4. *The Bible*, Revised Standard Version, New Testament, American Bible Society, New York, Matthew 6:24.
5. Ibid., Matthew, 10:39.
6. Ibid., Matthew, 5:44.
7. Ibid., John, 8:32.
8. Ibid., Revelation, 2;3.
9. Ibid., Revelation, 2:7.
10. Saddhatissa, p. 48.
11. Kosho Uchiyama, Roshi, *Approaches to Zen*, Japan Publications, San Francisco & Tokyo, 1973, p. 27.
12. D. T. Suzuki, *Zen Buddhism*, ed. William Barrett, Doubleday, Garden City, N.Y., 1956, p. 87.
13. Ibid., p. 88.
14. Ibid., p. 186.
15. Ibid., p. 206.
16. Ibid., p. 216.
17. Chogyam Trungpa, *Meditation in Action*, Shambhala, Berkeley, Calif., 1970, p. 55.
18. Ibid., p. 56
19. Joshu Sasaki, Roshi, *Buddha Is the Center of Gravity*, Lama Foundation, San Cristobal, N.M., 1974, p. 17.
20. *The Selected Poetry of William Blake*, ed. David V. Erdman, New American Library, New York, 1976, "Auguries of Innocence," p. 272.
21. *Dropping Ashes on the Buddha—The Teachings of Zen Master Seung Sahn*, compiled and edited by Stephen Mitchell, Grove Press, New York, 1976, p. 12.
22. Ibid., pp. 51–52.
23. *The Bible*, Revised Standard Version, Luke 15:24.
24. Ibid., Matthew 5:14.
25. Ibid., Matthew 5:16.
26. Ibid., Matthew 13:23.

27. Ibid., Matthew 17:20.
28. Ibid., Matthew 25:40.
29. Ibid., Mark 10:16.
30. Ibid., Mark 10:18.
31. Ibid., Mark 13:37.
32. Ibid., Luke 9:62.
33. Ibid., John 4:9.
34. Ibid., John 4:14.
35. Ibid., Matthew, 5:9.
36. St. John of the Cross, *Dark Night of the Soul*, Doubleday, Garden City, N.Y., 1959, p. 173.
37. *The Bible*, Revised Standard Version, Matthew 6:19.
38. *The Holy Bible*, King James Version, New Testament, World Publishing Company, Cleveland and New York, orig. pub. 1611, Luke 17:21.
39. *The Gospel According to Thomas*, trans. A. Guillaumont et al., Harper & Row, New York, 1959, p. 3.
40. *The Bible*, Revised Standard Version, Luke 14:6.
41. *The Holy Bible*, King James Version, Luke 21:19.

Chapter Five

Krishna, the Avatar

*H*INDUISM is a religion whose roots are ancient in India, the land of the Indus Valley. In the pre-Vedic times, going back as far as 4000 B.C., there were tribes, the Negritos, food-gatherers who followed a primitive animistic religion, and the Austric peoples, an agricultural culture whose creation myth held that the world was born from an egg.[1] Following these peoples were the more advanced Dravidians, immigrants from Mediterranean sources, who developed a rather advanced culture with fortresses, roads, wells, and agriculture. Their deities were "zoomorphic," including such gods as Ganesha, the "elephant-headed god."[2] The Vedic age began with the invasions of the Aryans, a family of Indo-European peoples. They crossed into India via the northwestern mountain passes around 1500 B.C.[3] The scriptures of the Aryans were formed in interaction with preexisting cultures, and came to be known as the *Vedas*. "Veda" comes from the Sanskrit root word "vid," which means "to know."[4] The four Vedas were completed in approximately the year 1000 B.C., and they consist of hymns which are essentially polytheistic in nature.[5] They worshipped many gods: Agni, the god of fire; Surya, the sun god; Ushas, goddess of the dawn; Yama, the god of death; etc. The *Brahmanas* which consisted of priestly and theological manuals were composed at the end of the Vedic period.[6] It was the Brahmanic religion into which Siddhattha Gotama was born, and to which he responded in ways which gave birth to Buddhism. Within Hinduism itself, there was a reaction to the polytheistic Vedas and Brahmanas in terms of the *Upanishads*. These consisted of discourses of a highly philosophical and mystical nature which were written between 600 and 200 B.C.[7]

The *Upanishads* teach of the all-encompassing, self-existent, and eternal Brahman, and his relation to the individual soul, or Atman, which is one of identity. The most famous teaching of the Upanishads is "Tat Twam Asi," which means, "Thou art That."

The next development of the Hindu religion took place somewhere between the years 200 B.C. and 200 A.D., and this was the writing of the great incarnational epics, the *Ramayana* and the *Mahabharata*.[8] In these, the idea is presented that a series of "avatars," or "saviors," come upon the earth at times of extreme crisis in order to assist humanity. The *Ramayana* is the story of the god-king, Rama, and his exploits. The *Mahabharata* is an epic poem of immense length consisting of eighteen volumes. It contains the legend of the avatar, Krishna, who is considered by Hindus to be the eighth incarnation of Vishnu,[9] the second person of the Hindu Trinity consisting of Brahma, the Creator, Vishnu, the Sustainer, and Shiva, the Destroyer. Krishna is, if you will, the Christ of the Hindu religion, and the story of his birth even bears some resemblances to the story of the birth of Christ. In both cases there was a wicked king, Herod in the case of Christ and Kamsa in the case of Krishna, who attempted to destroy the prophesied savior by the murder of innocents, and in both cases the infant savior was saved from premature destruction through the dreams of their earthly fathers.[10] There are other resemblances as well, among which is not historicity. There is considerable historical evidence of the existence of Jesus of Nazareth independent of the scriptural records, but this is not the case for Krishna, and Hindus care rather little for history in any case. Krishna may have been part fact and part legend; nobody really knows for sure. His name, which means "black one," and the date of his death which is given as 3102 B.C.[11] (in terms of our calendar), would place him in pre-Aryan Dravidic times which is beyond the range of recorded history. Whether he existed or not is not so much the point as the place he plays in the minds of the people as the carrier of the archetypal idea of an "avatar," or divine descent into the world. All that we know about him is found in the *Mahabharata*, the epic poem of the poet Vyasa, about whom very little is known, except that he lived and wrote somewhere between 200 B.C. and 200 A.D.[12] It is the sixth book of the *Mahabharata*, known as the *Bhagavad Gita*, or "The Song of God," which will concern us in this chapter. It consists entirely of a dialogue between the warrior, Arjuna, and his charioteer, Krishna, who just happens to be an avatar of Vishnu! In reading it, it flashed on me that, on the psychological plane, Arjuna was a universal "ego figure," and Krishna could be

viewed as the embodiment of the "Self." It begins with Arjuna in a
state of total despondency in the midst of a great battle to which his
fate as a warrior had led him. Suddenly the whole battle, and even life
itself, seemed pointless to him. This is what he has to say:

> Krishna, Krishna,
> Now as I look on
> These kinsmen
> Arrayed for battle,
> My limbs are weakened
> My mouth is parching,
> My body trembles,
> My hair stands upright,
> My skin seems burning,
> The bow Gandiva
> Slips from my hand,
> My brain is whirling
> Round and round,
> I can stand no longer:
>
> Krishna, I see such
> Omens of evil!
> What can we hope from
> This killing of kinsmen?
> What do I want with
> Victory, empire,
> Of their enjoyment?
> O Govinda,
> How can I care for
> Power or pleasure,
> My own life, even,
> When all these others,
> Teachers, fathers,
> Grandfathers, uncles,
> Sons and brothers,
> Husbands of sisters,
> Grandsons and cousins,
> For whose sake only
> I could enjoy them
> Stand here ready
> To risk blood and wealth
> In war against us?
>
> Knower of all things,
> Though they should slay me
> How could I harm them?
> I cannot wish it;
> Never, never,
> Not though it won me

The throne of the three worlds;
How much the less for
Earthly lordship!

Krishna, hearing
The prayers of all men,
Tell me how can
We hope to be happy
Slaying the sons
Of Dhritarashtra?
Evil they may be,
Worst of the wicked,
Yet if we kill them
Our sin is greater.
How could we dare spill
The blood that unites us?
Where is joy in
The killing of kinsmen?

Arjuna goes on in his discourse for some verses and he ends up by saying that he shall not struggle, and he shall not fight, and he will let the enemy, the evil children of Dhritarashtra, slay him, rather than go on fighting in this civil war. Having spoken thusly, Arjuna threw aside his arrows and his bow in the midst of the battlefield. He sat down on the seat of the chariot, his heart overcome by sorrow. He was filled with grief and self-pity.

This chapter of the Gita, "The Sorrow of Arjuna," ends in dejection and sorrow. It is a dark night of the soul. If we look at "the battle" from a symbolic standpoint, it is clearly an allegory of anyone's struggles in life, and the tendency, especially at mid-life, to sink into despondency and despair about the meaning and purpose of one's whole life and work. Sure, life looks pretty good to the brand new M.D. at age twenty-six or so, but what about ten or twenty years later, after thousands of patients, untold prescriptions, and routine housecalls, or the 1,000th appendectomy or whatever is the specialty of the physician? The career of a lawyer may sound promising at first, but there may come a time, after who knows how many cases, trials, and appeals, that the whole thing doesn't seem to make much sense anymore. It is supposedly a "distinction" to earn a Ph.D. in an academic field and to teach university students, but after twenty years of teaching the same old "Western Civilization" course to an uninterested bunch of people in their late teens, one could imagine Professor "So and So" throwing his notecards all over the floor, and sitting down on the floor and crying: "What does all this mean?" My cousin, Bruce, is a radio engineer, and I remember one day he took me to meet an older friend of his, a man in his forties or fifties, who said: "My life is half gone, and what has all this amounted to?" He was a television technician at a major network. I will make a confession: after finishing the fourth chapter of this book, the chapter on Buddha, and before beginning this one, I fell into a similar state of hopelessness and despondency about my life and work. I said to myself: "I am thirty-eight years old, and what has my life come to?" But then the "Krishna" in me began to stir, and he said: "Bob, get up off your butt, and get on with your work!" This is what Krishna had to say to Arjuna in his state of despondency:

Arjuna, is this hour of battle the time for scruples and fancies? Are they worthy of you who seek enlightenment? Any brave man who merely hopes for fame or heaven would despise them.

What is this weakness? It is beneath you. Is it for nothing men call you the foe-consumer? Shake off this cowardice, Arjuna. Stand up.

Arjuna goes on in his protest against taking action. He disguises his despondency as compassion:

Which will be worse, to win this war, or to lose it? I scarcely know. Even the sons of Dhritarashtra stand in the enemy ranks. If we kill them, none of us will wish to live.

Seeing through his alleged "compassion," Arjuna admits:

Is this real compassion that I feel, or only a delusion? My mind gropes about in darkness. I cannot see where my duty lies. Krishna, I beg you, tell me frankly and clearly what I ought to do. I am your disciple. I put myself into your hands. Show me the way.

Arjuna has placed himself in the traditional "disciple—Guru" relationship to Krishna, his charioteer. On another level, one could say that he has reached the limits of his ego's understanding, and he has turned within to the higher teacher, the Self. He has done a wise thing, and Krishna proceeds to teach Arjuna the way of Yoga, or "Union," in the remaining chapters of the *Bhagavad Gita*. When you ask the Self, or God-within, a question about what you should do in a given instance in life, such as in Arjuna's case, whether or not he should fight, you may find that you receive much more than you bargained for! God, in the form of Krishna, uses this opening in the mind of Arjuna to pass to him one of the highest spiritual teachings that humanity has ever known, the *Bhagavad Gita*'s Yoga. Krishna speaks first of the "Yoga of Knowledge," or "Jnana Yoga":

Your words are wise, Arjuna, but your sorrow is for nothing. The truly wise mourn neither for the living nor for the dead.

There was never a time when I did not exist, nor you, nor any of these kings. Nor is there any future in which we shall cease to be.

Just as the dweller in this body passes through childhood, youth and old age, so at death he merely passes into another kind of body. The wise are not deceived by that.

Krishna is speaking to Arjuna about the doctrine of the "Atman." The Atman is the true Self of man. Krishna is saying that not only for himself as the avatar of Vishnu, but for every human being who ever was or will ever be, there is no time "in which we shall cease to be." This is very much the same as the saying of Jesus, "Before Abraham even was, I am." In traditional Christianity, this is taken as referring to Jesus only, but Christian as well as Hindu mystics know that both Christ and Krishna are speaking of the true Self in every man. The ancient sages of India knew that the search for the supreme truth, or for the mystery of existence, must assume the form of the search for one's own true Self. The true Self is the "dweller within," the Atman.

This intuition can be reached through philosophical reasoning, as in the dialogues of Plato, but it is never settled through this method. We have philosophers to this day who believe in the soul and those who deny it. In fact, materialism has been very prevalent in the West for the last century, despite all arguments to the contrary. It has even been given the honorific aegis of "science," as in "scientific material-ism." This issue of the reality and immortality of the soul can be truly settled for each individual only through direct mystical experience. But mystical experience is not "democratic," and it does not come to all. To the contrary, in its true form, it is very rare. I have been through a very long inward journey during the past ten years, and I know very well both the personal and the collective unconscious, but the true mystical experience is beyond these, and I experienced it only once for about a half hour's duration. I would call the true mystical experience: Cosmic Consciousness, and I discussed my own experience in the chapter on Jesus (3). I will reiterate only one point, and that is that both Margaret and I (it was a shared experience) immediately and directly perceived that *there is no death*. That is to say, the Self we truly are, is, was, and always will be. I cannot "explain" this direct perception. It just was. It is why the mystics of most, if not all, of the great religions assert, in fullest confidence, the reality and immortality of the Self. If this Self is not much known in the modern disciplines of psychology and psychiatry, so much the worse for these disciplines. Among psychological schools, only the Jungians and the disciples of Assagioli affirm the reality of the higher Self. On the other hand, whether they view the Self in the same way the mystics see it, i.e., as the eternal spark of the Divine, I am not sure. Krishna (as Christ did as well) is asserting much more than "the Self is the archetype of wholeness." It *is* that, and much more than that. The Self can say: "There was never a time when I did not exist. . . ."

To those who would reject the Self as "unscientific" because it cannot be seen by the external senses, or be measured by scientific instruments, or even be "logically" defined, Krishna concedes: "This Atman cannot be manifested to the senses, or thought about by the mind." The Atman, or Self, cannot be known in the way that we know, for example, about the moons of Jupiter. Nor can it be known in the way that we know about electrons or protons. It is not an "object" at all either of sensory perception or intellectual conceptualization. About the Atman, Krishna says:

There are some who have actually looked upon the Atman, and understood It, in all Its wonder. Others can only speak of It as wonderful beyond their understanding. Others know of Its wonder by hearsay. And there are others who are told about It and do not understand a word.

Jesus spoke very similarly to his disciples when he told them that it was given to them to know of the Kingdom of Heaven because their eyes were open and their minds were awake. But it was not given to everybody to know of these Mysteries. Jesus said ". . . this people's heart has grown dull, and their ears are heavy of hearing, and their eyes have closed. . . ."[13] Jesus spoke these words 2,000 years ago, and Krishna is alleged to have spoken his words over 5,000 years ago, but the people have not woken up even to this day. I think that they have fallen into even much deeper sleep! Quite in contradistinction to the Western view of linear "progress," the Hindus view the history of humanity as a decline from a "Golden Age" known as the "Krita Yuga."[14] It has declined all the way from that age of spiritual enlightenment to the present "Kali Yuga," which is translated the "Iron Age," and is thought to be an era of moral evil and spiritual decay.[15] If you have any doubts about this, visit the Dachau concentration camp near Munich, Germany, and see what "modern" Western people did to their fellow human beings! Hindus believe that humanity fell into the Kali Yuga with the death of Krishna. They also believe that the Golden Age will be revived with the coming of the tenth avatar of Vishnu, who is called "Kalki."[16] This corresponds to the Christian concept of the second coming of the Christ, or Messiah, which will usher in a Messianic Age on earth. Orthodox Jews, Buddhists, Moslems, and practically every religion I have studied believe very much the same thing, i.e., the coming of a Blessed One who will restore humanity to Grace.

Krishna goes back to discussing Arjuna's duty as a warrior. He tells him that he should not hesitate to fight in a righteous war. If he refused to fight, he would be turning aside from his duty. Krishna says that he would be a sinner, if he did so, and he would be disgraced. He tells Arjuna: "Stand up now, son of Kunti, and resolve to fight."

Some have taken the *Bhagavad Gita* to be a book that favors war and killing and is antipacifistic. I think that this is a very superficial interpretation. The "war" that Krishna is talking about is life. In that war, everyone is a warrior. Whether you are a physician fighting disease, or an attorney fighting for your client in court, or a police officer fighting crime, or a salesperson fighting for another sale, or a scientist struggling to solve the riddles of nature, or a politician battling for the bill that he thinks is just, or an artist in the battle with paint, brush, and canvas, or a writer whose pen is his sword, Krishna would admonish you to: "Stand up . . . and resolve to fight."

Krishna, who has explained to Arjuna the nature of the Atman, tells him that he will tell him now of the method of "Karma Yoga." "Karma" is a Sanskrit word which means "deed" or "act." "Yoga" means "union," and in terms of the spiritual path it means "union with God." Hinduism is a religion which has a variety of Yogas, or Paths to God-Realization. The method of "Karma Yoga" is, as far as I know, the unique contribution of the *Bhagavad Gita* to the history of religion and spirituality. The Buddha emphasized, above all, a Yoga of meditation, but Krishna, in the *Bhagavad Gita*, teaches a "Karma Yoga," which is a "Yoga of Action." It is a Yoga that applies equally well to anyone who is pursuing his or her own path of life and work, whatever that may be, from sea captain to chimney sweep. It is the unique teaching of the Lord Krishna to the warrior Arjuna (although he teaches him all of the principal Yogas as well).

Krishna tells Arjuna that the method of Karma Yoga, if he can understand and follow it, will enable him to break the chains of desire which bind him to his actions. Furthermore, Krishna explains that with this Yoga, even abortive attempts are not wasted. He says that even a little practice of this Yoga will save Arjuna (and all of us "Arjunas") "from the terrible wheel of rebirth and death." Krishna states the method of Karma Yoga to Arjuna in the following manner:

You have the right to work, but for the work's sake only. You have no right to the fruits of work. Desire for the fruits of work must never be your motive in working.

This is a teaching in sharp contradistinction to both behavioristic psychology, e.g., Skinnerian, which teaches the control of behavior through reward, or "positive reinforcement," and the capitalist economic philosophy of our culture which assumes "profit" to be the chief motivation for productive work. The teaching of Krishna has nothing to do with "what can I get?" but everything to do with the doing of something for its own sake only. How quickly the factories and marketplaces of our society would empty if the "rewards" were removed! This would seem to indicate that the work in itself was of little value to the workers. In many cases, it is quite the opposite, an ordeal to be endured for the sake of the paycheck and food on the table. We have become a society of Skinnerian "rats" scurrying around pressing levers for our "positive reinforcement." Or perhaps we merely work to avoid punishment! What Krishna is saying is that the work that you do should flow from yourself, and it should be done *for the sake of itself*. For example, I enjoy gardening: I plant the seeds, and I water the plants, and so on. The growing, however, is not really my business; it is nature's business! Likewise, an artist can paint "in order to please" certain imagined customers, or art gallery owners, or critics. This will produce a rather "forced" result, as if the paintings were painted from the "outside in." You can also paint for the sake of painting itself, and put down on the canvas whatever arises within you. This is how great art happens. You need not worry about the gallery owners or customers or critics; they operate according to their own rules. If you are good, there will be an audience for your work. Krishna would tell you: "Don't worry about it; it will spoil your work." Likewise, for the writer, you can write what you "think" will sell, or what your publisher will want, or what will impress your reviewers, or you can write what you feel in your heart, and let God or the Tao take care of the rest. Do you see what I am saying? Krishna goes on to say:

Work done with anxiety about results is far inferior to work done without
such anxiety, in the calm of self-surrender. Seek refuge in the knowledge of
Brahman. They who work selfishly for results are miserable.

What Krishna says about "work done with anxiety about results"
applies to any skilled performance whatsoever from singing to skiing.
The singer who worries about what the audience "thinks of her" is
already projecting her center outside of herself, and is thereby losing
her capacity to "sing from the heart," as it were. In skiing, as in any
sport, one cannot really master it until one has, in effect, forgotten
about "doing it right," i.e., "checking" your performance against some
inner image of "correctness." When you forget about that, and just *do
it*, it works. In learning Judo, I found that if I worried about whether
or not I would be able to throw an opponent, it just did not work.
When I forgot about results completely, in one Judo tournament, and
entered into a state of "at-oneness" with my art, I beat seven oppo-
nents in a row. It is difficult to describe this state in words, but I am
sure that everyone has had it at one time or another in some activity
from dancing to jogging. This same principle of abandoning concern
for results applies very much to the creative arts. Whether you are a
dancer, or a sculptor, or a painter, or a writer, or whatever you are,
you will reach the perfection of your art only when you give up your
anxiety about results, and when you work "in the calm of self-surrender." Self-surrender is a way of saying "at-one with God."

When you "work selfishly for results," you will be "miserable" according to the Lord Krishna. This makes me think of those in our
society who enter the profession of medicine, for example, mainly
because of its high material rewards, and not because they are personally dedicated to the sacred calling of the healing arts. Such physicians
are replacing the "Hippocratic Oath" with the "Hypocritic Oath."
There is a Karmic Law of Justice in this Universe and those who
pervert the principles of their profession will find that they will sow
what they have reaped. The suicide rate in the medical profession is
quite high. Is it possible that what Krishna says is correct, that when
you work selfishly for results, you will reap a harvest of misery? Those
who feel "the call," in whatever their profession, be it medicine or the
ministry, and who work unselfishly for what they feel is *their duty*, will
receive in the nature of things the highest reward. Krishna, and the
Hindu saints, would call this "union with Brahman":

In the calm of self-surrender you can free yourself from the bondage of
virtue and vice during this very life. Devote yourself, therefore, to reaching

union with Brahman. To unite the heart with Brahman and then to act: that is the secret of non-attached work. In the calm of self-surrender, the seers renounce the fruits of their actions, and so reach enlightenment.

What is meant by "union with Brahman"? Hindu philosophy is nondualistic, and Brahman, or the Godhead, is not regarded as something "out there," or "wholly other" than oneself. Brahman is found, rather, in one's heart of hearts. It is we who have fled from Him; He is not apart from our true Selves. How we became separated from Him is more mysterious than the fact that *He is there*. Krishna would suggest to us that one way of becoming reunited with Brahman is to act without concern for the fruits of action. This is what he calls Karma Yoga. The Buddhists speak about "nonattachment," or "giving up desires." It is another way to talk about the same thing; the former is a way of self-less action, the latter a way of meditation.

Arjuna, by now fascinated with the discourse of his charioteer, Krishna, asks him:

Krishna, how can one identify a man who is firmly established and absorbed in Brahman? In what manner does an illumined soul speak? How does he sit? How does he walk?

Arjuna's questions seem a little "childish." He sounds like a little boy who asks his mother, "Mommy, where do we come from?" However, this childlikeness and innocence in spiritual matters are quite appropriate, for those who live in the ego-world truly know less about the Spirit than children know about their biological origins. Krishna answers his disciple, Arjuna, thusly:

> He knows bliss in the Atman
> And wants nothing else.
> Cravings torment the heart:
> He renounces cravings.
> I call him illumined.
> Not shaken by adversity,
> Not hankering after happiness:
> Free from fear, free from anger,
> Free from the things of desire.
> I call him a seer, and illumined.
> The bonds of his flesh are broken.
> He is lucky, and does not rejoice:
> He is unlucky, and does not weep.
> I call him illumined.

The teachings of Krishna sound very much like those of the Buddha on many points. Krishna seems almost to be expounding the Buddha's third noble truth when he says this about the illumined soul: "Cravings torment the heart: he renounces cravings." The Hindu poet Vyasa, who wrote the *Mahabharata* in which the Gita is contained, lived several hundred years after the time of the Buddha, and he may have been influenced by Buddhist ideas. On the other hand, the Buddha himself said: "All the Buddhas teach the same truth."[17] Nonattachment is a teaching common to both Buddhism and Hinduism. On the other hand, the terms "Nirvana" and "Brahman" are not used in identical ways. The term "Nirvana," in the Buddhist sense, means literally "extinction"; Buddhism is a "negative way." "Brahman" means something very much like our word "God." Hinduism is a "positive way." Whether these are the two sides of the same Truth has been argued in the affirmative and the negative. It is not my point to settle all religious disputes; there are indeed real differences between religions and there is also a *common core*. I tend to be more interested in the commonality than the differences, but this is a personal preference. Needless to say, in the Hindu context, enlightenment or illumination means "union with Brahman." This is the teaching of Lord Krishna.

After hearing what Krishna has to say about illumined souls who are united with Brahman, Arjuna is a little puzzled. "Union with Brahman" and "action" seem to him to be contradictories. He cannot understand why Krishna is urging him to go into battle, on the one hand, while he is saying that "Knowledge of Brahman" is the highest good, on the other hand. I suppose that Arjuna thinks that one can attain God-realization only by going off into some isolated cave and meditating for several years. Meditation and renunciation of the world is, indeed, the way of many seekers. Do we suspect that Arjuna is trying to escape from his duty when he asks Krishna: "But, Krishna, if you consider knowledge of Brahman superior to any sort of action, why are you telling me to do these terrible deeds?"

Krishna replies that enlightenment may be found by two different paths: the way of contemplation and the way of selfless action. This distinction would seem to be verified by the finding of the modern psychologist Carl Jung that people tend to fall into one of two different categories: the introvert and the extravert. Introverts (myself included) tend to live in, and pay more attention to, the inner world, the realm of ideas, and images, and feelings, and dreams, and so on. The outer world has meaning for them mainly in connection to their inner subjectivity. Extraverts (whom I know less directly), on the other hand, tend to pay little attention to their own subjectivity, but are fascinated by outer things, people, and the social world in general. It is quite likely that certain occupations and callings are more suited to the extravert, and others more to the introvert. I cannot see an automobile salesperson introvert, although it is possible, and being a writer, and knowing how lonely a calling it is, it is difficult for me to imagine an extraverted type being attracted to the literary profession, although I admit that there are some who are. The Hindu religion is almost uniquely diverse in the number of paths that it offers to the spiritual aspirant. For the Buddhist seeker, one is told: meditate, meditate, meditate! But the Hindu teacher will first consider the personality of the seeker. Is the seeker a person of action, or is the person more inclined toward contemplation? The teacher would also look at more subtle distinctions which relate closely to Jung's conception of the four functions: thinking, feeling, sensation, and intuition. There are Yogas which correspond to each of these, and we will speak more about them later.

Krishna goes beyond the mere distinction between contemplation and action when he states that freedom from activity is really impossible to achieve. He says that, "In fact, nobody can ever rest from his activity even for a moment." By activity, Krishna includes mental action, both conscious and subconscious, as well as physical acts. The meditator may appear to be "still" on the outside, but inside of his or her head there may be fantastic activity going on. Besides, who can just sit in meditation all of the time? Even the contemplative has to work to provide for his or her physical needs. Circumstances may even force the person to become a warrior! So action and contemplation are not really contradictory: there is action in contemplation and there is contemplation in action. The Shaolin Buddhist priests of old China were both monks and warriors. They knew, as Krishna did, that nonaction is impossible. Like the scientists of many millennia later, Krishna understood that everything is in motion, from the stars of the macrocosm to the atoms of the microcosm, and everything in between. The dichotomy between action and contemplation is not a real one. The real issue is *how* do you act? Is your action enslaved by attachment to the fruits of action, or is it action that is free from attachment to results? Even meditation itself is a form of action, and it is governed by the same principles. Many, in our culture, take up meditation in order to "gain something." This something is thought of as "in the future." It may be "relaxation," or "inner peace," or "psychic powers," or "enlightenment." Both Hindus and Buddhists would tell you that you are circumventing the very purpose of meditation in your concern with "results." The point of meditation is just that: meditation. Zazen is itself "satori" according to the Zen masters. Krishna would add that any form of action from meditation to cooking dinner is a possible way to enlightenment. In the Christian tradition, there was, in fact, a very enlightened monk named Brother Lawrence who was the cook for his monastery. He wrote a little book entitled *The Practice of the Presence of God*. Such "mundane tasks" as cooking and washing dishes was for him a "way of enlightenment." He was surely a Christian Karma Yogi if there ever was one! Krishna goes on to speak about action "performed as worship of God." He says:

The world is imprisoned in its own activity, except when actions are performed as worship of God. Therefore you must perform every action sacramentally, and be free from all attachment to results.

How is "action without concern for the fruits of action" equivalent to "action performed as worship of God"? What do we mean by God? If we think of him as "up there" somewhere, or "beyond the universe," we are thinking dualistically. But this was not the mode of thought of the Hindu sages any more than it was that of the Hebrew sages. For both Hindu and Hebrew, God has to do with the holy verb: *to be*. God has been called: *He who is*. He is perhaps *is* itself. If we think of God in this nondualistic way, then it makes perfect sense that action performed for its own sake is action that is "worship of God." If you have ever seen the Japanese tea ceremony performed by a master, you know what I mean. Prayer is not to a God "out there"; rather, the very act of praying is to make contact with the God who is everywhere! It is quite a beautiful thing when Krishna says that "You must perform every action sacramentally."

Krishna reiterates this point to Arjuna, who we can imagine is listening in rapt attention to his charioteer, when he says:

Do your duty, always; but without attachment. That is how a man reaches the ultimate Truth; by working without anxiety about results. In fact, Janaka [a royal saint mentioned in the Upanishads] and many others reached enlightenment, simply because they did their duty in this spirit.

How marvelous it is to think that one can attain to highest enlightenment not by any special meditations or spiritual practices, and not by withdrawing from the world and becoming a monk or sannyasin, but by merely performing one's work in life. Nothing need change except your inner mental attitude.

> The ignorant work
> For the fruit of their action:
> The wise must work also
> Without desire
> Pointing man's feet
> To the path of his duty.

One can carry out this Karma Yoga in any circumstance or station of life. One can be a Karma Yogi and be a police officer, fire fighter, baker, construction worker, engineer, scientist, dancer, farmer, doctor, housewife, or whatever is one's calling. Krishna says that "work is holy when the heart of the worker is fixed on the Highest." In this spirit, Krishna advises his pupil, Arjuna, to:

Shake off this fever of ignorance. Stop hoping for worldly rewards. Fix your mind on the Atman. Be free from sense of ego. Dedicate your actions to me. Then go forward and fight.

Arjuna's Karma-duty is that of a warrior, and that is what he needs to do. Each of us has his own Karma-duty, and it is up to us to perform it, for no one else can. Krishna says something very beautiful when he says:

It is better to do your own duty, however imperfectly, than to assume the duties of another person, however successfully. Prefer to die doing your own duty: the duty of another will bring you into great spiritual danger.

Some of us find out what it is we are meant to do very early in life. Pablo Picasso was already a master painter at the age of thirteen. Mozart composed great symphonies at the age of nine. These are the precocious. They are lucky. Many of us have to go through many false starts, and even come to the mid-point of our lives, before we find out what is undeniably our true path in life. Some come to the brink of suicide before they discover *who they are*, and what it is they are *meant to do*. The biographies of many great people contain this dangerous crossing between nonbeing and being. Sometimes one must overcome every obstacle, be it family, relatives, teachers, cultural expectations, and what have you, before one can come to the place that Martin Luther did, for example, when he said: "Here I stand, and I can do no other." It is something so important that you should bring it out in big letters and put it up on your wall: "It is better to do your own duty, however imperfectly, than to assume the duties of another person, however successfully."

This saying of Krishna's reminds me of another saying of that American sage Henry David Thoreau: "If a man does not keep pace with his companions, perhaps it is because he hears a different drummer. Let him step to the music which he hears, however measured or far away."[18] Thoreau lived for two years in the woods by Walden Pond to the puzzlement and sometimes scorn of his fellow Concordians. He lived really without much concern for the fruits of his actions. He sold very few copies of his book, *Walden*, in his lifetime. But Henry David Thoreau lived out his own Karma-destiny. I hope that I will do so, and I hope that you will too, for what Krishna means by "great spiritual danger" in doing another's duty, and not your own, is the loss of one's true Self. All the money in the world will not substitute for that.

Several of the modern sages and yogis of India have spoken about the path of the Karma-Yogi. Vinoba Bhave had this to say:

So the saints have pictured a Karma-Yogi God who rubs horses down, takes cows out to graze, drives a chariot, cleans dishes and mops floors. And they themselves have done the work of a tailor, or a potter, or a weaver, or a gardener, or a trader, or a barber, or a cobbler. *Doing these things, they have found themselves and become free.*[19]

The Hindu Swami Vivekananda, the disciple of Sri Ramakrishna, said this about Karma-Yoga:

Karma-Yoga is attaining through unselfish work of that freedom which is the goal of all human nature.[20]

The great pacifist and preacher Mahatma Gandhi said:

This is the unmistakable teaching of the Gita. He who gives up action falls. He who gives up only the reward rises. But renunciation of fruit in no way means indifference to the result. In regard to every action one must know the result that is expected to follow, the means thereto, and the capacity for it. He who, being thus equipped, is without desire for the result, and is yet wholly engrossed in due fulfillment of the task before him, is said to have renounced the fruits of action.[21]

Gandhi makes it clear that Karma-Yoga does not mean ignorance of the results of one's actions, but it does mean the renunciation of the desire for the fruits of one's actions. This means, for example, you may know that you are a good enough artist to win national recognition for your work, and that is well and good, but if you paint for the recognition rather than for the painting itself, you are subverting the process of Karma Yoga and your own possibility of happiness as well. Karma Yoga is a way to Self-realization. True Self and happiness are synonymous according to the Hindu saints. Ramana Maharshi, whom Carl Jung called the "embodiment of spiritual india," had this to say about the question: "What is happiness?"

Happiness is the very nature of the Self; happiness and the Self are not different. There is not happiness in any object of the world. We imagine through our ignorance that we derive happiness from objects.[22]

The Holy Kabbala, of which I have spoken, calls the Self, "Tifereth," which literally translated is "beauty." The true beauty within you is your Self. The realization of one's Self, according to all of humanity's spiritual traditions, is the greatest happiness that human beings can realize. Maharshi said, "We imagine through our ignorance that we can derive happiness from objects." Some of the most wealthy people are also the most miserable. True happiness lies within.

The *Bhagavad-Gita* teaches essentially four Yogas, or ways of Self-realization. These are: Karma Yoga, Jnana Yoga, Raja Yoga, and Bhakti Yoga. Relating these to modern psychology, these correspond respectively to the "four functions" of which Jung spoke: sensation, thinking, intuition, and feeling. If we say that Karma Yoga entails sensation, we mean by "sensation" the sensori-motor process. All action involves sensation, be it kinesthetic, tactile, visual, or auditory, etc. When you throw a baseball, for example, you experience tactile sensations from holding the ball, kinesthetic sensations from the action of your own muscles, visual sensations from seeing the ball in your hand and in flight, and even auditory sensations if the batter hits the ball, and so on. Sensation also entails action, even "seeing," which involves continuous and rapid eye-movements such as tracking, triangulation, focusing, etc. So the "sensation function" should really be called the "sensori-motor function," and, in this light, Karma Yoga, or the Yoga of Action, is the "sensation Yoga." Playing baseball, if done for itself, and not for its "fruits," could be a Karma Yoga.

We have also spoken briefly of Jnana Yoga, or the Yoga of Knowledge, and this would correspond most obviously to the Jungian "thinking function." It is the way of the philosopher, or the "thinking person," and it is a traditional Yoga with a venerable tradition in India. The *Upanishads* themselves can, I believe, be considered a "Jnana Yoga" par excellence. They were the product of the discussions and insights of forest sages and rishis who were every bit as wise as the Greek philosophers, such as, Socrates. The following discourse between a father and his son is contained in the *Chhandogya-Upanishad*:

"Put this salt into water, see me tomorrow morning," said Uddalaka. Shwetaketu did as he was told.

Uddalaka said: "Bring me the salt you put into water last night."

Shwetaketu looked, but could not find it. The salt had dissolved.

Uddalaka asked his son how the top of the water tasted. Shwetaketu said: "It is salt."

Uddalaka asked how the middle of the water tasted. Shwetaketu said: "It is salt."

Uddalaka asked how the bottom of the water tasted. Shwetaketu said: "It is salt."

Uddalaka said: "Throw away the water; come to me."

Shwetaketu did as he was told and said: "The salt will always remain in the water."

Uddalaka said: "My son! Though you do not find that Being in the world, He is there.

"That Being is the seed; all else but His expression. He is truth. He is Self. Shwetaketu! You are That."[23]

Krishna, in the Gita, teaches Arjuna essentially the same Jnana Yoga of the identity of the Atman and Brahman. It is another way, in the Hindu tradition, of Self-realization. Whereas Karma Yoga is the way for the person of action (and sensation), Jnana Yoga is a way for the intellectually and philosophically inclined. This is what Drishna says about Jnana Yoga to his pupil, Arjuna:

The form of worship which consists in contemplating Brahman is superior to ritualistic worship with material offerings.

The reward of all action is to be found in enlightenment.

Those illumined souls who have realized the Truth will instruct you in the knowledge of Brahman, if you will prostrate yourself before them, question them and serve them as a disciple.

When you have reached enlightenment, ignorance will delude you no longer.
In the light of that knowledge you will see the entire creation within your own
Atman and in me.

And though you were the foulest of sinners,
This knowledge alone would carry you
Like a raft, over all your sin.

The blazing fire turns wood to ashes:
The fire of knowledge turns all karmas to ashes.

Jnana Yoga, or the Yoga of Knowledge, has its counterpart in other
spiritual traditions as well. Jewish mysticism, or Kabbala, has its in-
tensely Jnana Yoga aspect in terms of the study of the Sephirotic
scheme of the Tree of Life, and the letter-number code which breaks
down the stories of the Bible into a metaphysical discourse of deepest
profundity. The Sufis have their Jnana methods in terms of the Sufi
teaching tales which are discussed in Sufi circles. Zen Buddhism has
its Jnana Yoga in the Koan tradition of Rinzai Zen which involves the
attempt to "solve" the unsolvable puzzle, such as the "Original Face"
Koan which we have discussed. The following Koan is called "Meeting
a Man of Tao on the Way":

Goso said, "If you meet a man of Tao on the way, greet him neither with
words nor with silence. Now tell me, how will you great him?"[24]

In the Zen Koan, as in other examples of Jnana Yoga, the mind is
pushed to the absolute limit until it is forced to *let go* of all pretensions
to understanding. At this point, the Spirit may break through. This is
quite unlike philosophy which actually believes in its own reasoning
products! The Jnana Yoga techniques are a way to break through the
"bubble" of the intellectual ego. "Satori" is not finding the "correct
theory" at all, but the sometimes startling revelation that all your
theories, and all the theories that have ever been created, are like
matchstick houses which are blown apart when the wind of the Spirit
begins to blow. Jnana Yoga is really a way for intellectuals to get
beyond the intellect. It pushes theory to the extreme unitl you *go
beyond.* It has been said, "Gray is all theory, green grows the Tree of
Life." Returning to the dialogue between Uddalaka and Shwetaketu in
the Chhandogya-Upanishad, we find that Shwetaketu did not really
grasp his father's teaching. "Explain once more, Lord!" said Shwetaketu. His father replied, "I will explain." This is what Uddalaka has to
say:

"My son! If a man were taken out of the province of Gandhara, abandoned in a forest blindfolded, he would turn here and there, he would shout: 'I have been brought here blindfolded and abandoned!'

"Thereupon some good man might take off the bandage and say: 'Go in that direction; Gandhara is there.' The bandage off, he would, if a sensible man, ask his way from village to village and come at last to Gandhara. In the same way the man initiated by his master finds his way back into himself. Having remained in his body till all his Karma is spent, he is joined to Himself.

"That Being is the seed; all else but His expression. He is truth. He is Self. Shwetaketu! You are That."[25]

Shwetaketu still doesn't understand, and he asks his father to "Explain once more, Lord!" His father, Uddalaka, attempts another story in his attempt to break through to his son about the nature of the Self.

"Relations gather round a sick man and say: 'Do you remember me? Do you remember me?' He remembers until his speech has merged in his mind, his mind in his life, his life in his light, his light in the one Being.

"When his speech is merged in his mind, his mind in his life, his life in his light, his light in the one Being, what can he remember?

"That Being is the seed; all else but His expression. He is truth. He is Self. Shwetaketu! You are That."[26]

His son, Shwetaketu, remains as unenlightened as before, so Uddalaka tries once again to communicate the nature of Self in the following story.

"My son! They bring a man in handcuffs to the magistrate, charging him with theft. The magistrate orders the hatchet to be heated. If the man has committed the theft and denies it, he is false to himself, and having nothing but that lie to protect him, grasps the hatchet; and is burned.

"If he has not committed the theft, he is true to himself and, with truth for his protector, grasps the hatchet; and is not burned. He is acquitted.

"The man that was not burnt, lived in truth. Remember that all visible things live in truth; remember that truth and Self are one. Shwetaketu! You are That."[27]

This story apparently got through to Shwetaketu: "Shwetaketu understood what he said, yes, he understood what his father said." Jnana Yogis have attained Self-realization via the way of the mind; Ramana Maharshi was a Self-realized one whose principal method was what he called "self-inquiry." He taught his students to reflect upon the ques-

tion "Who am I?" Am I this social role? Am I this body? Am I this set
of life experiences? Am I this inquiring mind? Am I "I"? Even that
concept will not do. The Self can never be contained in a concept. The
Chhandogya-Upanishad sees the Self as both a wall and a bridge:

Self is the wall which keeps the creatures from breaking in. Day and night do
not go near Him, nor age, nor death, nor grief, nor good, nor evil. Sin turns
away from Him; for Spirit knows no sin.

Self is the bridge. When man crosses that bridge, if blind, he shall see; if sick,
he shall be well; if unhappy, he shall be happy. When he crosses that bridge,
though it be night, it shall be day; for heaven is shining always.[28]

Krishna goes on to teach Arjuna a third Yoga, or bridge to Self, the
Yoga of meditation. It would correspond, I would say, to the "intuition function" in the Jungian system. Meditation is the way of *direct
seeing*. It is the way of the mystic. This is what Krishna says to Arjuna
about the way of the Raja Yogi:

The yogi should retire into a solitary place, and live alone. He must exercise
control over his mind and body. He must free himself from the hopes of
possessions of this world. He should meditate on the Atman unceasingly.

Unlike the Karma Yogi, the Raja Yogi follows a rather monastic
lifestyle. Zen monks in the Buddhist tradition typically withdraw from
the world, and follow an austere and secluded life for a period of
years. Zen monks are essentially "Raja Yogis." They meditate for
many hours every day. Hindu Raja Yogis do the same thing. Krishna
gives his student Arjuna the following meditation instructions:

The place where he sits should be firm, neither too high nor too low, and
situated in a clean spot. He should first cover it with sacred grass, then with a
deer skin; then lay a cloth over these. As he sits there, he is to hold the senses
and imagination in check, and keep the mind concentrated upon its object. If
he practices meditation in this manner his heart will become pure.

These meditation instructions (except for the necessity of sacred
grass and a deer skin) would be essentially those given to any student
of meditation today. It generally involves sitting in an upright position, on a meditation cushion or a straight chair, with the back straight
and the head upright. In Yoga, one generally meditates with eyes
closed, hence withdrawing from the world of the senses, whereas in
Zen the eyes are opened to a slight degree, although the sensory
stimulation is still kept to an absolute minimum (the Zennist usually

sits facing a blank white wall). The imagination, or the associative mind, is generally kept in check through the practice of concentrating the mind upon some "object." The object is usually an inward one, such as meditating upon a mantram, a koan, or one's breath. The most advanced meditators forgo any object at all, and engage in what is called "formless meditation." This is known as "Mahamudra," or "Great Form," in the Buddhist tradition. Krishna says that the Raja Yogi's "heart will become pure." Jesus said that the "pure in heart will see God." In verification of this, Krishna says that the Yogi who attains perfect control over his mind will "unite himself with Brahman."

This is a very slow process, however. I remember attending a lecture given by a Japanese Soto Zen monk, and a student who had been meditating Zen-style for three years asked the monk: "Why have I achieved so little even though I have been meditating for three years?" The monk said, "Three years? Come back and see me when you have meditated for ten years!" Krishna emphasizes the importance of patience when he tells Arjuna:

Patiently, little by little, a man must free himself from all mental distractions, with the aid of the intelligent will. He must fix his mind upon the Atman, and never think of anything else. No matter where the restless and the unquiet mind wanders, it must be drawn back and made to submit to the Atman only.

I remember the first time I practiced a simple form of meditation with the Arica group. For several hours afterwards, sights and sounds and other sensori-stimuli were so much sharper and clearer than they had every been before. The first time I practiced Zen Buddhist meditation, or Zazen, for forty minutes, I experienced a state of such profound peace for the rest of the day. One also experiences in insight (or "direct seeing") meditation a gradual journey through one's own unconscious, the pleasant and the unpleasant alike. One views whatever arises with nonattachment. Ten years later, I am still meditating, twice a day, morning and evening, in a "Christian-Zen" form of meditation, and continuing to progress along that infinitely slow Path. I'm not entirely sure that "progress" is the right word, though. When one meditates, one is always a beginner. There is a book by Shunryu Suzuki, Roshi, called *Zen Mind, Beginner's Mind*. It is in the *sacred now* that one can make the breakthrough to the Timeless. That can be very sudden. The "slowness" of the meditation path may be due to the fact that it takes many years of "training" to learn to attune oneself to the Timeless.

Scientists have looked into the neurophysiology of meditation during the last several years, and have found some interesting results in terms of the measurement of the EEG, or electroencephalogram, which measures "brain waves," or the periodic evoked potential of the cerebral cortex. In studying meditators, it would appear that the movement from beta to alpha to theta states on the EEG may correspond to a shift to progressively higher states of consciousness. Beta waves are defined as an EEG state of thirteen cycles per second, or higher, and this corresponds to the mental state that is outward and materially oriented toward external stimuli, or the state of associative thought and ideation. Most meditators can achieve an "alpha state," which is defined as the range from eight to thirteen cycles per second. The brain waves become less "jerky" and more "regular" in the alpha range. Meditators report a state of calm and tranquility at this point. Any sudden stimulus, such as a bright light or loud sound, will disrupt the alpha state and put the meditator back in the more active beta state. Theta waves, defined as the range from four to eight cycles per second on the EEG, seem to be associated with a state of inner exploration which moves through a world of images rather than words. It is the state associated with dreaming, or a waking consciousness in connection with the deep unconscious. It is seen in advanced Zen monks. I am not sure if it has been studied, but I would guess that it would be found in artists and writers and other highly creative persons while they were deeply engrossed in their creative work. As a writer, I can report that there is a stage of deep creativity when one is in connection with "the Muse." I am told that there is a "painter's Muse" as well, and I would assume that this is true for all of the creative disciplines from sculpture to musical composition. It is an area that merits investigation, and is a tie-in, as it were, between Karma and Raja Yoga. One's creative work can be as "meditative" as any traditional form of meditation.

There is an even deeper state than theta on the EEG, the delta stage, the range between zero and four cycles per second of cerebral evoked potential. If the progression from beta to alpha to theta produces steadily "higher states of consciousness," then we would expect the delta range to be the "highest of all." But it is the brain wave pattern found in the deepest stage of dreamless sleep. Sleepers who are awakened from this state of dreamless sleep associated with delta waves generally report nothing at all. It would appear to be a state of complete "unconsciousness." Yet, we all wake up profoundly "refreshed" and "renewed" when we have had a dreamless and deep sleep. It can be a very "healing sleep" indeed. Can it be that we make contact with the spiritual realm of consciousness during deep sleep, and that we forget about this completely upon awakening, as we often forget our dreams as well? Is this state so utterly different from waking consciousness that it is impossible to retain any memory of it in most cases? The Hindu tradition holds just this view, and, as contrary as it is to our Western thinking, it is worth considering what the *Mandukya Upanishad* has to say on the subject of dreamless sleep:

The third aspect of the Self is the Universal Person in dreamless sleep— *prajna* . . . He experiences neither strife nor anxiety, he is said to be blissfull. . . . *Prajna* is the Lord of All. . . . He knows all. . . . The sphere of *prajna* is deep sleep. . . .[29]

"Prajna" is, in my understanding from my Yoga practice, the Hindu term for the Universal Spiritual Energy which is called "Ch'i" in Chinese, "Ki" in Japanese, and "Ruach" in Hebrew, and so on. If one can attain to this state of consciousness in one's waking life, one has attained the highest enlightenment, or *turiya*. I imagine that it is identical to what Zen Buddhists call *satori*. Swami Rama, one of the authors of *Yoga and Psychotherapy*, a Hindu monk who was trained in the Himalayan monasteries, demonstrates his capacity to enter into not only the theta, but also the delta state at will, and moreover maintain his awareness of the external environment in this state of consciousness in studies at the Menninger Foundation.[30] Work such as that done at the Menninger Foundation begins to "bridge the gap," as it were, between science and spirituality. It is the beginning of the "convergence" that Pierre Teilhard de Chardin has spoken of in his writings. He himself was a Jesuit priest and a mystic, as well as a distinguished paleontologist who made basic discoveries in paleontology. He sees all things converging to what he called the "Omega point." The Omega point is the Christ. Krishna is the same concept in the Hindu religion. Concerning the true mystical experience, Krishna speaks these words to Arjuna about the Knowledge of God:

> Since you accept me
> And do not question,
> Now I shall tell you
> That innermost secret:
> Knowledge of God
> Which is nearer than knowing,
> Open vision
> Direct and instant.

Understand this
And be free for ever
From birth and dying
With all their evil.

Jesus told his disciples that "He who believes in me, though he were dead, yet shall he live." Krishna also confirms that the enlightenment of knowing God will free one from the cycle of birth and death. This is the great "Moksha," or liberation." It is what Jesus meant when he said: "Marvel not when I say unto you, you must be born again."

Krishna explains to Arjuna something of the nature of God in his Immanent Form. It is this direct knowledge that all mystics seek. It is the goal of all spiritual practice.

I am the sire of the world, and this world's mother and grandsire:

I am He who awards to each the fruit of his action:

I make all things clean, I am OM, I am absolute knowledge:

I am also the Vedas—the Sama, the Rik and the Yajus.

I am the end of the path, the witness, the Lord, the sustainer:

I am the place of abode, the beginning, the friend and the refuge:

I am the breaking-apart, and the storehouse of life's dissolution:

I lie under the seen, of all creatures the seed that is changeless.

I am the heat of the sun; and the heat of the fire am I also:

Life eternal and death. I let loose the rain, or withhold it.

Arjuna, I am the cosmos revealed, and its germ that lies hidden.

Krishna makes known to Arjuna that he is omnipresent in endless manifestations. Most important of all, Krishna reveals that he is the Atman:

I am the Atman that dwells in the heart of every mortal creature. I am the beginning, the life-span, and the end of all.

The Freudians' unifying entity is the "ego," which arises from the "id" originally, and is the mediator between the unconscious and the external world. The ego is the conscious self. The Jungians have for their centralizing concept the archetype of the Self, the prototype of Wholeness within each individual. In the Hindu concept, the Self is the Atman "that dwells in the heart of every mortal creature." It is the indwelling spark of the Divine Fire. Among Christians, the Quakers most clearly resemble the Hindus in their concept of the "inner light." In mysticism, the coming to the inward light is called the stage of "illumination." Saul of Tarsus, later to be known as St. Paul, experienced this inward light in a form so strong that it blinded him for three days. This *light* remained with him, and he regarded it as the indwelling Christ. Hindus would regard this interior light as the Atman. The Atman indwells all things, but there is an ascending order of manifestation of the Atman in this world from inorganic matter, to vegetable life, to instinctual animal life, to conscious human life. Among human beings, the light of the Atman is seen in its most advanced form in saints and sages. Medieval artists utilized the device of the "halo" which they painted around the heads of the saints. This was a way of pictorializing the inward light. In high saints, this "light" can actually be sensed as a kind of "aura." "Kirlian" photography has actually revealed a kind of "bioplasmic energy" which surrounds living things, and can be seen in different degrees in different people. Advanced Yogis, Zen monks, and other spiritual adepts seem to manifest this life-energy to a high degree. It may be enlightening to look at the experiences of the inward light in the lives of several well-known figures in Western spiritual history.

Blaise Pascal was a seventeenth-century philosopher, mathematician, and scientist. In the year 1654, at the age of thirty-one, something happened to him which altered his life. He describes the experience as follows on a piece of paper that he kept wrapped in parchment and sewn into the lining of his coat:

The year of grace 1654, Monday 23 November, day of St. Clement, Pope and Martyr. From about half-past ten in the evening until about half-past twelve, midnight, FIRE. God of Abraham, God of Isaac, God of Jacob, not of the philosophers nor of the wise. Assurance, joy, assurance, feeling, joy, peace. GOD OF JESUS CHRIST, my God and thy God. Thy God shall be my God. Forgotten of the world and of all except GOD. He is only found in the way taught in the Gospel. THE SUBLIMITY OF THE HUMAN SOUL. Just Father, the world has not known thee but I have known thee. Joy, joy, joy, tears of joy. . . .[31]

Jacob Boehme, a humble shoemaker by trade, was born in the year 1575 in a small village in Germany. At the age of twenty-five, he had an experience of the inward light while sitting in his room and gazing at a pewter dish. This is how his biographer describes it:

Sitting one day in his room his eyes fell upon a burnished pewter dish, which reflected the sunshine with such marvelous splendor that he fell into an inward ecstasy, and it seemed to him as if he could now look into the principles and the deepest foundations of things. He believed that it was only a fancy, and in order to banish it from his mind, he went out upon the green. But there he remarked that he gazed into the very heart of things, the very herbs and grass, and that actual nature harmonized with what he had inwardly seen. He said nothing of this to anyone, but praised and thanked God in silence. He continued the honest practice of his craft, was attentive to domestic affairs, and was on terms of goodwill with all men.[32]

The shoemaker-sage Boehme became one of the greatest figures of Protestant mysticism through his books, such as *The Way to Christ, Mysterium Magnum,* and *The Signature of All Things* etc. He had no university education whatsoever; his knowledge came from within. He continued his humble craft of shoemaking until he died.

The American poet and mystic Walt Whitman expressed his illumined vision in his poetry. These four lines from *Leaves of Grass* indicate an enlightenment experience similar to that of Pascal and Boehme:

> As in a swoon, one instant
> Another sun, ineffable-full dazzles me,
> And all the orbs I knew, and brighter, unknown orbs;
> One instant of the future land, Heaven's land.[33]

Blaise Pascal, Jacob Boehme, Walt Whitman, and many other mystics in human history have experienced illumination. This is the experience of the Shekhinah, or God in-dwelling in the soul, in nature, and in all things. One could call this the "pantheistic experience."

The light of God within the soul, or the "illuminative experience," is not the end of the Journey. For those "brave souls" who go on, there is another Dark Night of the Soul which follows the coming to the inner light. This is the Dark Night of the Spirit (as opposed to the earlier Dark Night of the Senses) as St. John of the Cross describes it. Almost all religious traditions, including the Hindu, the Jewish, and the Christian, etc., consider God to be greater than his Creation, in fact, infinitely so. The Creation is but One Ray of God's Infinite Light. The greatest mystics move on from the "illuminative experience" to the "unitive vision" of God as he is in himself. It is not really so much a conscious choice as a natural development of the spiritual path. When the "illuminative stage" passes over into the second Dark Night, and the blessed light is lost, it is a stage of unbelievable spiritual suffering.

The only "remedy" to this suffering is the coming to the "unitive life." Arjuna, after having realized what the Immanence of God is all about, requests Krishna to reveal himself in his Transcendent Form. Krishna does so, and Arjuna witnesses in awe and trembling, the "One without a second." Arjuna, bowing low before his God, speaks these words:

> Ah, my God, I see all gods within your body;
> Each in his degree, the multitude of creatures;
> See Lord Brahma throned unto the lotus;
> See all the sages, and the holy serpents.
>
> Universal Form, I see you without limit,
> Infinite of arms, eyes, mouths and bellies—
> See, and find no end, midst, or beginning.
>
> Crowned with diadems, you wield the mace and discus,
> Shining every way—the eyes shrink from your splendor
> Brilliant like the sun; like fire, blazing, boundless.

The *Bhagavad-Gita* uses a certain "anthropomorphic imagery" for the experience of the Unity which is essentially indescribable. What he experienced was the "One" to whom Jews refer when they utter the "watchword" of their faith, the *Shema:* "Hear, O Israel, the Lord our God, the Lord is One." This *One* is the goal of the mystic's quest. However, when one has found it, it is just too awesome and overwhelming, and one needs to return to ordinary consciousness again. After having "viewed" face to face the One in whom time and space are merely thoughts, Arjuna bows down and prostrates himself, asking pardon and forgiveness of his sins, and he literally pleads with Krishna to return once again to his more accustomed human form. Krishna complies with Arjuna's request, and becomes Arjuna's charioteer, as he was before. Arjuna is released from the terrible awe of "seeing God."

The great mystics report this experience of "cosmic consciousness," which is generally of short duration, but nonetheless utterly transforms their lives. Jacob Boehme, ten years after his "illuminative experience," describes his experience of "cosmic consciousness" as follows:

Suddenly . . . my spirit did break through . . . even into the innermost birth of Geniture of the Deity, and there I was embraced with love, as a bridegroom embraces his dearly beloved bride. But the greatness of the triumphing that was in the spirit I cannot express either in speaking or writing; neither can it be compared to anything, but with that wherein the life is generated in the midst of death, and it is like the resurrection from the dead. In this light my spirit suddenly saw through all, and in and by all the creatures, even in herbs and grass, it knew God, who he is, and how he is, and what his will is; and suddenly in that light my will was set on, by a mighty impulse to describe the being of God.[34]

Jacob Boehme describes this experience as being about a "quarter hour's duration." The soul, at least in this embodied form, cannot stand too much more of this experience of the Divine Unity. It is few, indeed, who are able to withstand this experience at all, and fewer still who return to tell about it. Just as Arjuna returned to his ordinary state of consciousness, so did Jacob Boehme. They returned to the world of people, and places, and everyday things.

Krishna goes on to teach Arjuna the "Yoga of Devotion," or "Bhakti Yoga." It is the war of ordinary religion, which consists generally of "worship of God," or "devotion." Krishna explains to Arjuna that it is "very difficult" for embodied souls to realize the unmanifest form of God which he has just experienced, but the Yoga of Devotion is a way which every person can follow. It is an "easy way."

> Quickly I come
> To those who offer me
> Every action,
> Worship me only,
> Their dearest delight,
> With devotion undaunted.
>
> Because they love me
> These are my bondsmen
> And I shall save them
> From mortal sorrow
> And all the waves
> Of Life's deathly ocean.
>
> Be absorbed in me,
> Lodge your mind in me:
> Thus you shall dwell in me
> Do not doubt it.
> Here and hereafter

A Bhakti Yogi will worship God in the form of Krishna. An ordinary Christian will worship God in the form of Christ. An ordinary Jew will worship God by practicing what it says in the Torah about loving God "with all your heart, and with all your soul, and with all your might." The ordinary Moslem also practices a devotional form of religion which involves prayer and worship, or devotion to Allah. What Krishna is saying is that ordinary devotional religion of prayer and worship is just as good a way to come to God as any other that he has discussed. It is even suggested that it is the best way! This would go along with what the Hebrew prophet Jeremiah had to say about the way to discover God: "You will seek me and find me; when you seek me with all your heart. . . ."[35]

Bhakti Yoga, the Yoga of Devotion, corresponds to what Carl Jung called the "feeling function." It is the opposite, as it were, of the "thinking function." Jnana Yogis, who engage in dialectical reasoning about the "nature of reality," and Bhakti Yogis, who merely worship Krishna with love and devotion, are the "opposite types" of the spiritual path. The "thinking type" and the "feeling type" are the bipolar opposites in human psychology. The "logician" is one example of the "thinking type," to whom "reason" is king. The "poet" is much more likely to be a "feeling type," and "the heart" is his or her center. The two other functional types are the "intuitive type" and the "sensation type," which correspond respectively to the Raja Yogi and the Karma Yogi, as we have already discussed. These are also bipolar opposites which cut in perpendicular fashion across the thinking-feeling bipolarity. These, then, are the four functional types, and the corresponding Yogas:

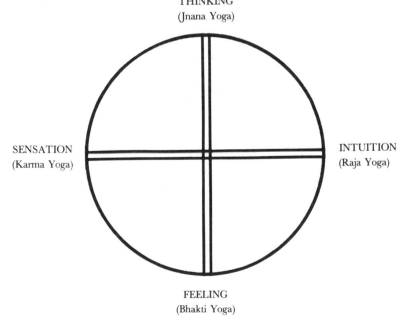

THINKING
(Jnana Yoga)

SENSATION
(Karma Yoga)

INTUITION
(Raja Yoga)

FEELING
(Bhakti Yoga)

According to Jung, we are either born with, or develop early in our lives, a primary function and an auxiliary function. In Jungian typology indicators, I come out very strongly an intuitive type, and secondarily a thinking type. Hence, I am an "intuitive-thinking type." During my academic years which were my twenties, I apparently "specialized" heavily in my auxiliary function of thinking in my pursuit of such intellectual interests as "cognitive psychology," "psycholinguistics," and "symbolic logic." Into the Journey for four years, the day after I met an important teacher on my Path, Robert Johnson, I had the following dream: there was a threesided cross, and from the "depths" arose a fourth side. Written on the fourth side was the word: FEELING. What this dream was telling me was this: "Bob, you have been a 'Jnana Yogi,' or a 'specialist' in the 'thinking function,' for many years now. That's fine and good. But if you wish to become whole, you will need to develop your currently neglected 'feeling function.' You will have to become a 'Bhakti Yogi.' "

It was only in the years since that dream that the "worlds of feeling" began to open up for me through poetry, music, and an appreciation of the "Bhakti," or devotional side of religion. I began attending worship services and I learned how to pray. The Christian Holy Communion service became my "Bhakti Yoga." Jewish worship and prayer is a very fine "Bhakti Yoga" as well, particularly in the ecstatic forms practiced by the Hasids. These are ways of "opening the heart," or "awakening the feeling function."

Really speaking, in the course of my Journey, I made the "circle," as it were, and engaged in "Yogas" of each of the four types. I went where the Inner Guidance led me. My long-term Kabbalistic studies engaged my "thinking function" in extraordinary ways; it was my "Jnana Yoga." I have spoken about how Christian Holy Communion involved me on the "heart level"; it was my "Bhakti Yoga." My "intuitive function," which is actually my primary function, was called into play in the highest degree via my practice of Buddhist "insight meditation." I presently practice what I call "Christian Zen." These were my forms of "Raja Yoga." The opposite of intuition is sensation, and it was long my "inferior function," so it has become my "latest specialty." I find that it is very well served by such everyday activities as cooking, washing the dishes, doing the laundry, plastering and painting the apartment, staining and varnishing furniture, and various other "odd jobs." Recently, I dreamed about doing clay animal sculptures. This relates to the "sensory function." I may take it up. Call these my: Karma Yoga. Whatever one does, from writing a book to climbing a mountain, if done for its own sake, can become a Yoga.

Krishna summarizes these "four ways" of realizing the Atman for Arjuna:

Some, whose hearts are purified, realize the Atman within themselves through contemplation. Some realize the Atman philosophically, by meditating upon its independence of Prakriti. Others realize it by following the yoga of right action. Others, who do not know these paths, worship God as their teachers have taught them. If these faithfully practice what they have learned, they also will pass beyond death's power.

Whatever spiritual practice suits you is your "way" up the "mountain" between earth and heaven. By "earth" and "heaven" I mean "material consciousness" and "spiritual consciousness." At the bottom of the mountain are different religious traditions, which are akin to different "villages." Each one seems quite separate and exclusive, and they even see each other as "rivals." There have, indeed, been religious wars throughout history: Christian against Moslem, Moslem against Hindu, and even Protestant against Catholic within Christianity. This is a narrow view. It is the external view of religion. Climbing up the mountain, one still goes along separate paths in the "uphill climb," but one notices other climbers along the way as you "narrow down" upon the summit. When you reach the top of the "mountain," something strange occurs. You all realize that you have reached the same summit! Whether you have called it the Buddha nature, or the Christ, or the Atman, or YHWH, or Allah, it is the same from the mountain top. It is here that you will "pass beyond death's power." Isn't this the whole point? Religions deal with names and forms: Christ, Buddha, Mohammed, Moses, and so on, and the teachings and practices that relate to each. But the Spirit "deals" with that which is beyond name and form. Such a man who has discovered the Spirit is one:

> Who sees his Lord
> Within every creature,
> Deathlessly dwelling
> Amidst the mortal:
> That man sees truly.

When you see God in all of his creatures, it is because you see Him within yourself. Such a man is Christ-realized in the Christian tradition, a Buddha in the Buddhist tradition, a Tzaddek in the Jewish tradition, and a Self-realized one in the Hindu tradition. The Self is the Atman. Krishna describes the Self-realized person in this way:

Thus ever aware
Of the Omnipresent
Always about him
He offers no outrage
To His own Atman,
Hides the face of God
beneath the ego no longer:
Therefore he reaches
That bliss which is highest.

Krishna says that it is the ego which "hides the face of God." It seems to be so that the ego, or "little I," in most persons is so highly "opaque" that the light of God is totally blocked out. This accounts for the materialism of our age. Man's state of Exile is made into a "philosophy" which denies the existence of the One from whom man is exiled. Even in this age, however, it is possible to break through the opaqueness of ego to the light of the Supreme. When you do, you will find both Self and God, Atman and Brahman. Krishna, the God-incarnate one, asks Arjuna whether he has "dispelled the delusions" of his ignorance. Arjuna replies in the affirmative that his delusions have been dispelled and his doubts have ended. He has found God.

NOTES

Primary Source:
   The Song of God—Bhagavad-Gita, trans. Swami Prabhavananda and Christopher Isherwood, New American Library, New York and Scarborough, Ontario, 1972, pages: 31–33, 35, 36, 38, 40, 41, 41–42, 44, 45, 46–47, 48, 54–55, 65, 66, 79, 82, 88, 92, 98, 104

Secondary Sources:
   1. Herbert Stroup, *Like a Great River—An Introduction to Hinduism*, Harper & Row, New York, 1972, p. 15.
   2. Ibid., p. 17.
   3. Ibid., p. 19.
   4. Ibid., p. 19.
   5. Ibid., p. 22.
   6. Ibid., p. 23.
   7. Ibid., p. 24.
   8. E. G. Parinder, *What World Religions Teach*, George G. Harrap & Co., London, 1968, p. 22.
   9. Stroup, p. 94.
   10. Geoffrey A. Barborka, *The Pearl of the Orient—The Message of the Bhagavad-Gita for the Western World*, Theosophical Publishing Hiuse, Wheaton, Ill., 1968, p. 138.
   11. Ibid., p. 152
   12. Parinder, p. 22.
   13. *The Bible*, Revised Standard Version, New Testament, American Bible Society, New York, 1971, Matthew 13:15.
   14. Barborka, p. 121.

15. Ibid., p. 122.
16. Parinder, p. 26
17. Paul Carus, *The Gospel of the Buddha*, Open Court Publishing Company, Chicago and London, 1915, C:2, p. 258.
18. Henry David Thoreau, *Walden*, College & University Press, New Haven, Conn., 1965, p. 347.
19. *The Spirit of Modern India, Writings in Philosophy, Religion, and Culture*, eds. Robert A. McDermott & V. S. Naravane, Thomas Y. Crowell Company, New York, 1974, p. 125.
20. Ibid., p. 126.
21. Ibid., p. 127.
22. Ibid., p. 210.
23. *The Ten Principal Upanishads*, trans. Shree Purohit Swami & W. B. Yeats, Macmillan Publishing Co., Inc., New York, 1965, p. 94.
24. Zenkei Shibayama, *Zen Comments on the Mumokan*, trans. Sumiko Kudo, New American Library, New York & Scarborough, Ontario, 1974, p. 259.
25. *The Ten Principal Upanishads*, p. 95.
26. Ibid.
27. Ibid., p. 96.
28. Ibid., p. 109.
29. Swami Rama, Rudolph Ballentine, MD., and Alan Weinstock, Ph.D., *Yoga and Psychotherapy—The Evolution of Consciousness*, The Himalayan International Institute of Yoga, Science, and Philosophy, Honesdale, Pennsylvania, 1976, p. 166.
30. Ibid., pp. 168–169.
31. Richard Bucke, M.D., *Cosmic Consciousness*, E. P. Dutton & Co., Inc., New York, 1969 p. 274.
32. Ibid., pp. 180–181.
33. Ibid., p. 228.
34. Ibid., p. 185.
35. *The Bible*, Revised Standard Version, Old Testament, American Bible Society, New York, 1952, Jeremiah 29:13.

Chapter Six

Muhammed, the Prophet

THE term "Islam" means "submission to God." The religion of Islam is the religion of surrender to the will of the omnipotent and omniscient Creator, the Only God. In the eyes of Muslims, or followers of Islam, Muhammed, like Abraham, Moses, and Jesus, is a *prophet of God*. Muhammed is not regarded as divine, but rather as a mortal man (like ourselves) who was called by God to fulfill a prophetic mission, namely, that of delivering his message to the idolatrous Arabs of the time. Unlike his illustrious predecessors, Muhammed lived and died in the full light of history, being born in A.D. 571 and dying in A.D. 632.

The Arabian peninsula, where Muhammed was born, is a land of sandy desert and barren steppes with little surface water except for a few scattered oases sustained by underground pools. The people of this region were, and are, Caucasians and Semites, who according to Islamic tradition were descendants of Shem, the oldest son of Noah. Furthermore, they believe themselves to be the descendants of Ishmael, the son of Abraham, and his handmaiden, Hagar. They called themselves "Arabs," meaning "nomads."[1] They were and are the "half-brothers," if you will, of the other descendants of Abraham, and his wife, Sarah, the "Israelites."

In this barren and hot desert land of Arabia, there was little agriculture, so trade was very important. The Bedouin tribes served as the "middlemen" in this crossroads between the East and the West. The key artery of trade in those days was the town of Mecca in West Central Arabia. The most powerful kin groups in Mecca were known as the "Quaraysh." Muhammed was born a member of an important family of the Quaraysh, the son of Abdullah and Aminah. However,

181

his father died before he was born, and his mother died when he was only six years old. He was turned over to the care of his grandfather, and after he died, to his paternal uncle, Abu-Talib.[2]

Muhammed grew up a caravan trader with his uncle, and he got to travel to places as distant as Syria, and to meet different kinds of people, such as Jews and Christians. He married a wealthy widow, whom he worked for as a caravan leader, named Khadijah, who was fifteen years his senior, when he was twenty-five. Their marriage was a happy one, and it lasted until Khadijah's death twenty-six years later. It produced two sons who died in infancy, and four daughters, only one of whom, Fatima, survived him.[3] His wife, Khadijah, was his loyal supporter, and the first convert to Islam following Muhammed's prophetic call. His uncle, Abu-Talib, never converted to Islam, but neither did he cease to remain a loyal kinsman, and protector of his nephew, Muhammed, against the persecutions which were to come.

The social situation of the day was one of the extremist contrast between wealth and poverty, and injustices existed at all levels of society. Wealthy landlords of the Quaraysh lorded it over the poor, and the helpless were at the mercy of the strong. Greed and selfishness were the order of the day. Intertribal warfare, and blood feuds, were rampant; it was a time of kill or be killed, rob or be robbed. Infanticide, especially the killing of infant girls, was commonplace. Pre-Islamic Arabia was an age which is known as *Jahilyya*, which was thought to mean the "age of ignorance,"[4] but it could more accurately be called an age of savagery, and the absence of social morality, rather than merely ignorance. It was a lawless and pagan society in which life was uncertain at best, and anxiety all-prevalent. The religious life at the time, even in the presence of the Jewish and Christian communities which existed in Arabia, could be described as a relatively primitive form of polytheism. No fewer than 360 gods and goddesses, often in the form of stone idols, were housed in the Ka'bah, a square stone sanctuary in Mecca. Among the popular gods and goddesses prior to the dawn of Islam were "al-Uzzah," or "Power," "al-Lat," or "the Goddess," and "Manah," or "Fate."[5] Surprisingly, even among this undeveloped pantheon of gods, existed "Allah," which simply means "the God." "Allah" is the Arabic word for the Babylonian "Il," and the Israelite, "El," and the South Arabian "Ilah."[6] So Muhammed's achievement was not the discovery of Allah, but the discovery that Allah was the only God, as is stated in the great prayer of Muhammed: "La illaha il Allah," which means "There is no god but God."

It occurred to me that the pre-Islamic time of Arabia was perhaps not all that different from our own time. We do have churches and synagogues in our midst where the true God, "Jehovah," is presumably worshipped, but he is more than drowned out by the multiplicity of pagan deities which are paid homage to, although not entirely consciously so. I spoke of some of these in the chapter on Moses (2): the gods Mammon, Moloch, and the Great God Science. There are many others on the American (and European) scene, not the least of which are: the gods of the celluloid and the electronic image (i.e., film and television), the machismo gods of the motorcycle and black leather jacket cults, the god of "humanism," the gods of the ersatz "new religions," and so on. Western people have long since ceased to be "theocentric," or God-centered, and have become "polycentric," if you will, or many gods-oriented. We don't generally speak of these things as "gods" anymore, but gods they are, nonetheless. One's god is, as Paul Tillich pointed out, one's ultimate concern. In our "pluralistic" modern age, ultimate concerns have become fragmented into as many "little gods" as were worshipped in the Ka'bah in Arabia at the time of the birth of the prophet, Muhammed. We even have the currently "fashionable" vogue of the "new polytheism" which has been extolled in recent books as the "liberating" wave of the future! The head of a religion department at one university described herself proudly to me as a "polytheist." It is strange that in our day the disease of a shattered universe is made into a "badge of honor." We may be, as one writer put it, a "polymorphous perverse" culture. Whether this is a sin or a virtue depends, I suppose, upon one's point of view. But the great theocentric cultures of the past believed in an Absolute Point of View, namely God, which transcended all relativities and gave meaning and purpose to existence. A culture such as ours, in which violent crimes are rampant, suicide, alcoholism, and drug addiction are commonplace, and all manner of other woes from schizophrenia to common neuroses are "the usual," should give some thought as to whether polycentrism is the virtue it is said to be in "liberated circles." Ancient cultures, such as the Israelite at the time of Moses, and the Arabic at the time of Muhammed, became integrated when they discovered, often with the help of a prophetic leader, the Unity which underlies the multiplicity. These diverse cultures who discovered God *found themselves* morally, spiritually, and psychically as a people. Warring tribes who spilled each other's blood for centuries became brothers under God as a result of Muhammed's work.

On a psychological level, and the chief purpose of this book is to explicate the psychological implications of the teachings of the World Masters, the "polycentric" state is the state of inner multiplicity and disharmony. The twentieth-century mystic G. I. Gurdjieff pointed out that the average man of our age, whereas he *thinks* that he is one self, is, in truth, a creature of many little "I"s coexisting in relative ignorance of one another. We are possessed, as it were, by many part-selves, each of which thinks, when it is in ascendancy, that it is the only self. This is to say that our behavior, thought, and emotion are as radically inconsistent and disharmonious as was the society of Mecca with its 360 different gods and goddesses to whom they paid homage in the time of Muhammed. The religious situation of the Meccans was a "polyidolatry" without, our psychic condition is a "polyidolatry" within. This is what Gurdjieff had to say about the fragmentation of people's being, as recorded in a book of recollections by his pupils:

Man is a plural being. When we speak of ourselves we speak of "I." We say "I did this," "I think this," "I want to do this"—but this is a mistake. . . . There is no such "I," or rather there are hundreds, thousands of little "I's" in every one of us. We are divided in ourselves but we cannot recognize the plurality of our being except by observation and study. At one moment it is one "I" that acts, at the next moment it is another "I." It is because the "I's" in ourselves are contradictory that we do not function harmoniously.[7]

We have deeply ingrained within us due to the fact that we use one name, and exist in one body, and give the social impression that we are one person, that we are one "I." But the facts belie this. Let me give you an example on the more obvious social or interpersonal level, and you will all identify with this. In myself there was the "I" who taught college; call him "Mr. Professor." There was also the "I" who was the "child" of my particular parents; call him "Bobby." And there were other social "I's" as well, but these two will do for the purpose of illustration. "Mr. Professor" was "wise," "strong," and "mature," and "knew all the answers to questions," etc. "Bobby" was the "little boy" in the eyes of his parents, and I still felt like this, especially in their presence. I am glad that they did not attend my classes! These two social selves are in obvious contradiction, and it is fortunate that the spheres of these social selves do not often overlap. A priest, and former World War II combat pilot, whom I know, told me that after flying many combat missions in the war, he went to his parents' home for a visit, and they were upset because he "stayed out late" that night! "Mr. combat pilot" and "Mr. child" do not fit too well together. But most of us occupy multiple social roles at the very same time: our profession as adults, the role of husband or wife, the role of father or mother of our children, the role of son or daughter of our parents, and so on. Let's imagine that we are police officer X on the beat, looking and feeling pretty "tough." We are "crime fighters." But then suppose we meet our old eighth-grade teacher, Miss Y, while walking our patrol that day. That brings back the "Johnny" mentality, and officer X momentarily switches off as we say, "Hi, Miss Y." Or suppose that we run into "dear old Mom." That will switch off Officer X mentality all the more! When we go home for the day to our wife, we may still keep part of our officer X "machismo," and a good wife is supportive of her husband's role in life. But we relate to our mate in a different, and, we hope, more personal way than we relate to the demands of our profession. Yet, isn't it unfortunate that our "modern culture" seems to almost "demand" multiple personality? Can we not imagine a simpler world in which we could simply be ourselves regardless of the circumstances? It is, in fact, the goal of the spiritual path to discover the true Self, and those few Self-realized ones I have met in the course of my travels were unique in their consistency of personality and behavior. They did not have a "public self" and a "private self" and a "self" for every occasion. They were *remarkably themselves* in whatever situation they happened to be in from giving a public talk to being with a few intimate friends. So we see that the persona, or social self, is capable of remarkable multiplicity in most people. In the few enlightened ones I have encountered, persona, or social self, was quite transparent, and merely reflected the single *I* that they have discovered through either Grace or much inner work.

On a deeper level than the social is the personal unconscious. Freud merely called this the "repressed." Jung elucidated the contents of the personal unconscious in his early work through the use of his "word association" test and other methods as well. He found that the unconscious contains distinct and separate "complexes," which are strongly emotionally charged and usually personified "subpersonalities" that exist within us, and may create neuroses or psychoses or psychosomatic symptoms in those so afflicted, and, in any case, govern the thoughts, feelings, and behavior of all of us, whether "normal" or "pathological." Freud made very much of one very important complex which he called the "Oedipus complex," and this has to do with the love-hate relationship between the little boy (and the "little boy" in us) and his mother and father. Jung's work demonstrated the mother and father complexes that are involved not only in neurosis, but in normal personality. He also demonstrated the existence of numerous other complexes through the word association methods and the analysis of dreams. If you keep a journal, and record your own dreams faithfully, you will note certain recurring figures, some of which evoke strong emotion. These are your "complexes." Among them, as Jung pointed out, is your ego itself, which Jung called the "ego complex." It is the conscious self that you *think you are*. In dreams in which you appear as "you," that is your "ego complex." If you frequently dream of your mother or father, that is your "mother complex" or "father complex." If you frequently dream of others taunting you, or ridiculing you, or chasing you, you may have a "persecution complex." The extreme of this is "paranoia." The phobic may frequently dream of the thing he is afraid of, for example, heights, closed spaces, dogs, or whatever, and these are "complexes" as well. In Jung's word association test, he read people a list of 100 common words and measured both reaction time and galvanic skin response (or GSR), both of which are measures of emotionality. These together with the contents of the associations can give you some idea of a person's complexes. Dreams are even more self-revelatory, and they indicate that we are by no means "alone" within our psyche at the level of the personal unconscious. We have many "inner neighbors."

Jung went a whole domain beyond Freud in his discovery of the archetypes of the collective unconscious. Whereas the personal unconscious contains "complexes" which relate generally to our own life-histories, the collective unconscious consists of "archetypes," or universal symbols which are "rooted in the universal history of mankind"[8] and are found in the myths of all cultures. I have discussed some of these in previous chapters, and a few examples should suffice us here. I spoke, for example, of the "anima," or the archetypal feminine, which exists within the deep unconscious of the male, and is a kind of "soul image." I spoke likewise of the "animus," or the archetypal masculine, which exists within the deep unconscious of females as a "spirit image." Jung discovered both in his work with patients, and in himself as well, many other archetypal figures such as "the wise man," "the trickster," "the muse," and so on. The Inner Journey, in its deeper phase, consists of the discovery of these great figures within one's psyche. But *one must not identify with them,* or make them into idols, for to do so is to become "possessed." This is the very nature of madness. I saw a woman in San Diego who marched around loudly shouting "I am Eve!" She made a general nuisance of herself, and in the truest sense was quite "mad." She had obviously identified with the archetypal figure of Eve, one personification of the universal fem-

MUHAMMED   187

inine, or the anima. It is almost a stereotype, the figure of the mad-man who says, "I am Napoleon," or "I am Christ." The proper rela-tion to the archetypes is one of *relationship,* not identification.

We have seen at the levels of social roles (first level), the personal unconscious (second level), and the archetypes (third level) there is multiplicity. Did the Ka'bah contain "stone images" of projected com-plexes and archetypal images of just about everyone in Arabia of the time? I think this was clearly the case. One could say that the stone images in the Ka'bah, all 360 of them, were a fantastic collective "projection" of the collective contents of the Arabian unconscious of that era. What happens when you "idolize" your complexes, or even the archetypes of the deeper unconscious? You become possessed by them! And, therefore, Arabia at the time of Muhammed was a land in a state of possession. Possession is madness. Would you not say that never-ending blood feuds, rampant murder and rape, banditry, and infanticide are "symptoms" of collective madness? I would say so. There were gods, in fact, such as "al-Uzzah," who required the sacri-fice of youths to sate their hunger.[9] Everyone acted out his or her particular possession or madness in those days of the age of igno-rance, or *Jahilyya,* in pre-Islamic Arabia. This was the collective "sick-ness" that Muhammed, the prophet, was called upon to try to cure. The extent and the rapidity by which he did so was remarkable in the religious history of humanity. The stages of the conquest of idolatry by Muhammed are remarkably parallel to the spiritual path of the individual seeker in the quest for Self. There is an outer, or exoteric, and an inner, or esoteric, story in all of this. As you recall, we said that Allah Himself was one of the gods in the Ka'bah, although He was not recognized as the Only God. Likewise, we all have experiences, de-spite our neuroses, of our true Selves. But we usually allow these brief moments of light to sink back into the darkness again. Muhammed was one who followed the light to its Source. He discovered the Unity amidst the multiplicity, and this changed the course of human history.

What is this Unity and where is it to be found? It is not to be discovered at the level of social roles, or persona, nor is it to be found at the level of the personal unconscious, and its complexes, nor is it to be found at the level of the collective unconscious, and its archetypes. You will not find the Unity in other words in the worlds of social psychology, or Freudian psychoanalysis, or even Jungian archetypal psychology. You will find *images* of the Unity, it is true, in the realm of the archetypes (just as you found images of "Allah" in the Ka'bah prior to the time of Muhammed), in dreams, inner visions, and religious symbols. But you will not find the *reality* of the Unity there. It is not found there, but rather it is to be found in the realm of the Spirit. It is the realm beyond name and form where you will find the Spirit. It is the Tao which cannot be named. It is the realm of God where no graven images are permissible. It is a silent realm. It is the realm about which the Hindus have said, "Neti, Neti," "Not this, Not that." It is what Moses discovered on Mount Horeb. It is what Jesus encountered at the River Jordan. It is what the Buddha experienced under the Bodhi tree. It is what Krishna showed to Arjuna. It is what Lao Tzu was talking about all along. And it is what Muhammed was gradually to become aware of during the years of his spiritual search. It is the reality of the One. Muhammed was to call this reality "Allah," "the God." His "image," whatever it might have been, I would guess a "star," existed among the many gods of the Ka'bah for centuries before Muhammed. His *reality* is what Muhammed rediscovered. It was a rediscovery of the same sacred reality which was revealed to Muhammed's ancestor, Abraham, in the ancient land of Mesopotamia, and which made him forsake the idols of his kinsfolk, and move to the "Promised Land" of Canaan. The discovery of the Unity made Muhammed, likewise, renounce idols, and commit himself to overthrow the idolatry of his time.

Muhammed's spiritual quest began at the age of twenty-five when he married Khadijah, his faithful supporter all along. There were fifteen years in Muhammed's spiritual preparation.[10] In order to get away from the idolatry and intrigues of Mecca, he retired to lonely caves on Mount Hira. Here he engaged in fasting, prayer, and meditation. During one all-night vigil in the month of Ramadan, when Muhammed was forty years old, he had the crucial experience of his life, a revelation of the archangel Gabriel, who commanded Muhammed to:

> Recite: In the Name of thy Lord who created,
>   created Man of a blood-clot.
> Recite: And thy Lord is the Most Generous,
>   who taught by the Pen,
> taught Man that he knew not.

When Muhammed came back to himself after this dream or trance, these words were as if inscribed upon his heart. When he left the cave in the morning, he heard that same awesome voice of the archangel say these words: "O Muhammed! Thou art Allah's messenger, and I am Gabriel."[11] Muhammed turned away from the brilliance of the vision, but no matter which way he turned, he saw the angel confronting him. Then the angel vanished.

Gabriel is considered to be in Judaism, Christianity, and Islam the "messenger of God." He appeared to the prophet Daniel, the Virgin Mary, and Muhammed. To Muhammed, Gabriel revealed the 114 *suras,* or chapters, of the Koran over the remaining twenty-two years of his life. Who or what is Gabriel? Is he a "heavenly being"? I would say yes, if we are willing to give up an "out there" conception of "heaven." Jesus said that "the kingdom of heaven is within." What does he mean by "within"? He means "within" your holy mind! And in some sense all minds are interconnected, as witness the phenomena of extrasensory perception, the communion between lovers, and spiritual experience which is shared, as on the day of Pentecost when the disciples received the Holy Spirit. Jung's concept of the "Collective Unconscious" would seem to speak to this issue. What kind of a "within being" is Gabriel? Clearly, Gabriel is a universal form who appears in different cultures, Jewish, Christian, and Islamic. We may take him to be an "archetype." Does this mean that I do not believe that he was "sent by God," as tradition holds? Absolutely not. If God created the physical universe, as believers (such as myself) attest, then surely he created the spiritual, archetypal, and psychological worlds as well. If He can, and does, at times, intervene in the physical world scene, as in the "parting of the Red Sea," He certainly can intervene in people's psychic world through dreams and visions. To say that angels are "archetypes" does not in any way lessen their reality. It merely says that they are not realities of a physical sort. If reality equals physical reality for you, we must part company here. To the mystic and visionary, his visions and spiritual experiences are as real as the physical objects in the "external world." At the age of thirty-two I had a vision of the Muse while standing on the beach at La Jolla, California. *She* was as real as real can be. She is still real for me today. But she is a reality of a different order from trees and rocks and flesh-and-blood human beings. The Muse is an archetypal reality of the sort that Plato spoke about, and Jung rediscovered. In the Kabbalistic metaphysics of the Jewish tradition, there are said to be four levels of "manifest reality": Azilut—World of Emanation; Beriah—World of Creation; Yezirah—World of Formation; and Asiyyah—World of Making. The World of Emanation is the Divine World, the World of Creation is the Archangelic World, the World of Formation is the World of the Psyche and Soul, and the World of Making is the World of the Body and Nature.[12] In this scheme of things, then, Gabriel, the Messenger of God, is a being of "Beriah," the World of Creation, the level of "Archangels." Gabriel mediated between the psyche of Muhammed and the Divine. Muhammed never reported the experience of "seeing God," as Moses experienced him at the "burning bush." The Divine World was mediated for Muhammed by the Archangelic World in the form of Gabriel. It was the same for the Virgin Mary in her experience of the "Annunciation" as reported in the Gospel according to Luke. The prophet Daniel also experienced Gabriel in a vision, as the giver of "wisdom and understanding." So Muhammed was in "good company!"

It takes a certain inner development to "see" these things, just as it takes the development of external perception for scientists in their respective fields to "see" what they do. We "believe in" the existence of viruses and bacteria, for example, although we probably have not "seen" them. It takes biologists who are trained in the use of microscopes years to learn to see these things. Likewise, we "believe in" molecules and atoms which chemists talk about even though we haven't "seen" them. It takes the special training of the chemist to adduce the evidence for their existence. Furthermore, we "believe in" subatomic particles which nobody has ever "seen," but physicists postulate in their theories to "make sense" of their experiments and observations. Astronomers, too, tell us about things that nobody has ever "seen," such as "black holes." Nevertheless, we do not hesitate to "believe in" them. On the other hand, when the mystics and sages report their experiences of "Angelic Beings" and "the Spirit," we in our materialistically biased culture of today find it hard to "believe." Believe it or not, there are specialists in the realm of the soul and Spirit, and Muhammed was one such. He was not "born that way," although he surely had a God-given gift. It was necessary for him to develop the use of his spiritual gift over many years. When revelation itself finally came, it was overwhelming even to Muhammed.

Following his first encounter with Gabriel, Muhammed was quite alarmed, as we might be, and thought that he might be "mad" or "possessed." His wife, Khadijah, assured him of his sound judgment and his sanity. Muhammed was a man who was "ready" for such an experience, but it is still a "heavy" experience to encounter the Archangel Gabriel and be informed that you are a prophet!

Khadijah had a blind cousin, Waraga, who was familiar with Jewish and Christian scriptures. He detected in Muhammed the signs of prophethood, and he predicted hardships. He said: "They will banish thee, and they will fight against thee."[13]

Muhammed's second revelation came shortly thereafter while he lay wrapped in his robe in a cave. The Voice of Gabriel said: "O thou enveloped in thy cloak, Arise and warn! Thy Lord magnify, Thy raiment purify, Pollution shun!"[14]

In subsequent days, Muhammed had further revelations and it became his increasing conviction that it was his mission to preach the message of Islam, or "submission to God," and to restore the pure monotheistic faith of Abraham to his descendants—through Ishmael—the Arabs. The call to prophesy is by no means unique among Semitic peoples. It began with Abraham, the patriarch, and it continued with many great examples in the Israelite line, among them, Isaiah, Jeremiah, Ezekiel, Daniel, Ezra, and so on. It seemed to "die" in the Ishmaelite line of Abraham's descendants until Muhammed "picked up the torch," as it were, and brought some light to those in darkness in Arabia in those days of the seventh century A.D. His audience, the powerful tribes of the Quaraysh, were by no means the most receptive audience, however, for what Muhammed preached was radically threatening to their status quo world of idolatry and social injustice. Like all prophets, Muhammed challenged most strongly the "powers that be."

Muhammed's first converts to the religion that came to be known as "Islam" were his wife, Khadijah, his cousin, Ali, his adopted son, Zayd, and Abu-Bakr, a respected merchant of Mecca.[15] Muhammed's progress went very slowly at first, and after three years of preaching in Mecca, his home city, he made only thirty converts, and these mostly from the deprived classes. The Quaraysh perceived that Muhammed was undermining their system of privilege, and was a threat to them. They tried to dissuade Muhammed at the outset through bribery, but he had this to say to them: "I will not forsake this cause until it prevails by the will of God, or I will perish instead."[16]

Muhammed's cause was the religio-social cause of bringing the message of the worship of the one God, Allah, and the teachings of brotherhood and justice, to the idolatrous and violent tribes of Arabia of that time. Muhammed could not be deterred by bribery, nor did he allow himself to become discouraged by the persecutions, almost to the death, which followed.

Does this story of Muhammed bear upon the individual seeker's spiritual quest? It most assuredly does, and Muhammed's saga forms another allegory, though as historical as the story of Moses and Jesus, of the Journey to Self. Along this Path, one meets with bribery, and with persecution, from the negating forces both within and without. It is really *too much* unless one can "cleave unto the Lord with all your might," as one Hasidic rabbi told me. Muhammed was evidently one of those who did just that. His one-man spiritual revolution in Arabia is a remarkable parallel to the spiritual revolution which needs take place within any single person's soul.

When the persecutions by the Quaraysh became too intense (and many of his followers were tortured and killed), Muhammed advised those who could not depend upon the protection of kinsfolk to seek refuge in Christian Abyssinia.[17] Muhammed and a small band of his followers remained behind in Mecca to continue the struggle against overwhelming odds. Perhaps his only protection against assassination was his family ties in the Quaraysh itself, the support of his uncle, Abu-Talib, and his wife, Khadijah, and, I would add, God's providence. When his wife and uncle died, he became the subject of increasing persecution, false accusations, and even death threats. One would-be assassin whose sword fell from his hand before he could strike Muhammed, fell to his knees and became an immediate convert.[18] This event increased his disciples' courage, but their situation in Mecca was all but intolerable.

As if it were "orchestrated" by God himself, a group of citizens from Yathrib—to be known as Medina—invited Muhammed and his followers to come to their city two hundred miles to the north of Mecca. Muhammed and about one hundred Muslim families left Mecca as unobtrusively as possible and moved to Medina where they were warmly received. Muhammed, the persecuted prophet and preacher in Mecca, became in Medina a religious leader of Muslims, a statesman, and eventually a military commander. The brotherhood of Islam superseded all ties of blood and kin. Here in Medina, Muhammed established a religious commonwealth comparable to the Israelite nation which Moses forged. This migration from Mecca to Medina is known in the Islamic tradition as the "Hegira," which means "Flight." The Hegira of 622 A.D. marks the beginning of the Muslim era.[19]

In the course of our own personal lives, we may find it necessary to make our own "Hegira" from the familiar place where we grew up, and have family and kinship ties, to a new place where we can establish our independent existence and identity. In Mecca, Muhammed was the "rebellious young man" subjected to the chastisements of the "elders" of the Quaraysh. In Medina, Muhammed became an authority unto himself and his own man, moreover, a leader among men. Is it not the same in all of our lives? We need to leave the *family mystique* in order to become persons in our own right. The Jungians would speak of this as the "individuation process."

Following the "Hegira," Muhammed's troubles with the Quaraysh were by no means over; in fact, there were a series of wars between the Meccan Quaraysh and the Medinan Muslims. In the first war, the Battle of Badr, the Muslims routed the Meccans, although they were outnumbered three to one. Muhammed's small band of holy warriors humbled the mighty of Mecca. In the following year, in the Battle of Uhud, the tide was turned and 3,000 Meccans of the Quaraysh defeated Muhammed's 700 men because 50 Muslim archers deserted at the time of battle. Muhammed himself was badly wounded. But the Quaraysh withdrew and did not take Medina because Muhammed's men fought so valiantly. Muhammed embarked on an expedition to encircle Mecca in the year 628 A.D., and he concluded a truce which granted Muslims permission to make a pilgrimage to Mecca in the following year. In accordance with the truce, Muhammed and his followers made a pilgrimage to Mecca in 629 A.D. The city was temporarily vacated for the three-day visit. Finally, in 630 A.D., or year eight of the Hegira, Muhammed resolved to end the resistance of the Quaraysh once and for all. He set out with 10,000 men for Mecca, and, when still a day's journey away, a delegation of the Quaraysh met with the prophet and offered to submit to Islam. Thus, without force or bloodshed, the Muslims entered Mecca in peace. Its inhabitants were treated with magnanimity and forgiveness, and thousands of Meccans converted to the new faith. Muhammed himself marched seven times around the Ka'bah, the former citadel of idolatry, and he personally destroyed all of its 360 idols with his staff. He proclaimed: "Allah Hu Akbar" ("God is great"). And he said that all true believers were brothers. In the two years that followed, from 630 A.D. to 632 A.D., all of Arabia, tribe after tribe, sent their representatives to Mecca to offer their submission to Allah. Muhammed, who was a persecuted outcast a mere ten years earlier, lived to see Islam triumph throughout Arabia.[20]

The series of wars and skirmishes, going first this way and then that way, in favor of Muhammed and against him, and finally resulting in his victory, first in Mecca, then in all of Arabia, reminds me of the inner battles which the seeker must fight against "the forces" which would block his development or destroy him. On the inward level, the battles of Muhammed against the Quaraysh resemble the battle of the hero against the negative archetype of the Terrible Father. The Terrible Father, you will recall from the chapter on Moses, represents the stagnant and stultifying aspect of culture in its most repressive form. In Moses' case, it was the Pharaoh and the power of Egypt; in the case of Muhammed, it was the Quaraysh, the ruling clan of Mecca.

Through his persistence and courage, and through his faith in God, Muhammed eventually triumphed over his old enemies. They even became his disciples! Likewise, it takes persistence and courage and trust in the power of Allah-within, or the true Self, to sustain the seeker in his quest, and, moreover, to empower him to defeat his enemies. And the greatest enemies are within. The Self = Wholeness; this is perhaps why under its power even former "enemies" become disciples. The Self is all-inclusive within the psyche, as God is "all in all" in the universe.

The time interval of ten years which worked such a miracle in religious history in Arabia is precisely the time span of most Inward Journeys as reported by the mystics of various spiritual traditions from Zen to Sufism. It was the time span that I experienced in my own Inward Journey cycle. The Journey of Ulysses in Homer's epic poem was exactly ten years. It took Ulysses ten years to overcome all the obstacles in his path from the cyclops to the witch, and then return to his *home port*. It seems to take at least this length of time to accomplish the immense task of defeating the inner enemies on the Path to Self.

Muhammed spoke of the wars which he had to fight as "Jihad," or "Holy War." Although he fought external wars against idolaters, Muhammed said that the "Greater Holy War" is within oneself.[21] This indicates that Muhammed was a psychologist as well as a prophet and statesman because anyone who has made the Journey knows that it *is* a holy war! The inner enemies, be they your complexes or the negative archetypes which underlie them at a deeper level, will put up a terrible battle against you. Symptoms such as depressions and anxiety attacks and phobias, etc., are your "inner enemies" acting up against you. When you become more conscious of them by paying attention to your dreams and inner imagery, you will become aware of just *who* these "inner enemies" are. When you know them in personified form, you can even "talk to them." This is what the Jungians call "active imagination." More than talking to them, you will really have to wage holy war against them! The real meaning of "Jihad" in Arabic is "Supreme Effort."[22] To overcome the inner enemies indeed requires a supreme effort. It is an effort that is long and drawn out, and may take as long as ten years of hard inner work, and yes, inner warfare! You will have to find out not merely who the "inner enemies" are, but who the "inner friends" are as well. The inner friends, some of whom I have spoken about already in previous chapters, are the positive archetypes. I found that I had to discover a "small army" of inner friends in my "holy war," including the "warrior," the "knight," the "wise man," the "warrior goddess," the "anima sister," and others. These "inner friends" even have their outer counterparts in most cases. Besides these various inner friends who make up your "interior army," one needs call upon, and rest in, the supreme inward power, the Self, or Allah-within, if you will. Jesus said that "the stone" which is the Christ, if you fall upon it, "you will be broken to pieces," but "when it falls upon any one it will crush him."[23] This hardly sounds "pacifistic," even coming from the Prince of Peace. There is a time for peace-making, and there is a time for Jihad, or Holy War. You will find that by far the greatest Holy War is within, but with trust in God, you, like Muhammed in his struggle, will win. "Winning" is simply this: *finding yourself.* This necessitates the destroying of your own inner idols, and the establishing of the true Self in their place as the "ruler" of your own inner house, or "Ka'bah."

You might try this "simple exercise." Get a set of crayons, or felt markers, and some paper, and draw in full color each and every one of your inner idols. Don't complain, "I can't do it." Just do it. Draw whatever comes to mind. It may be fear, or selfishness, or desire to dominate others, or your mother complex, or what have you. Draw them all in some personified or symbolic form, whatever image occurs to you. Greed, for example, might be pictured as a "pig," and fear as a "frightened monkey." Particular people who represent emotional complexes for you can be drawn as themselves. Use your own creative imagination in this task. When you have completed your set of "inner idols," draw a large square box around them: this represents your inner "Ka'bah." Now, draw a picture of your "inner Muhammed." He is your inner prophet and holy warrior. Then symbolize the "smashing" of each and every one of your "inner idols" by "X–ing" them out in red or black. You might repeat this whole project in modelling clay. Mold each of your inner idols into the "required shape." Let the clay idols harden. Then, place them in some square box; a shoe box will do. This is your "shrine" of inner idols. Now, simply take a hammer, and smash them! That is what Muhammed did in the Ka'bah after he marched into Mecca. Then, say this: "La illaha il Allah," "There is no god but God." This is to replace your inner idols with the Self, or Allah-within. This will not make you a capital "M" Muslim, but a small "m" muslim, which is to say, one who renounces idols, within and without. This is contradictory to nothing in Judaism or Christianity. If your god is God, then your self will be your Self "as God created you." I am not saying that this will "cure you," but it will make you aware of

the problem that needs be dealt with: the overcoming of inner idolatry.

In the year 632 A.D., his mission accomplished, Muhammed died
and was buried in Medina. His chosen successor Abu-Bakr said this to
the gathered multitudes: "O Muslims! If any of you has been worship-
ping Muhammed, then let me tell you that Muhammed is dead. But if
you really do worship God, then know ye that God is living and will
never die."[24]

Islam may be the most thoroughgoing monotheism that has ever
existed. It will brook no idolatry. It calls any "association" with Allah
in the process of worship a "shirk."[25] In Islam, it would be considered
a major shirk to confuse a prophet of God with God himself. The
Buddha always said that he was an ordinary man, like other men,
except that he realized the Truth. But certain schools (by no means
all) of Buddhism idolize the Buddha, and make him the object of
worship, rather than the Truth itself. I do not think that it was the
intention of Jesus, far from it, to set himself up as an object of worship, but only God himself. Jesus was the Messiah of God. The
"Christ," which Jesus realized within himself, is not a man, but the
"Universal Sonship," the Second Person of the Trinity. There is an
apparent difference between Christianity and Islam on the issue of
the Trinity versus the Unity of God. But true Christianity is as monotheistic as true Islam, for the "Three" are merely approaches to the
"One." It is not generally known in Christian circles, the ultimate
esteem in which Jesus is held in Islam, or by the prophet Muhammed
himself. The Sufis, who call Muhammed the "messenger of God,"
refer to Jesus as the "spirit of God." Yet, he is also considered to be a
man, like Adam, whom Allah called into being by saying, "Be!" Whoever can say, "There is no god but God," is a muslim in the universal
sense of renouncing idolatry. In this sense, Abraham can be viewed as
the "first muslim," as he is in Islamic tradition. Jews consider Abraham to be their father as well. St. Paul, the Jewish convert to Christ,
and apostle to the Gentiles, traced the religion of pure faith back to
Abraham. Abraham was the patriarch of three world religions; it
began by his renunciation of idolatry.

The psychological parallel of a "shirk" is the idolatrizing of the
archetypes. There is a tendency among certain neo-Jungians who "go
beyond" Jung to make a religion out of "archetypal psychology." This
was not Jung's intention. It is a reinstatement of Greek polytheism, as
is evident by reading some of the books by the "new polytheists." God
Himself (if they recognize Him at all) is reduced to one among the

many gods. The Self is simply one among the various archetypes. This is a level of confusion and a misunderstanding of the nature of both Self and God. The realm of the archetypes, as with the gods, is still the realm of "the many." It is a realm to be "gone beyond," in the language of the Buddhists, not a realm to be inhabited indefinitely and worshipped! The anima and the animus, the wise man and the wise woman, and so on, are the "helpers" along the way to the Self; they are not the "end" in themselves. The Self is the end of the Journey. It is impossible to discover the Self without discovering God, and vice versa. At the level of the Self and God, we are dealing with the level in which multiplicity has disappeared. It is the level of "the One." It is the "fourth level" which has been known throughout history simply as *the spiritual*. The *Shema* of Judaism and the *Shahadah* of Islam both testify to this level. The mystics of all traditions *know* it directly. In Sufism, or Islamic mysticism, the highest stage of the Path is known as "Tawhid."[26] It is the stage of Unity. Pure monotheism without is the correlative of Self-realization within. We will look, without interruption or interpretation, at a section of the second *sura* of the Koran known as "The Cow." It is a statement of pure Islamic monotheism, the "outer aspect" of the Unity.

The Cow

That is the Book, wherein is no doubt,
  a guidance to the godfearing
Who believe in the Unseen, and perform the prayer,
and expend of that We have provided them;
who believe in what has been sent down to thee
  and what has been sent down before thee,
  and have faith in the Hereafter;
those are upon guidance from their Lord,
  those are the ones who prosper.

As for the unbelievers, alike it is to them
whether thou hast warned them or hast not warned them,
  they do not believe.
God has set a seal on their hearts and on their hearing,
  and on their eyes is a covering,
and there awaits them a mighty chastisement. . . .

O you men, serve your Lord Who created you,
and those that were before you; haply so
  you will be godfearing;
who assigned to you the earth for a couch,
and heaven for an edifice, and sent down

out of heaven water, wherewith He brought forth
fruits for your provision; so set not up
    compeers to God wittingly.
and if you are in doubt concerning that We have
sent down on Our servant, then bring a sura
like it, and call your witnesses, apart from
    God, if you are truthful.
And if you do not—and you will not—then
fear the Fire, whose fuel is men and stones,
    prepared for unbelievers.

Give thou good tidings to those who believe
and do deeds of righteousness, that for them
await gardens underneath which rivers flow;
whensoever they are provided with fruits therefrom
they shall say, "This is that wherewithal
were were provided before"; that they shall be
given in perfect semblance; and there
for them shall be spouses purified; therein
    they shall dwell forever.

God is not ashamed to strike a similitude
even of a gnat, or aught above it.
As for the believers, they know it is the truth
from their Lord; but as for the unbelievers,
they say, "What did God desire by this
for a similitude?" Thereby He leads
many astray, and thereby He guides
many; and thereby He leads none astray
    save the ungodly
such as break the convenant of God
after its solemn binding, and such as cut
what God has commanded should be joined,
and such as do corruption in the land—
    they shall be the losers.

How do you disbelieve in God, seeing you were dead
and He gave you life, then He shall make you dead,
then He shall give you life, then unto Him
    you shall be returned?
It is He who created for you all that is
in the earth, then He lifted Himself to heaven
and levelled them seven heavens; and He has
    knowledge of everything. . . .

And We gave to Moses the Book, and after him
sent succeeding Messengers; and We gave Jesus
son of Mary the clear signs, and confirmed him
with the Holy Spirit; and whensoever
there came to you a Messenger with that your souls

had not desire for, you become arrogant,
and some cry lies to, and some slay? . . .

The Jews say, "The Christians stand not on anything";
the Christians say, "The Jews stand not on anything";
yet they recite the Book. So too the ignorant
say the like of them. God shall decide between them
on the Day of Resurrection touching their differences.
And who does greater evil than he who bars
God's place of worship, so that His Name
be not rehearsed in them, and strives to destroy them?
Such men might never enter them, save in fear;
for them is degradation in the present world,
and in the world to come a mighty chastisement.

To God belongs the East and the West;
whithersoever you turn, there is the Face of God;
        God is all-embracing, All-knowing. . . .

And they say, "Be Jews or Christians and
you shall be guided." Say thou: "Nay, rather
the creed of Abraham, a man of pure faith;
        he was no idolater. . . ."

        God
there is no god but He, the
Living, the Everlasting.
Slumber seizes Him not, neither sleep;
        to Him belongs
all that is in the heavens and the earth.
Who is there that shall intercede with Him
        save by His leave?

He knows what lies before them
        and what is after them,
and they comprehend not anything of his knowledge
        save such as He wills.
His Throne comprises the heavens and earth;
the preserving of them oppresses Him not;
He is the All-high, the All-glorious.

No compulsion is there in religion.
Rectitude has become clear from error.
So whosoever disbelieves in idols
and believes in God, has laid hold of
the most firm handle, unbreaking; God is
        All-hearing, All-knowing.

God is the protector of the believers;
He brings them forth from the shadows
        into the light

And the unbelievers—their protectors are
idols, that bring them forth from the light
    into the shadows;
those are the inhabitant of the Fire,
    therein dwelling forever. . . .

The Messenger believes in what was sent down to
    him from his Lord,
and the believers; each one believes in God
    and His angels,
and in His Books and His Messengers; we
    make no division
between any one of His Messengers. They say,
    "We hear, and obey.
Our Lord, grant us Thy forgiveness; unto Thee
    is the homecoming."

God charges no soul save to its capacity;
standing to its account is what it has earned,
and against its account what it has merited.

    Our Lord,
take us not to task
If we forget, or make mistake.
    Our Lord,
charge us not with a load such
as Thou didst lay upon those before us.
    Our Lord,
do Thou not burden us
beyond what we have the strength to bear.
    And pardon us,
    and forgive us,
    and have mercy on us;
    Thou art our Protector.
    And help us against the people
    of the unbelievers

"God charges no soul save to its capacity. . . ." This statement in
"The Cow" sura particularly struck me. We all have our troubles and
our "crosses to bear," it is true. I have mine, and you have yours.
Some have external wounds, and some have wounds of the soul. I
believe, from personal experience, that the latter are even more difficult to bear. The greatest wound that all of us have is our alienation
(or "exile") from God, and likewise, from our true Selves. The quest
for Self, or Wholeness, is what motivated me in my own Journey, and
what motivated me in writing this book as well. The quest for Wholeness is the quest for the Unity. The Unity is the ultimate healing of the
soul. In Islam, the Sufi mystics were the "specialists," as it were, of the

spiritual quest. We call it a "spiritual quest," and it is that, but it is just as surely a *healing quest*. And if "God charges no soul save to its capacity . . . ," then we may trust that God provides each soul with the means it needs to find its healing and its wholeness. The great Sufis of history found their various ways to help and guide souls on the Journey. This is the "inner side" of Islam.

The growth of Sufism was a reaction to the intellectualism and legalism of exoteric Islam, just as Hasidism was a reaction to the same tendency in orthodox Judaism. Sufism is the way of the mystic. Its three essential ingredients are light, knowledge, and love, as the means by which the divine presence is experienced. Divine union, known as "Tawhid" in Sufism, has two principal stages: (1)"Fana," or "extinction" of the neurotic or conditioned self, and (2) "Ba'qa," or "reintegration" in God. The tenth-century A.D. Sufi mystic Al-Hallaj said "I am He whom I love, and He whom I love is I."[27] He called himself "Al-Haqq," the Truth. He was condemned and crucified as a "heretic" by the Islamic authorities of his time for his claim of union with God. It was not until Al-Ghazali, the great Islamic scholar, theologian, and later Sufi mystic of the twelfth century A.D., that Sufism became "respectable" within orthodox Islam, He synthesized the inner and the outer ways, and succeeded in making orthodox Islam more mystical[28] (as the Hasids succeeded in making Judaism more mystical).

Jalaludin Rumi, who lived in the thirteenth century A.D., was the greatest Sufi poet (and one of the greatest poets who ever lived). He was also the founder of the Mevlevi order of "whirling dervishes."[29] In these dervish dances, the dancer whirls in a counterclockwise direction with right hand palm upward to heaven and left hand palm downward to earth. Another famous method devised by Rumi was the "dhikr," or "repetition" of the Name of God. The whirling dervish may also chant "Allah, Allah, Allah, Allah. . . ." Or he may chant one of the other ninty-nine names of God. Rumi, the poet-mystic, said this about "the Way":

> The Way has been marked out.
> If you depart from it, you will perish.
> If you try to interfere with the signs on the road,
> you will be an evil-doer.[30]

What Rumi says is reminiscent of what Krishna said about one's "Karma duty." It also reminds me of what Lao Tzu said about discov-

ering your "proper place." To find and follow our own unique "Way"
that God has set out for us is probably the most important thing that a
human being can do. It is, in my opinion, what it means to "follow
Christ."

Rumi said this about where the true Self, or God, is to be found in a
poem entitled "He Was in No Other Place":

Cross and Christians, end to end, I examined. He was not on the Cross. I
went to the Hindu temple, to the ancient pagoda. In none of them was there
any sign. To the uplands of Herat I went, and to Kandahar. I looked. He was
not on the heights or in the lowlands. Resolutely, I went to the summit of the
(fabulous) mountain of Kaf. There only was the dwelling of the (legendary)
Anqa bird. I went to the Kaaba of Mecca. He was not there. I asked about him
from Avicenna, the philosopher. He was beyond the range of Avicenna. . . .
I looked into my own heart. In that place, I saw him. He was in no other
place.[31]

This poem by the Sufi-mystic Rumi reminds me of the passage in
the Bible about the great Hebrew prophet Elijah and the "still small
voice":

And there he came to a cave, and lodging there; and behold, the word of the
LORD came to him, and he said to him, "What are you doing here, Elijah?" He
said, "I have been very jealous for the LORD, the God of hosts; for the people
of Israel have forsaken thy covenant, thrown down thy altars, and slain they
prophets with the sword; and I, even I only, am left; and they seek my life, to
take it away." And he said,"Go forth, and stand upon the mount before the
LORD." And behold, the LORD passed by, and a great and strong wind rent the
mountains, and broke in pieces the rocks before the LORD, but the LORD was
not in the wind; and after the wind an earthquake, but the LORD was not in
the earthquake; and after the earthquake a fire, but the LORD was not in the
fire; and after the fire a still small voice.[32]

The poet-mystic Rumi and the prophet Elijah found the Lord in
the same place—within their own heart or soul, the place of the "still
small voice." The Sufis were and are masters of the soul; I would call
them "psychologists" in the truest sense, the word "psychology" having to do with psyche, or soul. The word has been debased in the past
one hundred years of "scientific psychology," which has as much to do
with the soul as the atheist has to do with God. With the possible
exception of the Jungian school, "modern psycholgy" has been singu-
larly unrevealing about the soul. it has even denied the existence of
the soul. The Islamic writer Seyyed Hossein Nasr has this to say about
the "modern behavioristic sciences":

The careful "scientific" study of fragmented human behavior is incapable of revealing the profounder aspect of human nature precisely because of an *a priori* limitation that so many branches of the modern behavioristic sciences of man—veritable pseudosciences if there ever were any—have placed upon the meaning of the human state itself.[33]

Nasr states that a vision of human nature will never come from the study of "fragmented behavior." He says that it is like going "around the rim of the wheel indefinitely without ever entering upon the spoke to approach the proximity of the axis and the Centre."[34] Our academic psychology departments in this country (which I know all too well from personal experience) with their "studies" of the ever more trivial reflect what Nasr says about the "modern behavioristic sciences." Whether the student investigates the intricasies of "reinforcement schedules" of rats or pigeons in the Skinnerian laboratory, or "learning curves" in the memorization of "nonsense syllables" in human experimental psychology, or "Gestalt" experiments in the "perception of dots," or "responses" of "subjects" to "Rorshach ink blots" in clinical-oriented psychology, or the statistical results of group-administered "personality tests" in factor-analytic psychology, he will, as Nasr puts it, be going "around the rim of the wheel indefinitely. . . ." Such approaches to human behavior are doomed, in the nature of the case, to approach indefinitely the asymptope of superficiality. Such "experiments" will *fill up* "scholarly journals," but will not *add up* to an understanding of the human soul, or psyche.

Sufism is the direct study in oneself of "the Centre." According to Nasr, the Ultimate Reality, or Allah, is both Inward (al-Batin) and Outward (al-Zahir).[35] The Sufi sees God as Inward, the Center. We in the "modern" West encounter very few people who live life in the deeper levels of their being. Our behavioral sciences reflect this. Nasr states that the sacred books of humanity such as the Koran contain "a history of the human soul." The prophets of humanity are a source of information about human beings *vis a vis* the Center. The prophet of Islam himself said, "He who knows himself knows his Lord."[36]

Islam sees the human being as "the image of God." The rebellion against God occurs not at the level of the body, but at the level of the soul. It is not the body, but the soul that needs healing. The fragmented "gods" of the Ka'bah, in conflict one with the other, represent the fragmented state of the human soul. Healing involves the disintegration (Fana) of the inner idols, and the reintegration (Ba'qa) of the soul in God, the One. God cannot be harmed, but the human soul *can* be destroyed. Witness the sickness of modern society! People today are in need, perhaps more than in any other time of history, of the sacred tradition of healing.

All Muslims believe in the Unity as it is expressed in its most universal sense by the *Shahadah*: "La illaha il Allah." But, it is only the Sufi who has realized the mysteries of the Unity within himself. The whole discipline of Sufism, with its many different schools, is a spiritual way whose goal is to cure humans of their inner idolatry, or hypocrisy, and to make them whole. People in Western culture confess God with their speech, but actually live and behave as if there were many gods. We pay homage to the outer gods of materialism, war, science, and hedonism, and to the inner gods of anxiety, depression, anger, lust, and addiction. Sufism seeks to cure humans of this deadly malady of psychic polytheism. Its aim is to make humans integrated. God the Creator is One, and so must each human being become one. To be fragmented and compartmentalized is to be lost in the world of psychic complexes and inner conflicts. Psychic health is Wholeness, and Wholeness is Unity. The Integrated Man according to the Sufis reflects the Divine Unity and the Divine Qualities. There is a "spiritual fragrance" about such a person in all he says and does. Pierre, whom I have spoken about in previous chapters, was this kind of man. There was something about him which was simply indescribable. He was in touch with that spiritual energy, or *barakah*, as the Sufis call it, which animates the universe. Pierre described himself as a Christian Sufi, but he was no stranger to Islamic Sufi circles in the Middle East either. Adnan Sarhan, who was a Sufi teacher I encountered a couple of years later, said that he had known an enlightened Frenchman named Pierre who travelled through the Middle East. He described him as "that man with the luminous blue eyes."

F. Schuon, celebrated author on world religions, says that "There is in every man an incorruptible star, a substance called upon to become crystallized in Immortality; it is eternally prefigured in the luminous proximity of the Self."[37] One who has realized this "star" within himself has found peace. Sufi psychology involves the purifying of one's consciousness of inner idols, untruths, hypocrisy, and negative emotions so that it regains its original quality of "mirror-likeness" to reflect the *sacred reality* that is within. The Sufis seek to strip away all that is false within people, including their psychological and social conditioning, to attain to the "void" or "nothingness" which the Sufis call "Fana." But the Sufi does not stop at nothingness. He empties himself only in order that he can be filled with *everything-ness*. This is the meaning of "Ba'qa." The Fana/Ba'qa cycle is very much analogous to the Crucifixion/Resurrection cycle in Christian mysticism. The Christian mystic needs to go through his or her own "crucifixion," in the psychic sense, in order that he or she may attain to the "resurrection," or spiritual rebirth.

Dreams which play so large a part in both Freudian and Jungian psychology were always considered of great importance by both the Sufis and the Kabbalists. It is to Freud's and Jung's credit that they discovered these things, but they were not the "pioneers" they are thought to be. They merely "rediscovered," as it were, knowledge that was long known in the mystical traditions of both East and West. There are, in general, two kinds of dreams: "little dreams" and "big dreams." Little dreams are the dreams of the personal unconscious, and these consist of persons, events, and themes of our personal life histories. Such dreams uncover unconscious conflicts and traumas, some dating from early childhood. Freud specialized in this area, but, as Bakan has shown, it was well known in the Jewish mystical tradition.[38] Jung discovered that certain dreams contain universal or archetypal themes that transcend the individual's life history. These are "big dreams." I had a dream of this sort concerning my anima figure about a year ago. In it, I met her at college, and then we were both transformed into ducks! We flew together toward the "home pond." It was a very powerful dream. I was later to learn that there is a fairy tale very much like this. At the level of the "big dream" archetypal themes present themselves in the same way that they arise in the minds of the writers of myths and fairy tales: *from the deep unconscious.* In my dream, as in the very similar fairy tale, the meaning is: one must meet the inner feminine being, or anima, before one can "fly home," which is to say, come to the Self. The Sufi masters of the past were well aware of archetypal dreams and their importance on the Journey. Professor A. Reza Arasteh, a scholar of Sufism, states that: "The dream . . . reveals the signs of the path."[39]

Sufi methods are among the most varied of any spiritual traditions, and include such practices as meditation, the "Dhikr," or "repetition of the Names of God," movement exercises, sacred dances, and the telling of Sufi teaching tales.

I was a member of a Sufi group led by a dervish from Baghdad, Iraq, named Adnan Sarhan, for about one year. I attended weekend workshops for many months culminating in a ten-day workshop in rural upstate New York. Sufism was actually the first traditional spiritual discipline which I practiced following my work with the "Arica group" (Arica claims to be a "modern mystical school" somewhat analogous to the Gurdjieff work). My year with Adnan's group was in some ways one of the most powerful experiences of my Path. Let me tell you about it. I'll begin with Adnan.

Adnan is a swarthy Bedouin Arab born in Baghdad. Somewhat shorter than average in height, he is gifted with a truly athletic physique, and a dynamic quality one rarely sees in our culture. Adnan was a champion swimmer, wrestler, and boxer, as well as a master of Sufi dancing, one of the best in the world, I have been told. Besides his athletic prowess, he is an initiate of four Sufi orders. Adnan was more a man of action than a man of words, but when he did speak, he always had something very special to say. He had a "life energy" about him that one sees in people who are very close to nature such as American Indians. His eyes were full of life. Adnan was one of the "rainmakers" whom I have known.

Adnan's teaching methods were so spontaneous and varying that it would be impossible to repeat them. Students tried to take notes, at first, on everything that went on. Eventually, they realized that this was senseless. Sufism has nothing to do with academia. You become a Sufi by becoming a Sufi. One day, a professor of Islamic studies at a major university came to visit Adnan while he was conducting a workshop. We were having a "rest break." The professor talked on and on about all he "knew" about Sufism. Adnan didn't say a thing. Finally, Adnan fell asleep! It was his "comment" apparently on the professor's one-sided intellectualism. Sufis can be very direct.

My first contact with Adnan was in San Francisco during the summer of 1972 while I was taking the "Arica training." Adnan gave a workshop there one evening. These were my comments in my diary about the Sufi workshop:

In the evening we had a class by a whirling Dervish named Adnan—wonderful man—a beautiful natural physique. We chanted "Allah," and did Sufi dancing. Then we went around in a circle for hours saying "Ya Hadi" to the point of exhaustion.

Chanting "Allah" again and again is what is known as the "Dhikr." It is analogous to the "mantram" in Yoga. The dancing we did was spontaneous and self-expressive. Adnan's instruction for the dancing was simply "Move as you will." We danced to Adnan's Sufi drumming, and he is one of the most remarkable drummers I have ever heard.

He literally makes the drums take on a life of their own. For the last "exercise" of the evening, we all got into two large circles, the women in an inner circle, and the men in an outer circle, and we held hands dancing around the circle in reverse directions, the men counter-clockwise and the women clockwise. We chanted "Ya Hadi," which means: "Come, O Holy Spirit." Another translation is: "Come, Divine Guidance." We did the circle dance and chanted for six hours from 8:00 P.M. to 4:00 A.M. the next morning. According to Adnan, this was a relatively short session. Sometimes the dervishes go on dancing for twenty-four hours! It produced in general a very relaxed, and even loving, state among the participants.

I moved to New York after completing the Arica training in San Francisco, and whom did I meet there, but Adnan! He was apparently to be my teacher for the coming year. In the first workshop I took with Adnan in New York City, we did the whirling dervish dance of the Mevlevi school. This produced in me a trance state which lasted for several hours. The next day a T.V. crew shot some pictures of the Sufi group doing the "Ya Hadi" dance with Adnan in full dervish "regalia." During this session, I experienced some profound postural changes that released energy repressed since childhood. A neo-Reichian psychologist at a later workshop said that the Sufi "body discipline" so far exceeds any known Western "body psychologies" as to make the latter seem like "kindergarten." He described the Sufi "body work" as "postgraduate studies." Wilhelm Reich, in his writings, speaks as if he "discovered the body" as much as Sigmund Freud sounds as if he "discovered dreaming." The ethnocentrism of Western psychology is something to behold!

About a month into the Sufi sessions with Adnan, I had a dream in which I was slipping down a steep mountain, but Adnan stretched out his hand and pulled me up to safety. I had another dream in which Adnan looked at me and said: "You are a Sufi." Quite a compliment coming from him. I usually had a dream about each and every significant teacher on my Journey.

I will move ahead to the summer of 1973 when I went up to a farm in Cornwall, New York, to take a ten-day Sufi workshop with Adnan's group. Let me point out that this was a ten-day fast. We ate nothing whatever from dawn to sunset, and then had only a single cup of home-made soup at about 10:00 P.M. before retiring for the night. And we ate nothing till the next bowl of soup! Fasting is very important in the Sufi tradition. Adnan said, "Allah does not hear your prayers when your stomach is full!" Let me indicate what the Sufi camp was like by quoting my diary notations from day 1 to day 10, adding some commentary as well:

Day #1: I packed and took a bus to Cornwall and the Sufi camp. I felt out of touch with the country vibration coming from the big city. I felt rather tense. We listened to tape recordings by Idries Shah that evening. I shared a room on the ground floor of the farm house with Dr. Linc Wildner, a physician from Washington, D.C.

Day #2: We got up early and did morning exercises for several hours led by Adnan. That afternoon, a group of us drove to a lake and went swimming. Feel quite good. At 7:00 P.M., we had our "coffee shop" discussion and readings from Sufi tales. Later we had a game of ball. Then we listened to a tape recording by Doris Lessing. Getting into a higher vibration. (We didn't drink any coffee during what Adnan called our "coffee shop," but rather we engaged in group discussions, and we read Sufi teaching tales.)

Day #3: Nice morning session of exercise and meditation. That afternoon I went swimming at Lake Stillmin with Jeanne. The swimming was good. That evening we did the whirling dervish dances, and we did readings. This is really ascetic! Three days with practically no food. (How we maintained such high energy levels with so little food, I don't know.)

Day #4: The morning exercises were a little odd. I snuck away for the afternoon and had lunch (illegal) with Jeanne. We returned in time for the outdoor "coffee shop" and indoor chanting of "Allah" after dark. I went into a trance state while chanting and was criticized for that. One is supposed to remain awake and conscious.

Day #5: I feel a bit estranged from the group in the morning. Remember myself (as Gurdjieff said). The morning exercises were excellent. We ended them with free dancing and I became very involved. That evening we read "Teachers of Gurdjieff." The outdoor "coffee house" was good.

Day #6: I am feeling a little "out of syntony" with the group. It's OK. Very strenuous exercise session. Went swimming with Kurt, Mike, Lisa, Julie, and Surge at Lake Sebago. Evening "coffee shop"—we read stories of the Arabian desert. Also did whirling dervish dances. Later we had "dinner." Feel pretty good.

Day #7: Strenuous exercises and whirling dances in the morning. Felt quite peaceful during the afternoon in the shade. Helped prepare a salad for dinner. Enjoyed this. I am peaceful inside. "Coffee house," then drumming. "Jam session." Good dinner of soup and salad.

Day #8: Morning exercises, and surprise: we ate lunch! Long break, and then then 6:00 P.M. "coffee shop." I read the story of the "Streaky Sand" to the group. Then we scattered for solitary contemplation in the woods. Following this we did a deep-breathing exercise, and then we had a dinner of soup.

Day #9: I feel I have a purpose to be a part of a movement to higher consciousness and the Spirit. Help in raising the level of mankind's consciousness in some way. To help others as a healer. After the morning exercises, I felt tired and fell asleep. My whole life seemed to spin around in my head. When I woke up, I took a walk in the woods. I returned to the farm house, and I looked at a large tree. I had a UNITIVE EXPERIENCE. I saw the whole earth as one living being—visually. I could see the energy flowing from the earth through a tree into the atmosphere and into outer space. I saw the whole universe as one being. I told no one about this experience. That evening we had the "coffee shop," and I read a Sufi tale called "The Travellers and the Grapes" to the group. Adnan interpreted the tale. Then we chanted and had dinner. (I experienced something of what the Sufis call "Tawhid," or "The Unity," that afternoon.)

Day #10: Last day. Cleaning up. Lunch. Discussion of the problems of America with Adnan. I felt very good about Sufism at this point and would have gladly gone on for another two months. Drove back to New York City with Linc Wildner.

I spoke about the "coffee shops" and the Sufi teaching tales which we read and discussed. These all came from the books by Idries Shah which contain teaching stories of the Sufi masters from over the past thousand years. On Day #9 of the workshop, the day I had the UNITIVE EXPERIENCE, I read a Sufi tale called "The Travellers and the Grapes,"[40] to the group at the evening "coffee shop." This tale is about four travellers from four different countries who have a certain sum of money among them. They each want to buy something with the money. The Persian wishes to buy "angur," the Turk, "uzzum," the Arab, "inab," and the Greek, "stafl." They were unable to resolve the seeming disagreement. Another traveller, passing by, who happened to be a linguist, said, "Give the coin to me and I will undertake to satisfy the desires of all of you." He went to the shop of a fruitseller and bought four small bunches of grapes. The Persian said, "this is angur"; the Turk objected, "no, this is uzzum"; the Arab demurred, "this is inab"; the Greek said, "this in my language is stafl." But they shared the grapes among themselves, and each realized that the disharmony had been caused by his faulty understanding of the language of the others. The "travellers" are the ordinary people of the world; the linguist is the Sufi. Adnan made the following comments about the tale which I recorded on tape:

This explains the situation of the people in the world in their various beliefs and religions. Each thinks "theirs" is the one, while actually, in essence, it's all the same, leading to the same, because religions came for that purpose, to show the people, to lead the people to the right direction. But when people get simple in the mind, they become prejudiced, believing what they have is

right, and the others are not. Only take people who are deep in their thinking, and understanding, people who have had experiences, people who have
been through experiences, and they find the reality that is hidden behind the
faith, beliefs, religions. They all stem from the same Source. All have one
message: it is to know the Self. If a person knows the Self, or if he is going in
that direction, everything becomes simple and easy, and all the problems that
exist in the world will be solved. The further that people are away from the
Self, the more greedy, selfish, nervous, angry at each other, fight each other,
kill each other. All these problems come. The more they go in the direction of
the Spirit and consciousness, the more harmony and beauty they will have,
the more they enjoy the time, the days, the relationships, the relationship of
human being to human being, within the family, within friendships, within
the human race in general.

Sufis believe that we all belong to the human race like one family, and that
there is a duty for every person. The Sufis believe that whenever you can
teach something that you know, you should teach it to others. An older
brother will teach the younger brother, a teacher will teach the kids, a mother
will teach the children; a relative, a stranger, if you have something to teach
should do it. And that way there will be always growth or evolution.

The goal of the Sufi is the "Complete," or the "Perfect Man," or the "Superior
Man." To get away from all the negative, to use what is in this world to be
complementary to the Spirit and consciousness; not to have a human being
who is complementary to what is in this world as far as the "material."

"Material" in this world is to satisfy the needs of the human being, and to use
it, but not to be used by the material, where it will be overwhelming in its
power, and the human being will be sunk under it, and will lose all his value.
The understanding is important, and this comes from the Spirit. If people
have Spirit all over the world, regardless of the different nations, they will
communicate better. The language will not hinder the world, as we saw in this
story. They are all fighting over "the grape." Each of them has a different
name for it, and they all want "the grape," but each one thinks the word he's
using for it is the "right word," and that the other one is all wrong. Then
someone came and brought the grapes, and said, "that's what you all
wanted." So this situation actually exists today, on a big scale, and on a small
scale; in families, in villages, in big cities, in countries, and in the rest of the
countries of the world. It's the same problem. They are all fighting for "the
grape," all wanting "the grape," but all are going about it differently.

In the Sufi tradition, "grapes" and "wine" are usually metaphors for
spiritual experience. The Sufi is not satisfied with "names" and "de-
scriptions" of *the wine*. He wishes to drink it! This is analogous to the
contrast between theology and mysticism; theology has to do with
belief, mysticism with direct experience. Going along with the metaphor of the "grapes" and the "wine," the Sufi, Bayazid Bistami speaks
about the "The Seed of Sufi Knowledge":

The true seed was made in Adam's time. The miracle of life, existence.

It germinated in the period of Noah. The miracle of growth, rescue.

By the time of Abraham it had sent forth branches. The miracle of spreading, maintenance.

The epoch of Moses saw the making of the grapes. The miracle of fruit.

The time of Jesus was that of the ripening of the yield. The miracle of tasting, joy.

Mohammed's time saw the pressing of the clear wine. The miracle of attainment, transformation.[41]

Sufi teaching tales are more than just "stories"; they are tools, just as meditation, for the transformation of consciousness. With this in mind, we will end our little "coffee shop" with a Sufi tale that is current in the oral tradition in many languages in Sufi circles all over the world. It is my favorite Sufi tale, and it is a magnificent allegory of the Spiritual Path.

THE TALE OF THE SANDS

A STREAM, from its source in far-off mountains, passing through every kind of and description of countryside, at last reached the sands of the desert. Just as it had crossed every other barrier, the stream tried to cross this one, but it found that as fast as it ran into the sand, its waters disappeared.

It was convinced, however, that its destiny was to cross this desert, and yet there was no way. Now a hidden voice, coming from the desert itself whispered: "The Wind crosses the desert, and so can the stream."

The stream objected that it was dashing itself against the sand, and only getting absorbed: that the wind could fly, and this was why it could cross a desert.

"By hurtling in your own accustomed way you cannot get across. You will either disappear or become a marsh. You must allow the wind to carry you over, to your destination."

But how could this happen? "By allowing yourself to be absorbed in the wind."

This idea was not acceptable to the stream. After all, it had never been absorbed before. It did not want to lose its individuality. And, once having lost it, how was one to know that it could ever be regained?

"The wind," said the sand, "performs this function. It takes up water, carries it over the desert, and then lets it fall again. Falling as rain, the water becomes a river."

"How can I know that this is true?"

"It is so, and if you do not believe it, you cannot become more than a quag-mire, and even that could take many, many years; and it is certainly not the same as a stream."

"But can I not remain the same stream that I am today?"

"You cannot in either case remain so," the whisper said. "Your essential part is carried away and forms a stream again. You are called what you are even today because you do not know which part of you is the essential one."

When he heard this, certain echoes began to arise in the thoughts of the stream. Dimly, he remembered a state in which he—or some part of him, was it?—had been held in the arms of a wind. He also remembered—or did he?—that this was the real thing, not necessarily the obvious thing, to do.

And the stream raised his vapour into the welcoming arms of the wind, which gently and easily bore it upwards and along, letting it fall softly as soon as they reached the roof of a mountain, many, many miles away. And because he had had his doubts, the stream was able to remember and record more strongly in his mind the details of the experience. He reflected, "Yes, now I have learned my true identity."

The stream was learning. But the sands whispered: "We know, because we see it happen day after day: and because the sands extend from the riverside all the way to the mountain."

And that is why it is said that the way in which the Stream of Life is to continue on its journey is written in the Sands.[42]

The word for "wind" and "spirit" in Arabic is the same: "ruh." The "wind" in this tale is the "Ruh Allah," the Spirit of God. The stream is you and I, the human being seeking to make his or her journey through life. Being "stuck" at the desert, and unable to cross, has two possible meanings: physical death or spiritual death. I think both interpretations are acceptable. In either case, *we have no choice* but to surrender to the "arms of the wind," the Ruh Allah, if we are to continue on our Journey. It is he who "performs this function" of Spiritual Rebirth and Renewal.

NOTES

Primary Source:
   The Koran Interpreted, trans. by A. J. Arberry, Macmillan Publishing Co., New York, 1955, Sura II, "The Cow," pages: 30, 31–33, 39, 42, 45, 65–66, 71–72, Sura XCVI: "The Bloodclot," p. 344.

Secondary Sources:
   1. Caesar E. Farrah, Ph.D., *Islam,* Barron's Educational Series, Woodbury, N.Y., 1968, p. 19.
   2. Ibid., p. 38.
   3. Florence Mary Fitch, *Allah The God of Islam,* J. C. Dillon & Co., New York, 1950, p. 21.

4. M. S. Seale, *Quar'an and Bible,* Croom Helm, Ltd., London, 1978, p. 13.
5. Farah, p. 28.
6. Ibid.
7. *Views from the Real World, Early Talks of Gurdjieff as Recollected by His Pupils,* E. P. Dutton, 1975, p. 75.
8. Jolande Jacobi, *The Psychology of C. G. Jung,* Yale University Press, New Haven, Conn., 1973, p. 39.
9. Tor Andrae, *Mohammed the Man and His Faith,* Harper & Row, New York, 1960, p. 17.
10. Farrah, p. 38.
11. Andrae, p. 44.
12. Z'ev ben Shimon Halevi, *Kabbalah and Exodus,* Shambhala, Boulder, Co., 1980, p. 18.
13. Farrah, p. 41.
14. *The Meaning of the Glorious Koran,* trans. Mohammed Marmaduke Pickthall, New American Library, New York and Scarborough, Ontario, p. 420.
15. Farrah, p. 42.
16. Ibid., p. 44.
17. Ibid., p. 45.
18. Fitch, p. 27.
19. Geoffrey Parrinder, *The Faiths of Mankind,* Thomas Y. Crowell Co., New York, 1965, p. 15.
20. Ibid., pp. 16–17.
21. Martin Lings, *What Is Sufism?,* University of California Press, Berkeley and Los Angeles, 1977, p. 29.
22. Fitch, p. 55.
23. *The Bible,* Revised Standard Version, New Testament, American Bible Society, New York, 1971, Luke 20:18.
24. Farrah, p. 60.
25. *God and Man in Contemporary Islamic Thought,* ed. Charles S. Malik, American University of Beirut, Centennial Publications, Beirut, Lebanon, 1972, p. 144.
26. Farrah, p. 211.
27. Ibid.
28. Ibid.
29. Ibid., p. 217.
30. Idries Shah, *The Way of the Sufi,* E. P. Dutton, New York, 1970, p. 103.
31. Ibid., p. 105.
32. *The Bible,* Revised Standard Version, Old Testament, American Bible Society, New York, 1952, Kings 19:9–12.
33. Seyyed Hossein Nasr, *Islam and the Plight of Modern Man,* Longman, London & New York, 1975, pp. 5–6.
34. Ibid.
35. Ibid., p. 6.
36. Ibid., p. 7.
37. F. Schuon, *Light on the Ancient Worlds,* trans. Lord Northbourne, Perennial Books, London, 1965, p. 14.
38. David Bakan, *Sigmund Freud and the Jewish Mystical Tradition,* Van Nostrand, Princeton, N.J., 1958.
39. *Sufi Studies: East and West,* ed. Prof. L. F. Rushbrook Williams, E. P. Dutton & Co., New York, 1973, Ch. IX, "Psychology of the Sufi Way to Individuation," by Prof. A. Reza Arasteh, p. 109.
40. Idries Shah, *The Sufis,* Doubleday, Garden City, N.Y., 1964, pp. 21–22.
41. Shah, *The Way of the Sufi,* p. 242.
42. Idries Shah, *Tales of the Dervishes,* E. P. Dutton, New York, 1967, pp. 23–24.

Epilogue

A Synthesis

WE have come a long way from the *wei wu wei,* or "action of nonaction," of the poet-sage Lao Tzu to the *jihad,* or "holy war," of the prophet-warrior, Muhammed. In between, we have seen the reluctant-liberator, Moses, the carpenter-turned-Messiah, Jesus, the prince who renounced the world to find enlightenment, Gotama Buddha, and the God-incarnate charioteer, Krishna. What do these very different stories of very different individuals from very different cultures have in common? Do you recall what Chuang Tzu, the disciple of Lao Tzu, said about "getting lost in Tao"? He said that all people need to do is to "get lost in Tao." Tao is as natural to humans as water is to fish. But somehow humans have gotten alienated from the Tao. They have become disconnected from their Source. It is something that happened in every culture on earth at some time in human history. We in our Judeo-Christian tradition have the myth of the original Garden of Eden where man lived in harmony, and of man's subsequent exile from Eden when he ate of the "Tree of Knowledge of Good and Evil." It is as good a myth as any, and it speaks very deeply to our Unconscious Psyche.

The goal, then, of each of the World Teachers was to instruct us human beings in exile on *the way* back home! "Home" depending upon the language is "the Tao," "the Promised Land," "the Kingdom," "Nirvana," "Brahman," or "Allah." "Home" is the Source. It is from the Source that our "true Selves" were created, as it were, in the "Source's image." It is to the Source that we need go for "spiritual rebirth." Jesus spoke about this to his disciple Nicodemus when he said, "You must be born again." Each and every one of the world religions has its own concept of being "born again." The Buddhists, for example, speak of it as "Nirvana," or "enlightenment," the Hindus as "Moksha," or "liberation," and the Sufis have their own term, "ba'qa," or "reintegration in Allah." Are these different realities? I don't think so. Malachi Martin, former Jesuit priest and author, speaks of the "Castle" (or Grail). He says this about it:

One characteristic of the Castle is always underlined by those who genuinely perceive it and report about it; it owes nothing to any particular race of men, group of individuals, individual man or woman; rather, it is the object of all humankind and in that sense belongs to all—individually and collectively. But (there's the rub), while it is perceived in its totality, it comes in time and in each particular place to be expressed fragmentarily. Whole as each vision may be in the instant of opening to spirit, each attempt to tell the vision breaks into parts under the weight of words. For human expressions (words, actions, images, symbols, thoughts) are all particular and limited. All take on the shape of culture, are tied with the strings of syntax, reflect the hues of schools of logic that filter into and color every effort to share unfettered vision.[1]

Let us look at a quotation from the book of each World Teacher about the Ultimate Reality in the light of this truly "catholic" vision:

The Tao that can be expressed is not the eternal Tao;
The name that can be defined is not the unchanging name.

Lao Tzu

. . . say unto the children of Israel: I AM hath sent me unto you.

Moses

. . . lo, *I am* with you alway, even unto the end of the world.

Jesus

. . . let every one be wedded in holy love to the truth.

Buddha

I am the place of the abode, the beginning, the friend, and the refuge.

Krishna

God, there is no god but He, the Living, the Everlasting.

Muhammed

This *breakthrough* to Spiritual Reality is the goal of all sacred traditions. Some of the stories of the World Teachers in this book give us great examples of what this breakthrough is like. One of the most awesome in our Judeo-Christian tradition is the "burning bush" experience of Moses. Another spiritual breakthrough was the "baptism" experience of Jesus when the "heavens opened" and the Holy Spirit descended upon him like "a dove." The Buddha had this breakthrough after sitting in meditation for forty days under the Bodhi tree. He called this "enlightenment." Krishna seems to have just "appeared." We do not know about his breakthrough. The details of Lao Tzu's life are little known (except that he was a historian of the Chou court). His poems would indicate, however, that he *knew* whereof he spoke. Muhammed had his "night of power" when the Archangel Gabriel appeared to him and commanded him to "Recite!" None of these men just remained in his spiritually enlightened state; each "returned to the marketplace" to fulfill a mission in the world. Moses, for example, did not just sit on the mountaintop contemplating the "burning bush" forever; rather, he came down from the mountain and returned to Egypt to free his people!

How can we relate these teachings about the Spiritual Reality, and humans in the light of the Spiritual Reality, to psychology? "Religion" and "psychology" are usually viewed as "separate compartments," one having to do with "faith" and the other with "science." I do not like this dualistic view. I see what we call "religion" and "psychology," rather, as *levels of one continuum*. The Kabbalists would call this continuum the "Tree of Life." I am myself a student of Kabbalistic mysticism, but rather than present the "Kabbalistic Tree" per se (many fine books exist on it), I would like to share with you a vision I had many times during the fall of 1979. It was a vision of a "pyramid" with an "all-seeing eye," very much like the one you will see on any one-dollar bill (on the side which says "In God we trust"). It is called the "Great Seal," and I understand that it is a Rosicrucian mystical symbol. In my vision of the pyramid with the all-seeing eye, there were "four levels." Each had to do with a level of the psyche. I call the whole scheme the "pyramid of understanding." This is what it looked like with each level labelled as I saw it:

The first realm, or Ego Consciousness, would be the realm of psychologies such as that of Adler's "individual psychology." Both Freudian and Jungian psychology also deal with this level in their own way. Jung defines the ego in this manner:

We understand the ego as the complex factor to which all concious contents are related. It forms, as it were, the center of the field of consciousness. . . .[2]

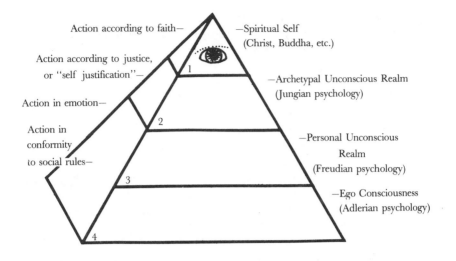

Even Jung has some difficulty "defining" the ego because this is the self we "always are." It is the omnipresent "little I." It is the "I" which looks out on the "world of things." It can also look inward at the inner realm of thoughts and feelings. The ego seems to "possess" a body in which we live. In most of our waking hours, we exist in the "world of the ego." It is the base of the pyramid which rests upon the "real world." It is our connection with material and social reality, and without this connection we are lost. Action on this level tends to conform to the social rules of the culture in which we live.

The second realm is what I call the "Personal Unconscious." This area was the specialty of Freud, who spent his whole lifetime elucidating its contents and laws. To Freud, the Personal Unconscious equals the Unconscious. There is nothing beyond it for him. It consists, for Freud, of ideas and impulses of the individual which were once conscious and became repressed due to traumatic circumstances of life (generally in early childhood), and also of contents which were never conscious (presumably innate). Freud speaks of the Unconscious (i.e., Personal Unconscious) in the following way in his book *The Ego and the Id:*

. . . we obtain our concept of the unconscious from the theory of repression. The repressed is the prototype of the unconscious for us. We see, however, that we have two kinds of unconscious— the one which is latent, but capable of becoming conscious, and the one which is repressed and which is not, in itself and without more ado, capable of becoming conscious.[3]

I think Jung's concept of the Personal Unconscious is more interesting. It involves the idea of the "complex." Freud himself borrowed this concept. A "complex" is a "feeling-toned" idea or mental content which operates, in certain respects, like an "independent personality." There are many kinds of complexes. Freud made the most of what he called the "Oedipus complex," which is the love-hate relationship between a boy and his mother and father. The "Electra complex" is the similar situation for the girl. Many other things can be complexes as well, and Jung was the inventor of the "word association" test which was an early means of "getting at" complexes. Among the words comprising the test were "death," "woman," "to kiss," "sick," and "mountain." Any of these might touch upon "complexes." For example, one might be obsessed with the fear of dying, and this would be a "death complex." The word "to kiss" might touch on sexual complexes. And the word "mountain" might elicit complexes having to do with fear of heights, or "acrophobia." We all live with the realm of the Personal Unconscious, and we experience it every night in our dreams. Both Freud and Jung would consider dreams to be the "royal road to the Unconscious." Action in this level coming from the Personal Unconscious tends to be irrational and emotional in quality as in phobic reactions, or violent rage, and so on.

Jung discovered the "Archetypal Unconscious Realm" in his own Night Sea Journey, and he confirmed it in the dreams and inner visions of his patients. It is a domain which has been known to human beings of all cultures and times in history through their myths and fairy tales. You will meet such figures in this realm as the Wise Man and the Wise Woman. The Wise Man appeared to me in a dream about a red-robed monk who "opened the door" to the Holy of Holies. Virgil performed this role of Wise Man to Dante on his Journey through Hell, Purgatory, and Heaven in the *Divine Comedy*. Women tend to meet first the Wise Woman. A woman friend of mine had a dream of a nun who "pointed the way" down a "golden ladder" into a "deep pond." In fairy tales, the "fairy godmother" seems to perform this role of Wise Woman for the heroine in question, as in the tale of *Cinderella*. Following the meeting with the Wise Man or Wise Woman, one tends to meet the "countersexual figure" within. Jung called these the "Anima" and the "Animus." Jung describes the Anima in this way:

Whenever she appears, in dreams, visions, and fantasies, she takes on personified form, thus demonstrating the factor she embodies possesses all the outstanding characteristics of a feminine being. She is not an invention of the conscious mind, but a spontaneous production of the unconscious. Nor is she a substitute for the mother. On the contrary, there is every likelihood that the numinous qualities which make the mother imago so dangerously powerful stem from the collective archetype of the Anima, which is incarnated anew in every male child.[4]

Both Anima and Animus are universal figures of myth and literature. In the King Arthur legend, Queen Gwenivere is one Anima figure. Sir Lancelot of the Lake is the Animus figure, and his life becomes entwined with Gwenivere; they are Anima and Animus for each other (and for us as well). In Dante's *Divine Comedy,* Beatrice is the Anima figure who "descends from heaven" (arises from the Unconscious). Hero, Heroine, Wise Man, Wise Woman, Witch, and Ogre, King, and Fool, these are some of the "characters" of the Archetypal Unconscious Realm. It is a realm in which the "archetype of justice" tends to prevail, as, for example, the "evil witch" in fairy tales and myths is usually "burned to death," or in other ways killed, which is what she richly "deserves," the "ogre" is "cut down," and the "dragon" is slain. The hero usually "rights all wrongs" and "establishes justice" in the kingdom. Behavior coming from this "level" has the aspect of "justice," or "self-justification."

The Self is a concept found in Jung's psychology. It is his "ultimate concept." Jung would call the Self the "archetype of wholeness." It is signified in dreams by the coming of the "Mandala." Speaking of his own "individuation process," Jung states:

My mandalas were cryptograms concerning the state of the self which were presented to me anew each day. In them I saw the self—that is, my whole being—actively at work.[5]

Dreams or visions of this sort are very powerful and they are *symbols of the Self.* But I wonder whether a symbol of the Self *is* the Self. If so, then everyone who has had a dream or vision of a Mandala is a Self-Realized person. I do not think that this is the case. Self-Realized ones are far rarer on this planet than you may realize (despite all the glib talk about "self-realization" in "human potential" circles).

A Self-Realized person is one who, as William Blake puts it, "sees a World in a grain of sand and a Heaven in a wild flower. . . ."[6] He is one who can strip himself naked and walk out into the wilderness trusting himself fully to the care of God as St. Francis of Assisi did. He is like the "wind," as Jesus put it, and "you do not know whence it comes or whither it goes; so it is with every one who is born of the Spirit."[7]

Another aspect of my vision of the pyramid with the all-seeing eye was this: the tip of the pyramid "made contact" with the Divine Reality. I picture it thusly:

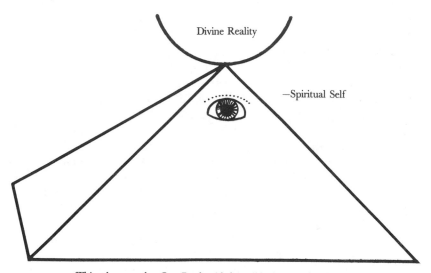

(This relates to what Otto Rank said about "the 'cosmic unity' which the man of Antiquity knew and expressed in his religions" —see Prologue)

The person of Self-Realization has awakened to the "Inner Eye" of the Spirit. Such a person is "in contact with" God. This person is one who is "born again," in the sense of Jesus, "enlightened," in the language of the Buddha, or "liberated," in Krishna's meaning of the word. It is at this "level" that true prayer is possible. It is at this "level" that miracles are commonplace. The lives of the saints were filled with miracles. It is at this "level" that revelation is possible. Revelation is quite simply "communication" between God and man. It takes place at the level at which the human person "touches" God, that is, at the level of the Spiritual Self. Most (there are notable exceptions) clergy in our modern West hardly operate at this level, but rather at the level of conventional prayer and rituals. One does not often feel "contact with God" in our twentieth-century churches and synagogues. What is this "contact" like? I'll relate to you a little story.

I once attended a "peace conference" at a synagogue in New York City. It was attended by both Jewish and Christian clergy. Several of these clergy recited standard prayers of their faith before the congregation. Nothing much happened. There was an American Indian contingent who attended this peace conference as well. A chief and medicine man from a West Coast tribe, I am not sure which, came up to the podium. I think his name was "Crazy Bear," or something like that. The conference took place several years ago. "Crazy Bear" stood silent for almost a minute in front of the assemblage and entered into a rather meditative state. He seemed to "center down" to what the Quakers call the "Deep Center." In this state, he spoke not "standard prayers" at all, but he began to address God spontaneously as "Grandfather." I don't really remember the content of what he said exactly except that it had to do with his prayers for peace for all peoples, for the animals, and for the whole earth. I remember more the effect it had upon the audience to have before them a man who *was actually* in contact with the Divine Reality as he spoke. It was an electrifying feeling, and it was also a feeling of profound peace which seemed to be shared by everybody in the synagogue that evening. He really "brought us together."

You might say that if one person is operating from the level of the Spiritual Self, everybody around that person (and perhaps people all over the world) will share this experience to some degree. The Spiritual Self is that which is within us which unites us with our fellow human beings. It is strange that what is most unique to each person is also what is most universal. Between the true Self of one individual and the true Self of another, a "spark" can jump which illumines the vision of both persons to the Kingdom. The Sacred Dimension is *between* as well as *within*.

NOTES

1. Malachi Martin, *The New Castle*, E. P. Dutton, New York, 1974, pp. 8–9.

2. C. G. Jung, *Psyche and Symbol*, Doubleday, Garden City, N.Y., 1958, pp. 1–2.

3. Sigmund Freud, *The Ego and the Id*, W. W. Norton, New York, 1960, p. 5.

4. Jung, p. 12.

5. C. G. Jung, *Memories, Dreams, Reflections*, Vintage Books, Random House, New York, 1963, p. 196.

6. *The Selected Poetry of Blake*, edited David V. Erdman, New American Library, New York, 1976, p. 272, "Auguries of Innocence."

7. *The Bible*, Revised Standard Version, New Testament, American Bible Society, New York, 1971, John, Chapter 3:8.

Bibliography

Primary Sources:
CHAPTER 1: Lao Tzu, *Tao Te Ching*, trans. Ch'u Ta-Kao, Samuel Weiser, New York, 1973.

CHAPTER 2: *The Holy Scriptures* according to the Masoretic Text, Jewish Publication Society of America, Philadelphia, 1955.

CHAPTER 3: *The Bible*, Revised Standard Version, The New Testament, American Bible Society, New York, 1971.

CHAPTER 4: Paul Carus, *The Gospel of the Buddha*, Open Court Publishing Company, Chicago and London, 1915.

CHAPTER 5: *The Song of God—Bhagavad-Gita*, trans. Swami Prabhavananda and Christopher Isherwood, New American Library, New York and Scarborough, Ontario, 1972.

CHAPTER 6: *The Koran Interpreted*, trans. A. J. Arberry, Macmillan, New York, 1955.

Secondary Sources:
Adler, A., *Social Interest*, Capricorn Books, New York, 1964.

Ansbacher, H. L., and Ansbacher, R. R., eds. *The Individual Psychology of Alfred Adler*, Harper & Row, New York, 1965.

Barborka, G. A., *The Pearl of the Orient—The Message of the Bhagavad-Gita for the Western World*, The Theosophical Publishing House, Wheaton, Ill., 1968.

Barclay, W., *The Beatitudes and the Lord's Prayer for Everyman*, Harper & Row, Publishers, New York, 1964.

Bible, The, Revised Standard Version, New Testament, American Bible Society, New York, 1971.

Blake, W., The Selected Poetry of, David V. Erdman, New American Library, New York & Scarborough, Ontario, 1976.

Bucke, R. M., *Cosmic Consciousness*, E. P. Dutton, New York, 1969.

223

Butterworth, E., *How to Break the Ten Commandments*, Harper & Row, New York, 1970.

Capra, F., *The Tao of Physics*, Shambhala Publications, Berkeley, Calif., 1975.

Chen, W. C. C., *Tai Chi Chuan*, William C. C. Chen School of T'ai Chi Chu'an, 161 West 23rd Street, New York, 1973.

Cloud of Unknowing, The, trans. Clifton Wolters, Penguin Books, New York, 1961.

Course in Miracles, A, Copyright by the Foundation for Inner Peace, Tiburon, Calif., Coleman Graphics, Huntington Station, N.Y., 1975.

Dante, The Portable, The Divine Comedy, trans. Clifton Wolters, Penguin Books, New York, 1961.

Dropping Ashes on the Buddha—The Teachings of Zen Master Seung Sahn, compiled and edited by Stephen Mitchell, Grove Press, New York, 1976.

Eckhardt, M., *Meister Eckhardt, A Modern Translation*, trans. R. B. Blakney, Harper & Row, New York, 1941.

Errico, R. A., *The Ancient Aramaic Prayer of Jesus "The Lord's Prayer,"* Science of Mind Publications, Los Angeles, 1975.

Falls, C. B., *The First 3000 Years*, Viking Press, New York, 1960.

Farrah, C. E., *Islam*, Barron's Educational Series, Woodbury, N.Y., 1968.

Fitch, F. M., Allah—The God of Islam, J. C. Dillon & Co., New York, 1950.

Freud, S., *The Ego and the Id*, W. W. Norton, New York, 1960.

Freud, S., *The Future of an Illusion*, Anchor Books, Doubleday, New York, 1967.

Freud, S. *Leonardo da Vinci—A Memory of His Childhood*, W. W. Norton, New York, 1964.

Freud, S. An Outline of Psychoanalysis, W. W. Norton, New York, 1940.

Freud/Jung Letters, Bollingen Series XCIV, Princeton, N.J., 1974.

Gibran, K., *The Prophet*, Knopf, New York, 1980.

God and Man in Contemporary Islamic Thought, ed. Charles S. Malik, American University of Beirut, Centennial Publications, Beirut, Lebanon, 1972.

Gospel According to Thomas, The, trans. A. Guillaumont et al., Harper & Row, New York, 1959.

Guignebert, C., *The Jewish World at the Time of Jesus*, University Books, New York, 1959.

Halevi, Z., *Kabbalah and Exodux*, Shambhala, Boulder, Colo., 1980, p. 18.

Holy Bible, King James Version, World Publishing Company, New York, 1611 edition.

Houston, J., *Lifeforce: The Psychohistorical Recovery of the Self*, Delacorte Press, New York, 1980.

Jacobi, J., *The Psychology of C. G. Jung*, Yale University Press, New Haven, Conn., 1973.

Jastrow, R., *God and the Astronomers*, Warner Books, New York, 1980.

John of the Cross, St., *Dark Night of the Soul*, Doubleday, Garden City, N.Y., 1959.

Johnson, R., *HE*, Perennial Library, Harper & Row, New York, 1977.

Jung, C. G., *Memories, Dreams, Reflections*, Vintage Books, Random House, New York, 1963.

Jung, C. G., *Psyche and Symbol*, Doubleday, Garden City, N.Y., 1973.

Lao Tzu, *The Way of Life*, trans. R. B. Blakney, New American Library, New York and Scarborough, Ontario, 1955.

Lings, M., *What Is Sufism?*, University of California Press, Berkeley & Los Angeles, Calif., 1977.

Martin, M., *The New Castle*, E. P. Dutton, New York, 1974.

Meaning of the Glorious Koran, The, trans. Mohammed Marmaduke Pickthall, New American Library, New York & Scarborough, Ontario, 1970.

Meltzer, M., *Slavery: From the Rise of Western Civilization to the Renaissance*, Cowles Book Company, New York, 1971.

Mentor Books of Major American Poets, eds. Oscar Williams and Edwin Honig, Mentor Books, New American Library, New York and Scarborough, Ontario, 1962.

Merton, T., *Love and Living*, Bantam Books, New York, 1979.

Merton, T., *The Way of Chuang Tzu*, New Directions Publishing, New York, 1965.

Nasr, S. H., *Islam and the Plight of Modern Man*, Longman, London and New York, 1975.

Newsweek, "Pesticides' Global Fallout," August 17, 1980.

Parinder, E. G., *What World Religions Teach*, George G. Harrap & Company, London, 1968.

Parrinder, G., *The Faiths of Mankind*, Thomas Y. Crowell Company, New York, 1965.

Ouspensky, P. D., *In Search of the Miraculous*, Harcourt Brace Jovanovich, New York and London, 1977, p. 130.

Rama, S., Ballentine, R., and Weinstock, A., *Yoga and Psychotherapy—The Evolution of Consciousness*, Himalayan Institute of Yoga, Science, and Philosophy, Honesdale, Pa., 1976.

Rank, O., *Beyond Psychology*, Dover Publications, New York, 1958.

Saddhatissa, H. *The Buddha's Way*, George Braziller, New York, 1971.

Sanford, J. A., *The Kingdom Within*, Paulist Press, New York, 1980.

Sasaki, J., *Buddha Is the Center of Gravity*, Lama Foundation, San Cristobal, N.M., 1974.

Schuon, F., *Light on the Ancient Worlds*, trans. Lord Northbourne, Perennial Books, London, 1965.

Seale, M. S., *Quar'an and Bible*, Croom Helm Ltd., London, 1978.

Shah, I., *The Sufis*, Doubleday, Garden City, N.Y., 1964.

Shah, I., *Tales of the Dervishes*, E. P. Dutton, New York, 1967.

Shah, I., *The Way of the Sufi*, E. P. Dutton, New York, 1975.

Shakespeare, W., *Hamlet*, Pocket Books, New York, 1958.

Shibayama, Z., *Zen Comments on the Mumokan*, trans. Sumiko Kudo, New

American Library, New York and Scarborough, Ontario, 1974.

Spirit of Modern India, The—Writings in Philosophy, Religion, and Culture, Eds. Robert A. McDermott and V. S. Naravane, Thomas Y. Crowell Company, New York, 1974.

Stroup, H., *Like a Great River—An Introduction to Hinduism,* Harper & Row, New York, 1972.

Sufi Studies: East and West, ed. Prof. L. F. Rushbrook Williams, E. P. Dutton, New York, 1973.

Suzuki, D. T., *Zen Buddhism,* ed. William Barrett, Doubleday, New York, 1956.

Teilhard de Chardin, P. *The Heart of Matter,* Harcourt Brace Jovanovich, New York and London, 1978.

Thoreau, H. D., *Walden,* College & University Press, New Haven, Conn., 1965.

Toynbee, A., 1976 magazine clipping.

Trungpa, C., *Meditation in Action,* Shambhala, Berkeley, Calif., 1970.

Uchiyama, K., *Approaches to Zen,* Japan Publications, San Francisco and Tokyo, 1973.

Unger, M., *Unger's Bible Dictionary,* Moody Press, Chicago, 1966.

Upanishads, The Ten Principal, trans. Shree Purohit Swami and W. B. Yeats, Macmillan, New York, 1965.

Views from the Real World—Early Talks of Gurdjieff as Recollected by His Pupils, E. P. Dutton, New York, 1975.

Watts, A., *TAO: The Watercourse Way,* Pantheon Books, New York, 1975.

Wittgenstein, L., *Tractatus Logico Philosophicus,* Routledge and Kegan Paul, London (New York: Humanities Press), 1961.

Index

DISCARD